Praise for
Magnifeco

Kate Black's *Magnifeco* is a wonderful and relevant book that we need to reference whenever we go shopping! Full of information on complex issues, *Magnifeco* identifies the problems in beauty and fashion products with clarity and a sense of purpose. Most importantly, Kate provides hope and real-life solutions that we can all act upon. *Magnifeco* helps us (fashionistas and shoppers alike!) make better choices in our shopping decisions and discover brands that are doing it better. A phenomenal resource for our #buybetter toolbox.

— Amber Valletta, fashion icon, actress, and founder, Master & Muse

A powerful case for change combined with a much-needed guide to buying into the kind of future we simply must create. In *Magnifeco*, Kate offers a useful guide to anyone interested in aligning their values to choices we make every day. A stirring invitation to a life beyond mindless consumption and the enormous potential we each hold for good.

— Andrew Morgan, director, *The True Cost*

Finally, a book that cuts through the noise and shows us exactly how to shop ethically and sustainably, from our hair and makeup down to the shoes on our feet.

— Elizabeth L. Cline, author,
Overdressed: The Shockingly High Cost of Cheap Fashion

Want to be an environmentalist but look hip and fashionable while you're marching? Kate Black's *Magnifeco* is the most comprehensive buyer's guide I have seen yet.

— Colin Beavan, No Impact Man

In today's world, where we cannot always be guaranteed transparency when it comes to the products we are buying and brands we support, this book is a thoroughly researched and refreshing resource. It is all you need to know when it comes to protecting yourself, the planet, and your unique sense of style!

— Anna Griffin, publisher and editor-in-chief, *Coco Eco* magazine

The Magnifeco blog has been a consistent and reliable point of reference for the sustainable fashion community, and Kate Black is a compulsive sharer of information, a curator of thoughts, unafraid to throw anything into the mix. She has been conducting articulate and relevant conversations on the topic of ethics and sustainability in the fashion industry, and this book is a powerful condensation of her experience and observations. The definitive guide on how and why we should shop more responsibly, this book will make the journey to alternative buying both more compelling and more relevant.

— Orsola de Castro, co-founder, Fashion Revolution Day

Kate Black's breadth of knowledge — and passion — make this book a must-read for anyone interested in where our future is inexorably headed: a new industry standard of ethical, sustainable fashion and nontoxic beauty. A smart, lively, eye-opening guide to what we all need to know about what we put on our bodies every single day.

— Rona Berg, editor-in-chief, *Organic Spa Magazine*

Kate Black's new book is beyond *MAGNIFECO!* Unveiling the human and environmental impacts of the fashion and beauty industries, her comprehensive and important array of explanations, resources and tips is a must-read for every fashionista with a conscience.

— Marci Zaroff, ECOfashion pioneer and founder, Under the Canopy

We want to make smart and conscious choices. We aim to support responsible brands and companies with our decisions. Because we are all both citizens and consumers, at the same time. This book is a lighthouse to help us navigate the oceans of our fashion, beauty and jewelry choices

— Maria Eugenia Girón, co-author,
Sustainable Luxury and Social Entrepreneurship: Stories from the Pioneers and
executive director, IE Business School Premium and Prestige Observatory (Madrid)

At last, a simple, easy-to-understand explanation of the link between jewelry and the environmental and social costs of mining. Black explains how harnessing the Earth's resources has resulted in inequality, abuse and environmental havoc, and offers a different way forward. Consumers have choices, and *Magnifeco* lays out how consumers can chose to support solutions to intractable problems like slave labor in mining camps or permanent poisoning of waterways.

— Jennifer Krill, Executive Director EARTHWORKS

KATE BLACK

MAGNIFECO

your head-to-toe guide to ethical
fashion and non-toxic beauty

new society
PUBLISHERS

Cover design by Diane McIntosh.

Middle lower model image (cover and internal pages): Fashion by Study NY, photographer: Mathieu Fortin (L'Eloi, Montreal), creative direction: Françoise Cournoyer & Isabelle Allard-Gendron, stylist: Sabrina Deslauriers (L'Eloi, Montreal), hair & make-up: Jessica Lablanche (Folio Montreal), model: Annie Claude MB (Folio Montreal)

From top left down: Handbag: product and photograph © Kempton & Co. Towels and bottles © iStock Marsbars. Belt © iStock Roman_Gorielov. Scarves © iStock enviromantic. Make-up © iStock Spanishalex. From lower right up: clothing tag © iStock knape. Jeans © iStock dstaerk. Shoes: Brother Vellies, image © Jason Eric Hardwick. Bracelet © by/nataliefrigo 2014.

Printed in Canada. First printing October 2015.

New Society Publishers acknowledges the financial support of the Government of Canada through the Canada Book Fund (CBF) for our publishing activities.

Paperback ISBN 978-0-86571-797-8
Ebook ISBN 978-1-55092-590-6

Inquiries regarding requests to reprint all or part of *Magnifeco* should be addressed to New Society Publishers at the address below. To order directly from the publishers, please call toll-free (North America) 1-800-567-6772, or order online at www.newsociety.com

Any other inquiries can be directed by mail to:
New Society Publishers
P.O. Box 189, Gabriola Island, BC V0R 1X0, Canada
(250) 247-9737

New Society Publishers' mission is to publish books that contribute in fundamental ways to building an ecologically sustainable and just society, and to do so with the least possible impact on the environment, in a manner that models this vision. We are committed to doing this not just through education, but through action. The interior pages of our bound books are printed on Forest Stewardship Council®-registered acid-free paper that is **100% post-consumer recycled** (100% old growth forest-free), processed chlorine-free, and printed with vegetable-based, low-VOC inks, with covers produced using FSC®-registered stock. New Society also works to reduce its carbon footprint, and purchases carbon offsets based on an annual audit to ensure a carbon neutral footprint. For further information, or to browse our full list of books and purchase securely, visit our website at: **www.newsociety.com**

Library and Archives Canada Cataloguing in Publication

Black, Kate, 1969-, author
    Magnifeco : your head-to-toe guide to ethical fashion and non-toxic beauty / Kate Black.

Includes bibliographical references and index.

Issued in print and electronic formats.
ISBN 978-0-86571-797-8 (paperback).--ISBN 978-1-55092-590-6 (ebook)

    1. Fashion--Moral and ethical aspects. 2. Beauty, Personal--Environmental aspects. 3. Clothing and dress--Moral and ethical aspects. 4. Clothing and dress--Environmental aspects. 5. Shopping--Moral and ethical aspects. 6. Consumer education. 7. Sustainable living. I. Title.

GT511.B63 2015   391   C2015-905201-7
                                         C2015-905202-5

MIX
Paper from
responsible sources
FSC® C016245

Contents

Introduction

WHEN I STARTED THE MAGNIFECO BLOG IN 2008, it was on the heels of *Vanity Fair*'s annual green issue and just before *Vogue*'s first green issue. I fell in love with eco-fashion, the ethos and all the designers striving to make fashion better. I was living in Tokyo at the time and thought women like me and conscious consumers everywhere needed a "daily eco-fashion find." I picked a name that might resonate in many languages. "Magnifeco" is an exclamation of delight in finding something that is "extraordinarily fine, superb and *eco*." The blog features products from around the globe and is read in 120 countries.

Since then, even though fashion and beauty are now regularly prefixed with words like "green," "natural," "environmentally friendly," "eco," "healthy" and "sustainable,"[1] the industry is not as healthy as it should be. There are still dark sides to both industries: dangerous chemicals in everyday personal care products, deadly pesticides used to grow cotton, child labor in gold mining and stone cutting, deforestation to make fashion, and toxic leather facilities. Consumers have the power to change these situations, if only they knew. Many of those issues could be easily avoided and then eradicated.

That's why I wanted to write this guide. Until consumers — you — know more about the dirty secrets of each of these sectors, and can start shifting your dollars towards brands and designers doing things differently, nothing will change.

The content in the coming pages can be a little heavy. It's laid out to share the research that NGOs and activists are conducting, research that we as consumers should know, but that rarely makes the pages of beauty or fashion magazines. The Rana Plaza factory collapse in Bangladesh in 2013 brought to light some of the hazardous working conditions that are a result of fast fashion, but there's more to know.

For those who just want to know what to buy, each chapter has a shopping guide of suggested brands, and some details about why they are "better." Plus, in the fashion chapters there are selected "game changers" — designers who are breaking the mold and offering products that are truly "magnifeco."

No one paid to be in the shopping guides. The brands listed were chosen because they represent a cross-section of values, style, price and availability. The lists could have gone on and on, and new brands are popping up daily. However, in the interest of not making this book any heavier, come to Magnifeco.com for more.

Chapter 1

Beauty

"For the first time in the history of the world,
every human being is now subjected to contact
with dangerous chemicals, from the moment of
conception until death."[1]

— Rachel Carson,
citizen-scientist and author of *Silent Spring*

A SWIPE OF A LIPSTICK or a pass of deodorant, most of us are thinking about the external effects of those efforts: if the latest lip color will make our eyes "pop" or the underarm scent will cover body odor. Yet how many of us can honestly say we think about the effects of those products on us internally — the possible lead in the lipstick[2] or whether our deodorant contributes to breast or testicular cancer?[3] Although we are growing more conscious about what we put *inside* our bodies, we often overlook what we put *on* our bodies, next to our largest organ (our skin). However, with the emergence of medicinal applications like nicotine patches, we know the medical profession recognizes how absorbent skin is. Maybe it's time we gave this a second thought.

Although US Food and Drug Association (FDA) was set up to regulate cosmetic products and their ingredients in 1938,[4] the cosmetic provisions have been amended just three times since then.[5] Even though it was after then that the chemical age really emerged and synthetic chemicals entered every aspect of our life, including our personal care products. Most of the products we know and love for their ability to make our life easier, from hair spray and brushless shaving cream to plastic and polyester, are all based on synthetic chemicals and were all created *after* the FDA. We learned to love what chemicals could make; we just didn't consider if there could be a downside.[6] When 20,000 people lost their lives in Bhopal, India, after a chemical gas spill from a pesticide factory,[7] we started to understand what occurs from too much rapid exposure to chemicals. However, what we don't know are the long-term effects of small doses of chemicals on our health or the environment.[8]

If we are to make any changes to our health, and for the health and safety of future generations, the choices we make in beauty (and fashion) matter. So, while we don't really get to choose *if* we opt in, we do get to choose *how* we opt in — and where we are willing to change.

I say this because some things you won't want to change (we all have our favorite product or cosmetic that we can't imagine parting with). This chapter is meant to give you the tools to make informed decisions and choose products that are better for you (and the environment) — when you are ready. Some you will change immediately — you might drop the book and run to the bathroom and start right away — while others might be a challenge. Do what you can, when you can.

Who's Protecting Us?

A common misconception is that personal care and beauty products are "FDA tested" or "FDA approved," that the FDA monitors these products and there is a safeguarding process to test and register the safety of all the products we use.

This is true for pharmaceuticals and drugs but not personal care products. Medicines are actively monitored and require several stages of safety testing. Chemical additives in personal care products, on the other hand, require no premarket testing. When it comes to personal care products, the FDA states quite clearly on its website homepage, "The FDA does not approve cosmetics." This includes shampoos, soaps, shaving creams, perfumes, colognes and makeup.

Rather, the role of the FDA is to compile the lists of chemicals and additives that companies use, and wait for complaints. Since its 1938 launch, the FDA has banned only 8 ingredients, and restricted 3, bringing the total of banned or restricted to 11.[9] Compare this to Canada that has a hotlist of over 600 banned or restricted ingredients or the European Union (EU) that has stricter rules and regulations and has banned or restricted 1,300 chemicals from cosmetics. It's a large disparity and concern, given that diseases and illnesses seem to be on the rise and exposure to chemicals is thought to be a contributing factor.[10] For example, published statistics in the United States show that:

- 1 in 2 men and 1 in 3 women will be diagnosed with cancer in their lifetimes.[11]
- 1 in 8 women will be diagnosed with breast cancer. Only about 10 percent of these women carry a gene for the disease.[12]
- Just under half of all pregnancies end in miscarriage or produce a child born with a birth defect or chronic health problem.[13]
- There is a rise in genital birth defects such as hypospadias (the opening of the urethra develops on the shaft, not at the tip, of the penis) and cryptorchidism (undescended testicles, a risk factor for poor semen quality and testicular cancer).[14]

The numbers aren't noticeably better in Canada:

- Testicular cancer is the most common cancer among young men between 15 and 29 years old.[15]
- On average, every day 67 Canadian women will be diagnosed with breast cancer and 14 will die.[16]
- Asthma is the most common chronic disease of children in Canada, affecting 12.5 percent of children,[17] and it's rising.

Personal care and beauty products use about 12,000 different chemicals, and nearly 90 percent of them have never been assessed for their impact on long-term health.[18] Chemical ingredients, for which there is no safety information publicly available, are found in almost every product on the market. In addition, ingredients known to be linked to cancer can be found in over one-third of cosmetics and personal care products.[19] No one is protecting us. It's up to the consumer to decide what is safe. It's up to you.

This isn't just a "girl" problem. While I call this chapter "Beauty" and the FDA considers everything from soap to shaving cream to makeup to be "cosmetics," this affects us all. This is a personal care product problem. Think about your bathroom, the products lining your shower, around the sink, in your cosmetic case or your shaving kit. It is estimated that the average man uses six personal care products a day, containing more than 85 different chemicals, while women use double, averaging around 168 chemicals.[20] Chemicals that get absorbed into our skin, inhaled, even ingested. What doesn't get into us either contributes to the toxicity of our home or we wash them down the drain and send them into our waterways.

The Body Burden

In 1962, American marine biologist and conservationist Rachel Carson published *Silent Spring*, a book credited with advancing the global environmental movement. In it, Carson suggested that the planetary ecosystem was reaching the limits of what it could sustain.[21] While recognizing modern chemistry had created powerful tools for society, she urged caution. In doing so, she became one of the first to sound the alarm on the long-lasting effects of chemicals, not just to the environment, but to all living organisms (including humans). She was speaking, in particular of pesticides like DDT, which was later banned in 1972, but she knew she had to speak up when she testified before Congress (in 1963) that it should be a basic human right to be protected from poison. She urged the committee to give serious consideration to a "much neglected problem. That of the right of the citizen to be secure in his own home against the intrusion of poisons applied by other persons." She implored that this freedom from chemical intrusion should a basic human right.[22]

Carson was attacked by the chemical industry and called out as an ignorant and emotional woman.[23] It took a full decade after her testimony before Congress for the government to pass, and begin to enforce, pollution controls in factories and hazardous waste dumps.[24] But it turns out she was right to worry.

Not only can we not secure our homes from toxic chemicals, but we can't keep unwanted chemicals out of our *bodies* either. In 2004 the

Environmental Working Group (EWG), with the help of the Red Cross, measured pollutants from blood taken randomly from the umbilical cords of newborns across the US. The researchers detected a total of 287 chemicals, including 180 that cause cancer in humans or animals.[25] Many of the chemicals we worry about today were already present in infants before they are born.

This is commonly referred to as the *body burden*: a stockpile of chemicals that are in your body without your knowledge or idea of source. In 2001 the Centers for Disease Control and Prevention (CDC) began a large-scale body burden study to "determine which chemicals get into Americans and at what concentrations."[26] The first year, researchers tested for 27 chemical compounds; two years later, they tested for 116. This is one of the ways we know that certain chemicals are *persistent*. For example, polychlorinated biphenyls (PCBs), odorless mixtures of chlorinated compounds used for coolants in transformers and fluorescent bulbs, contaminated air, water and soil during their manufacture, use and disposal. PCBs became so ubiquitous that they were banned in 1977.[27] Yet body burden studies reveal not only are they are still found in us but they have proven to be world travelers, showing up in geographic locations far from where they started.[28] For example, Inuit nursing mothers in Canada's North measure the highest PCB levels in their milk of any women in the world.[29] Body burden studies can show us which chemicals bioaccumulate in the human body, but they can't show any connections between exposure and source or exposure and illness.

In Europe and Canada, this has been enough to prompt radical changes in the way toxic chemicals are regulated. But in the US? it's different; even with Rachel Carson's forewarning and the results of the CDC's body burden studies, the US has been slow to ban or restrict chemicals. As McKay Jenkins puts it, in his book *What's Gotten Into Us?* "Chemicals in Europe are considered guilty until proven innocent. Here in the United States, it is the other way around."[30]

Sadly, there is no general agreement about useful or safe methods for reducing body burdens. The wisest strategy is prevention and overall chemical reduction. Reducing the toxicity of the air we breathe, the water we drink and the food we eat will take collective, legislative efforts. But reducing your toxic load from personal care products can start now.

Conventional Products

Some of the issues with conventional products can be changed; firstly, our usage — or over-usage. When was the last time you read the instructions or used a "pea-sized" amount of product as directed? Some products should never be used on open skin; some should be used in a well-ventilated area. When toxicology studies are done, they are done on recommended usage that consumers often do not follow.

Then other issues are more difficult to avoid. For example, even if you are armed with all of the latest chemicals to avoid — the "toxic ten,"[31] the "dirty dozen,"[32] etc. — personal care products do not always display ingredients on their labels. Plus, numerous studies have revealed dangerous ingredients within products that were *not* listed on their labels, from the lead in lipsticks[33] to phthalates in popular perfume brands[34] and in conventional men's products.[35]

Lastly, there is the concern about chemical combinations. For example, what happens when you combine using your favorite aftershave with the face moisturizer of another brand? Or a foundation with a different brand moisturizer? Even if someone is in the lab of the manufacturer testing for safety, you can bet no one is testing how safely their chemicals interact with chemicals of other brands. Conventional products and their synthetic chemicals react with each other and affect our bodies in ways that scientists haven't even begun to map out.[36]

Given the potential interactions between chemicals, added to our body burden and mixed in with our individual genetics, it is nearly impossible to know all of the effects they will have on us. We are counting calories and steps and lessening our body burden with our food choices but completely overlooking what might be the most toxic-laden room in the house: the bathroom. It's time to start counting chemicals.

The Watchdogs

Before we get to the nasty ingredients, first you should take comfort and know there are external watchdogs who are keenly interested in safeguarding consumer safety. Most of the information that follows comes from them. They are brave name shamers — when they do toxic studies on products, they are not afraid to share the brands or the names, and their research and efforts offer hope for the future of this industry and our personal health and wellness. At the very least, the tools they have developed and the reports they write provide more information for consumers.

The **Environmental Working Group (EWG)** is an American public interest group dedicated to using the power of information to protect public health and the environment. Its mission is threefold:

1. To protect the most vulnerable segments of the population — children, babies and infants in the womb — from health problems attributed to · toxic contaminants.

2. To replace federal policies, including government subsidies that damage the environment and natural resources, with policies that invest in conservation and sustainable development.

3. To give consumers the tools they need to make the best product buying decisions for their family.

True to its word and supporting the third mission, the EWG has developed one of the best tools for consumers to look deeper into the chemical makeup and toxicity levels of everything from toothpaste to perfume. The Skin Deep® Cosmetics Database (ewg.org/skindeep) launched in 2004, provides online profiles of over 69,000 personal care products. The EWG team of staff scientists compare ingredients on personal care product labels and websites to information in nearly 60 toxicity and regulatory databases. The result: a product hazard rating of 0 to 2 (low hazard), 3 to 6 (moderate hazard) and 7 to 10 (high hazard).

In 2002, EWG, Health Care Without Harm and Women's Voices for the Earth released a groundbreaking report called *Not Too Pretty*. It scientifically tested a wide range of personal care products and found concerning chemicals in more than 70 percent of the products, including shampoos, deodorants, hair gels and fragrance — chemicals that weren't listed on the label.

Presuming that this was just the tip of the iceberg, the "Campaign for Safe Cosmetics" was launched as a coalition of non-profit health and environmental organizations (including the EWG) to further everyone's access to safer personal care products and smarter laws governing cosmetic safety. Its mission is to protect the health of consumers and workers. It is challenging the personal care products industry to phase out the use of chemicals linked to cancer, birth defects and other serious health concerns and replace them with safer alternatives.

In 2007 the Campaign for Safe Cosmetics released two more scientifically tested studies. Using independent lab testing, it tested 33 lipsticks for lead and proved the urban myth true: lead is found in two-thirds of the samples.[37] The second study, on children's bath products, found 1,4-dioxane, a petroleum by-product and carcinogen that was not listed on any product labels.[38]

The **Environmental Defense** could be called the Canadian equivalent to the EWG. Heralded for leading the way to getting BPA banned from baby bottles, it focuses on critical environmental and health issues in Canada: climate change, toxic chemicals, pollution, endangered species, to name a few. In 2010, the Environmental Defense launched "Just Beautiful." Similar to the Campaign for Safe Cosmetics, the Just Beautiful campaign has two aims: to educate consumers about the toxins found in everyday cosmetic and personal care products and to challenge Canadian cosmetic laws to ensure all products are clean and safe for use.[39]

In 2012, the Environmental Defense published *The Manscape: The Dirt on Toxic Ingredients in Men's Body Care Products*. It tested 17 men's grooming products and found that some of these popular products contained carcinogens and chemicals known to harm male reproductive health: 1,4-dioxane plus phthalates and parabens (which mimic estrogen) that have been linked to risk factors for testicular cancer.[40]

The **Silent Spring Institute** (SSI) is a non-profit research organization in Cape Cod, Massachusetts, working to identify links between chemicals in our everyday environments and women's health, especially breast cancer. The SSI was launched in 1994, after members of the Massachusetts Breast Cancer Coalition called for investigation into elevated breast cancer rates on Cape Cod. The only scientific research organization dedicated to breast cancer prevention, SSI is staffed and led by researchers dedicated to science that serves the public interest. They partner with physicians, public health and community advocates, and other scientists to propel progress in breast cancer prevention. It is named in tribute to Rachel Carson (author of *Silent Spring*) who died of breast cancer just two years after her book was published.

The SSI 2012 study, *Endocrine Disruptors and Asthma-Associated Chemicals in Consumer Products* examined 213 products across 50 product types (shampoo, toothpaste, etc.) and found many detected chemicals were not listed on product labels.[41] It also found well-known endocrine-disrupting phthalates were not present, but less-studied phthalates were, indicating substitution.

The **David Suzuki Foundation** was founded in Canada in 1989 as a solutions-based organization that aims to conserve the environment by providing science-based research, education and policy work. This includes preventing pollutants and toxic chemicals from entering bodies and the environment. In 2010, it published a list of cosmetic chemicals to avoid; the *Dirty Dozen* is available as a printout and consumer guide.

The **Women's Voices for the Earth** (WVE) was formed in Montana in 1995. Identifying that many environmental organizations at the time failed to include women in leadership positions and did not fully recognize the systemic connections between health, class, race and the environment, WVE sought to create a new environmental organization led by women. It works to amplify women's voices to eliminate toxic chemicals that harm health and communities.

In 2010, WVE released *Dirty Secrets*, a report that exposed the dangers of fragrance in cleaning products. It was updated in 2013 to include personal care products, and its 2013 *Chem Fatale* report was the first to explore the health effects of toxic chemicals in feminine care products.

All of these watchdogs are concerned about the overarching topics of environment and human health, but often from different angles, exposing new risks and highlighting conventional products that are affected. Their combined research has significantly shaped this chapter, and when new bodies of research are added, you will find them on Magnifeco.com.

Chemical Soup

The primary concern of a personal care brand, and the FDA, to be fair, is the immediate safety of the product on the consumer: will it cause reactions or adverse effects? As consumers, we hope, and expect, that products are safe to use in the day to day. But of deeper concern of late are the long-term or lasting effects of chemicals and bioaccumulation. Are our products safe to use over time? Chemicals are in the air, in our food, in our water and in our bodies before we even choose our beauty or grooming regimen. It's the chemicals we add through our purchasing decisions that we do have control over.

The biggest issues in conventional personal care products are:

- Carcinogens — chemicals that cause cancer
- Teratogens — chemicals that cause birth defects
- Developmental/reproductive toxicants — chemicals that damage the normal development of the fetus, infant or child or damage our reproductive tissues
- Endocrine disruptors — chemicals that can cause damage through their ability to interfere with normal hormone function as the body manages growth, tissue repair and reproduction
- Persistent and/or bioaccumulative chemicals — these resist normal breakdown in the environment, building up in wildlife, the food chain and people, and lingering in body tissues for years or even decades after exposure
- Allergic/immunotoxicity — can manifest as allergic reactions or an impaired capacity to fight disease and repair damaged tissues in the body

The Nasty Truth

The list of the "worst of the worst" varies slightly among the different watchdogs. Not that they differ in perspectives but rather in the timing of the studies and who has the most current information. Gathering research is an expensive and independent endeavor. Each product test can cost between $100 and $200, and labs need to know what they think they are looking for and go from there. Each year, new hypotheses get tested and verified, and both the scientific bodies and the watchdogs get more precise about which chemicals are the worst.

As mentioned before, the EU has phased out 1,300 chemicals, almost 1,300 more than the US. As a result, multinational brands use different formulations for products made in Europe and North America, even for the same brand. Since conventional brands already make safer versions for Europeans consumers, the question becomes why don't they do the same here? Some say the change rests on consumers and our lack of outcry. It's also based on cost: synthetic and chemical ingredients are considerably cheaper than natural ingredients. Why change to a more expensive formula if consumers aren't demanding it? However, everyone agrees the worst are the chemicals that serve as fragrances, surfactants and preservatives.

Fragrance, or parfum, is a corporate catch-all for ingredients that may or may not have to do with scent. Due to an antiquated trade-secret law, brands and products are not required to disclose what is in this "special sauce." The word "fragrance" can indicate the presence of up to 4,000 different unlisted ingredients.[42] This proves problematic when you are trying to steer clear of specific chemicals. Sadly, "unscented" products are not necessarily a safer alternative. Often, chemicals used to "un" the scent (of chemicals) are more harmful than the ones that make the scents. The following nasties can lurk in "fragrance":

- Phthalates (pronounced thal-ates): These are common plasticizing ingredients that usually make plastic softer (like your shower curtain). But in fragrance, some phthalates bind to the "scent" and help it linger. Linked to birth defects in the reproductive system of boys at exposure levels typical for about one-quarter of US women, they also lower sperm-motility in adult men. Studies in laboratory animals show significant developmental toxicity and damage to adult reproductive, adrenal, liver and kidney organs.[43]

- Synthetic (artificial) musks: Environment Canada has categorized several synthetic musks as persistent, bioaccumulative and/or toxic, and others as human health priorities.[44] Artificial musks accumulate in our bodies and are often detected in breast milk and blood. They are linked to skin irritation, sensitization and even cancer in laboratory studies and are linked to reproductive and fertility problems in women at high levels of exposure. Separate laboratory studies also suggest that they affect hormone systems. While the European Union has banned use of some synthetic musks in cosmetics and personal care products, in the US all musk chemicals are still unregulated, and safe levels of exposure have not yet been set.[45]

- Styrene: This is a new discovery in the fragrance chemical soup; reports assert it is reasonably anticipated to be a human carcinogen.[46]

Surfactants lower water's surface tension, permitting it to spread out and penetrate more easily.[47] Used to make products foamy, sudsy or creamy, they are in shampoo, skin cleanser, body wash, shaving cream, toothpaste, mouthwash, moisturiser, sun cream, mascara and more.

- 1,4-dioxane: This carcinogen linked to organ toxicity is not added to products directly but rather is a petroleum-derived contaminate that is formed when ingredients react to each other. It is generated through a process called ethoxylation, in which ethylene oxide, a known breast carcinogen, is added to other chemicals to make them less harsh. Avoid sodium laureth sulfate, PEG compounds, chemicals that include the clauses xynol, ceteareth and oleth.[48] Ethylene oxide and 1,4-dioxane are prohibited on Health Canada's Cosmetic Ingredient Hotlist. However, the Hotlist does not control for the presence of these chemicals as contaminants.[49]

Preservatives are another controversial catch-all. If a product has any water in it — it needs a preservative. Water, over time, equals bacteria and mold. But the corporate incentive to have a long product shelf life comes at the expense of our shelf life.

- Formaldehyde: Some cosmetic chemicals are designed to react with water in the bottle to generate a little formaldehyde, which keeps the product from growing mold and bacteria. A 2010 study found that nearly one-fifth of cosmetic products contained a formaldehyde releaser. Formaldehyde is a carcinogen.[50]
- Parabens: This family of chemicals are used as antimicrobial preservatives in personal care products, pharmaceuticals and foods. These suspected endocrine disruptors have been detected in human breast cancer tissues, suggesting a possible association between parabens in cosmetics and cancer. Studies indicate that methylparaben applied on the skin reacts with UVB, leading to increased skin aging and DNA damage. Long-chained paprabens — isopropylparaben, butylparaben, methylparaben and isobutylparaben — act as estrogens and disrupt hormone signaling.[51] A recent study by scientists at the Harvard School of Public Health linked propylparaben to impaired fertility in women.[52] Parabens may also interfere with male reproductive functions.[53] To top

it all off, since parabens are used to kill bacteria, they inherently have some toxicity to cells.

- Triclosan and triclocarban: Triclosan is used as an antibacterial agent and a preservative to resist bacteria, fungus, mildew and odors. Also found in products that are advertised as "antibacterial." It can pass through skin and has been shown to interfere with thyroid signaling and male and female sex hormone signaling (endocrine disruption). Triclocarban is the active ingredient in some antibacterial bar soaps. Researchers have linked it to reproductive abnormalities in laboratory animals.[54]

It's becoming more common to see items in the shopping aisles listed as "-free," for example, "paraben-free" or "fragrance-free." Some brands have taken this as a new marketing opportunity. According to the watchdogs, "free" is not necessarily better. It often signals a switch to a different "new" chemical — one that perhaps hasn't been tested or explored.

Given all the research coming to light, it might seem odd that brands still use these formulations. Especially when, in the case of 1,4-dioxane, it has been shown that a single additional step in the creation process could eliminate that toxin. The Environmental Working Group reports:

> In a review conducted in 1982, the industry-funded Cosmetic Ingredient Review panel noted that the cosmetic industry was aware of the problem of 1,4-dioxane in cosmetics and was making an effort to reduce or remove the impurity. But decades later, FDA expresses continuing concerns about 1,4-dioxane, noting its potential to contaminate a wide range of products, and its ready penetration through the skin. FDA notes that 1,4-dioxane can be removed "by means of vacuum stripping at the end of the polymerization process without an unreasonable increase in raw material cost," but such treatment would be voluntary on the part of industry.[55]

Ignoring this simple safe-guarding step shows why it is essential for consumers to take caution. Our health and well-being are in our hands.

Know Your Labels

The first step to reading labels is looking at the ingredients. As mentioned earlier, this is not always the most ideal way, since many of the nastiest ingredients can be hidden in the fragrance. You can use the Skin Deep® Cosmetics Database (erg.org/skindeep) to get a rating — both on ingredients and products.

Another challenge to reading labels is that many conventional brands have co-opted terms like "pure," "natural," "healthy," "hypo-allergenic" — that are very loosely regulated. Even "organic" can be confusing, as it is occasionally part of the brand name or product name, hiding under name-not-claim confusion.

Here's a hypothetical example that highlights the confusion:

1. A manufacturer makes some body lotion.
2. The lotion contains some organic lavender essential oil but also contains 1,4-dioxane, the carcinogen formed by the reaction of common ingredients mixed together.
3. Certified United States Department of Agriculture (USDA) organic body care products are not allowed to contain harmful ingredients or chemicals. (However, they are allowed to contain a synthetic if there is no organic substitute.) Since the lotion contains 1,4-dioxane, it does not meet certification standards under the USDA organic certification process.
4. But since no one regulates the term "organic" and because the product does contain organic lavender oil, the manufacturer decides to label the lotion "Organically Herbal Lavender Lotion."
5. The new lotion heads to the shelves, where a consumer sees the product name, assumes it's safe and organic because it says "Organically Herbal" and chooses it.[56]

You can seek popular certifications like USDA Organic (see Figure I) and other European certifications. (Not only does Europe have higher chemical restrictions but they also have a greater array of recognizable certification and consumer labels for brands.)

Lastly, you can write the brand. Non-toxic beauty brands want users to have a closer relationship with them than just through their ingredient list. The list is a good place to start, but many non-toxic makers and manufacturers want consumers to be curious. Many share not only their full list of ingredients, but also why they choose to use them. While researching this book, I found many happy to discuss not only their formulations but why (and how) they are non-toxic. And why certifications (Figure I) are chosen or not chosen. There isn't one harmonizing certification for non-toxic beauty brands. Here are some of the most common and what they mean.

Figure I

1. The Soil Association 2. ECOCERT 3. NATRUE the International Natural & Organic Cosmetics Association 4. BDIH 5. COSMEBIO the French Professional Association for Natural, Ecological and Organic cosmetics 6. ICEA, Environmental and Ethical Certification Institute 7. USDA Organic Seal 8. NSF "contains organic ingredients" mark 9. Vegan Society 10. PETA Cruelty-free 11. The Leaping Bunny 12. Period After Opening (PAO)

Although the USDA[57] doesn't certify cosmetics or personal care products, if brands are using agricultural ingredients and follow the USDA food-grade guidelines, they can use the **USDA Organic label**. To say "organic," products must contain at least 95 percent organically produced ingredients. They may display the USDA Organic Seal and must include the certifying agent's name and address. To say "Made with organic ingredients," products must contain at least 70 percent organic ingredients and product labels can list up to three of the organic ingredients or "food" groups on the principal display panel. Products with less than 70 percent organic ingredients cannot use the term "organic" on the principal display panel.

Since the agricultural-based USDA mark isn't always appropriate for personal care products, the American National Standards Institute (ANSI) created a mark that allows for limited chemical processes that are typical for personal care products (but not allowed for food products). The voluntary standard **NSF "contains organic ingredients"** covers products with 70 percent or more organic ingredients.

Similar to USDA, the **Soil Association Organic Standard** is a UK-based certifying body that awards its seal to products whose total contents are 100 percent certified organic, 95 percent certified organic or whose contents contain at least 70 percent certified organic ingredients, where the remaining 30 percent are non-toxic, plant-based, GMO-free ingredients that pose no known risk to health or environment.

ECOCERT, another organic certification organization, was founded in France in 1991. Although based in Europe, it conducts inspections in over 80 countries, making it one of the largest organic certification organizations in the world. ECOCERT prohibits the use of synthetic perfumes and synthetic preservatives like parabens, mineral oil, propylene glycol and other synthetic ingredients.

BDIH, a German private sector label for "Certified Natural Products," does not allow synthetic fragrances, dyes and petroleum products or commonly used paraben preservatives.

NATRUE, by the International Natural & Organic Cosmetics Association, a non-profit based in Brussels, Belgium, guarantees that the product has been created using a manufacturing process that avoids unnecessary synthetic processing; uses environmentally friendly practices;

has no synthetic fragrances and colors, no petroleum-derived products (paraffin, PEG, -proplyl, -alkyl, etc.), no silicone oils and derivatives, no genetically modified ingredients (complying with EU organic regulation); and has not been tested on animals. About 1,400 products carry this seal.

Quality Assurance International (QAI), a USDA-accredited organic certifier (also owned by NSF), has made an agreement with NATRUE to streamline the certification process for companies interested in pursuing certification to both standards. Under the agreement, companies certified to NSF in the US now have the option to simultaneously garner NATRUE certification in the EU.

COSMEBIO® is the seal from the Professional Association for Natural, Ecological and Organic Cosmetics in France. Since 2002, COSMEBIO has been working to promote natural and ecological cosmetics made with ingredients from organic farming and developed using green technologies (green chemistry). All 9,000+ products with this seal have been paraben-free since 2002.

ICEA, the Environmental and Ethical Certification Institute in Italy, is a consortium that certifies 170 companies and 3,000 products that are safe and natural products, without chemical substances harmful to humans, animals or the environment.

The words "cruelty-free" or "not tested on animals" do not always guarantee that the chemicals or other ingredients, in their pure or original state, were not tested on animals.[58] Cruelty-free wording often refers to voluntary pledges by brands that their final formulation (the product itself) is not tested on animals. The **Leaping Bunny** program is more robust. Companies sign a pledge not to test on animals during any stage of product development. The company's ingredient suppliers make the same pledge, assuring that the entire product is free of animal testing. The **PETA Cruelty-free** bunny certification is similar.

If You Can't Eat It

Dr. Pratima Raichur, a New York City-based Ayurvedic physician, chemist and botanist and doctor of naturopathy, is the creator of Pratima Skincare. Ayurveda, a 5,000-year-old system of medicine that originated in India, focuses on natural healing and stresses the use of plant-based medicines and treatments. Dr. Raichur's advice, and the principle behind her Ayurvedic line of skincare products at her SoHo spa, coincides with what we have said: "When you buy a beauty product, read the label." She goes one step further and advises, "If you cannot eat what is in the bottle, do not put it on your skin."[59]

Dr. Raichur began, like many of the brands on the following pages, trying to make a "better" product. In her case, it was for relief of acne and skin irritation for friends at work. She, like many of the skin care brands listed in the shopping guide, believes that rather than stripping the skin, what the skin really needs is to be fed. And, since skin is such an absorbent organ, it should be fed healthy food: herbs, oils — even probiotics.

Treating your personal care products like food and considering how they contribute (or detract) from your health may seem like an impossible standard. For some, it may even feel like a diet, a host of things you "can't have." But the reality is non-toxic brands are, in many cases, not only better than conventional brands but better *for* you.

I asked makeup artist Katey Denno, whose client list includes celebrities with stellar skin like Julianne Moore, Amanda Seyfried, Christy Turlington and Amber Heard, for some advice. Katey is frequently asked to speak at makeup and skin care events and often teaches large and small groups about "green" makeup and skin care options. Her beauty direction has graced the pages of *Vogue*, *Glamour*, *ELLE*, *InStyle* and *Nylon*. She shares this:

> The majority of the products in the green beauty world are, at this point, on par with those you'll find in the mainstream mass market — particularly when it comes to skin care. Additionally helpful are the countless blogs devoted to honest, ruthless reviews of these "green" skin care product lines. Doing a little research will get you just the right regimen to get your skin to look and feel gorgeous.[60]

The following pages will highlight some of the best and cleanest brands around. This journey towards cleaner, greener products will require some trial and error. Luckily, almost every brand listed in the shopping guide sells travel sizes — your opportunity to try, for a smaller investment, and decide if a new product will be right for you.

Hair

Given the size of your scalp in relation to your body, you might think shampoo and conditioner can't be that bad. However, don't forget that, as you rinse, all those chemicals run down your body and then right into the water systems. Ugh. Not to mention how close styling products come to your face for inhaling and possibly ingesting.

Shampoo was created in the early 20th century, and the surfactants and chemicals that make it do what it does — feel silky in our hand, lather and foam and rinse out without too much residue — haven't changed much since the 1930s. However, back then, hair washing was a once-a-week activity, not the daily ritual for so many today. Also, take into account all the added products we have incorporated into our habits. For some, hair care can involve four or five products. Our obsession with hair is contributing to our toxic load and body burden in ways we need to examine.

Surfactants, additives, preservatives and fragrance are all at play here, and recently the watchdogs have noticed by-products of concern. For example, DEA, a foam booster, is not a known toxicant, but when it sits on the shelf for some time, it can react with other chemicals to form nitrosamines. These potent and easily absorbed carcinogenic by-products are linked to stomach, esophagus, liver and bladder cancer.[61]

Hair Dyes and Relaxers

Many women (and men) use hair dye, so it's surprising that green chemistry is lacking when it comes to coloring, straightening and otherwise changing our hair. Cancer.org stays on the fence about dye and posts on its website, "It's not clear how much personal hair dye use might raise cancer risk, if at all."[62] Not very definitive, but what is definitive is that dyes, highlights, straighteners, relaxers and perms all carry their own toxic load.

We've spent so much time trying to rid the world of lead and being cautious about lead poisoning, it's shocking that it is still in some products, like gradual hair dyes for men. You know, the soft "natural-looking" color that allows men to step back from grey in three weeks? Those may contain lead acetate, which can increase the body's lead level. Because lead is a potent neurotoxin, lead acetate has already been banned in Canada and the European Union. However, it is not banned in the US.[63]

For other kinds of dyes, the greatest concern is coal tar, a mixture of petroleum-derived chemicals. Coal tars and coal tar pitches are known human carcinogens. The specific components of coal tar used in hair dyes, aromatic amines, have been shown to mutate and cause cancer in animals. P-phenylenediamine, another coal tar used in many hair dyes, has been linked to tumors in laboratory tests conducted by the US National Cancer Institute. Bad news for brunettes: darker hair dyes tend to contain more phenylenediamine than lighter colours.[64] If you are a regular hair dyer, be aware that an increasing number of studies of humans link long-time hair dye use with cancer, including bladder cancer, non-Hodgkin's lymphoma and multiple myeloma.[65]

Remember the Brazilian blow-out? Almost as soon as it came to North America, the keratin-based hair-smoothing treatment was outed for its toxicity, containing high levels of formaldehyde, also called methylene glycol (up to 10 percent), even when labeled "formaldehyde-free." But, little has been said or done for other relaxers. Products marketed to black women (like hair relaxers and skin lighteners) contain some of the most toxic chemicals used by the cosmetics industry. Many have never even been assessed for safety.[66] African Americans have a 41 percent greater rate of invasive breast cancer than white women (21 percent). African American women under 40 not only have a higher incidence of breast cancer than white women under 40, they are more likely to die of the disease at any age. Risk factors don't necessarily explain ethnic variations.[67] Here are some of the nasties in relaxers and their health concerns:

- BHA: immune system toxicity, cancer, hormone disruption, organ toxicity buildup in our bodies
- Coumarin: immune system toxicity, reproductive harm, cancer, cell damage
- Hydroquinone: immune system and skin toxicity, cancer, reproductive harm
- Octoxynol-40: mutagen, cancer, immune system toxicity; may be contaminated with 1,4-dioxane or ethylene oxide: linked to cancer[68]

This would be a good chance to talk about the societal and cultural pressure we all feel to change our hair and try to deconstruct that, but let's move on. If you dye, relax or both, none is best and less is better. Perhaps consider decreasing your chemical load in other areas. Let's look at shampoo, conditioners and styling aids; they offer some great non-toxic alternatives.

The Alternatives

Changing to a healthier hair care line might fill you with dread. Finding products that work can be a long, expensive and time-consuming process. Some are opting out of shampoo altogether. Perhaps you have heard of the No Shampoo movement (**No Poo**). It's been around since the 1970s or even earlier. Hair fashion trends such as beach hair or bed head are basically advocating less wash for better, fuller hair. No Poo-ers agree, rejecting conventional shampoo hair washing altogether.

Some think that conventional hair washing is a societal norm that harms rather than helps hair, believing that shampooing every day removes sebum, the oil produced by the scalp. This causes the sebaceous glands to produce oil at a higher rate, to compensate for what is lost during shampooing. We wash every day because the hair is greasy; but the hair is greasy because we wash every day.

No Poo-ers proclaim that by not using conventional shampoos they are saving money, saving the environment and reducing their toxic load. The Internet is full of techniques, video how-tos and blogs, but in a nutshell, the purest way to No Poo is to only rinse your hair. Others swear by washing with dissolved baking soda, using vinegar to balance the pH and then some add honey or oils like coconut or olive. Advocates swear that it leads to fuller, shinier hair.

An alternative to No Poo is **Co-Washing**, washing only with conditioner, which is preferred by those with thick or curly hair. Like vinegar used by No Poo-ers, conditioner acts as a pH balancer for Co-Washers. The Internet abounds with different techniques and strategies. Those with curls say it produces the best curls of their lives.

Then there's the possibility that we've been doing it all wrong. When researching for their book *No More Dirty Looks*, Siobhan O'Connor and Alexandra Spunt sat down with Horst Rechelbacher, dubbed the Father

of Safe Cosmetics,[69] who advised them to wash hair "backwards,"
saying:

> When you wash your hair, try using your conditioner first. If
> you want to go all the way, put oils on your scalp, give your-
> self a nice massage, and then comb it through. Next, wet it
> down, put conditioner all over your hair and then also all
> over your body. Wash yourself with the conditioner, then
> rinse it all off. Then, you use shampoo.[70]

Rechelbacher was referring to his "so clean you can eat it" product
line: Intelligent Nutrients. (Please don't coat your body with a conventional products.)

If you want the traditional shampoo and conditioner combina-
tion, you might have to try several to find one that's a fit. Without the
(chemical) foam boosters, non-toxic shampoos don't all lather the way
conventional ones do. Without the silicone and plastics in conditioners, you won't have the same tangle-free experience you are used to.
But, fingers crossed, you'll find one that works. When I moved on to my
current favorite, the friend who recommended the brand warned that it
would "take a while" to get accustomed. She was right — it took over a
month of stringy, lifeless, yet frizzy hair for my hair to finally look and
feel "normal."

Shopping Guide

- **Acure Organics**, acureorganics.com, is a family-owned and operated
  company founded on sustainable principles. Each product is free from
  animal testing, parabens, sulfates, phthalates, synthetic fragrances,
  harmful preservatives and artificial colors. Acure uses plant stem cell
  technology coupled with avocado, lemongrass, quinoa protein, acai
  and argan oil and as many certified organic ingredients as possible.
  Many products bear the USDA organic seal. Shampoo, conditioner and
  hair oil. Also active in skin care, body care and lip balms.

- **Aubrey® Organics**, aubrey-organics.com. Aubrey Hampton, a phy-
  tochemist and herbalist, founded Aubrey Nature Labs in 1967 and is
  a pioneer offering plant-based, synthetic-free personal care products.

Aubrey's list of "firsts" in the industry is impressive: the first to use coconut fatty acids in hair and skin care; first to formulate cosmetic products with jojoba oil, evening primrose, blue camomile and more; first to develop a natural preservative with citrus extract and vitamins A, C and E; and the first cosmetic manufacturer to be certified as an organic processor. Nearly every health food store in the United States and Canada carries the products, which are also sold throughout Europe, Asia and South America. Certified Leaping Bunny, NSF, USDA Organic and BDIH. Aubrey has a complex Hair Care Matrix to help you find the perfect product for your hair type. Also makes organic styling aids and a dark brown hair dye. Also active in skin care, bath and spa, body lotion, fragrance, deodorant, makeup, baby and men's products.

- **Desert Essence®**, desertessence.com, founded in 1978, was one of the first companies to introduce jojoba oil and tea tree oil to the US. Certified Leaping Bunny, and several products are certified to NSF standard. Shampoo and conditioners by ingredient (shea butter, jojoba, red grape), plus styling products. Also active in skin care, bath and body oils, dental care and baby products.

- **Intelligent Nutrients**, intelligentnutrients.com, was founded by Horst M. Rechelbacher, perhaps better known for founding Aveda Corporation in 1978, which he later sold to Estée Lauder. Intelligent Nutrients uses 100 percent food-based and organic certified ingredients. The son of an herbalist, Horst was a hairstylist, an active environmentalist, artist and organic farmer. His organic farm in Wisconsin, which is solar, wind and geothermal powered, grows plant ingredients for Intelligent Nutrients products. The company mission is "Everything we put in and on our bodies must be nutritious and safe." Products are USDA Organic, Soil Association Organic, Cosmos Organic, ICEA and Leaping Bunny certified. Shampoo, conditioner, hair treatments, style and finishing products as well as a range of tools and accessories. Also active in skin care, body care, aroma, nutraceuticals and lip care.

- **John Masters™ Organics**, johnmasters.com. Also a hairstylist, John Masters became concerned about the chemicals he was working with and became committed to a toxic-free salon. He created his first product in 1991. All product ingredients must be harvested in an environmentally friendly manner (wild-crafted), have no artificial colors, fragrances or fillers and undergo no animal testing. Everything is made with 70 to 100 percent organic content, and organic ingredients are certified organic by ECOCERT, QAI, California Certified Organic Farmers or Organic Crop Improvement Association. Several items are USDA certified. Line includes shampoos, conditioners, styling products and tools. Also active in skin care, body care, men's grooming and pet care (shampoo and conditioner).

- **Shea Moisture**, sheamoisture.com. Perfect for kinky, curly and wavy hair, Shea Moisture relies on the recipes of Sofi Tucker, the daughter of healers in Sierra Leone. Widowed at 19, Sofi made handmade shea butter, African black soap and other natural remedies, selling them in local villages to support her family. Four generations later, her grandson is committed to including natural, certified organic and ethically sourced ingredients that help solve hair and skin concerns. Cruelty-free hair products include shampoos, conditioners, co-wash, hair color, hair kits, kids' hair kit, leave-ins, masques and men's products. Also active in skin care, body and baby lines.

- **skinnyskinny**, skinnyskinny.com. Those not ready to No Poo might like to transition with organic dry shampoo. Clara Williams, owner and founder, is an aromatherapist who started her soap and skincare line more than a decade ago. The organic product line is *skinny* of all filler ingredients. Talc-free dry shampoo and styling waxes. Also active in skin care, soaps, body scrubs, bath soaks, aromatherapeutic room sprays and soy candles. Vegan (with the sole exception of a beeswax lip balm) and Leaping Bunny certified.

Skin Care

Another relatively easy switch might come in your skin care regime. Katey Denno advises:

> If you're new to the world of green beauty and feeling overwhelmed with the many options — none of which are from brands you've ever seen in commercials, or attached to celebrity endorsers, it can be daunting enough to make you go back to your mainstream drugstore or beauty counter

purchasing. I always encourage women to start cleaning up their makeup bags with the addition of natural skin care and lip color since those two categories have absolutely arrived.[71]

Non-toxic brands are often started by women who are trying to fill a void. Like Dr. Raichur concocting an Ayurvedic remedy of herbs and oils for her colleagues to help battle acne, many of the women at the forefront of non-toxic skincare started trying to fix a skin ailment. California-based chemist Marie Veronique Nadeau (founder of Marie Veronique) shares,

> Twelve years ago I got fed up battling rosacea and throwing hope and money at dozens of products that didn't work. So I took matters into my own hands. My kitchen became my lab, and I started experimenting with the best and healthiest ingredients I could find. My final formula not only relieved my rosacea, but also grabbed the attention of friends needing solutions to their own skin conditions. Before long, I had new products and a new business that supported my philosophy — promoting personal well-being and an eco-conscious lifestyle. I love talking with my customers about the formulation process — and could talk for hours about research, and the ingredients we use — and why. It's all about finding out what my customers need and creating safe, healthy solutions that really work.[72]

All the brands listed here share the same motive. Each has concocted different formulas and different regimens, but with the same aspect at their core: healthy skin without chemicals or additives.

Shopping Guide

- **Beauty Counter**, beautycounter.com, dedicated to producing products as lush as conventional ones, has a list of over 1,500 ingredients it won't use (a list more extensive than the EU's restricted list). Plus, for women who love to evangelize their products (and make money doing so), Beauty Counter is a member of the Direct Selling Association. Certified B Corporation. The website is dedicated to transparency, and every product lists EWG's Skin Deep Rating. Skin care line includes cleansers, moisturizers, toners, oils, eye treatments. Also active in body, hair and makeup and has a line of hair and bath products called Kids Counter.

- **The Body Shop®**, thebodyshop.co.uk, has included natural and organic ingredients for many years, but its Nutriganics™ products represent the first certified line. Nutriganics also includes organic ingredients provided by organic Community Fair Trade producers; The Body Shop's global network of fair trade producers ensure that ingredients are grown sustainably, with respect for the environment and the people who cultivate and harvest them. Nutriganics' Community Fair Trade ingredients include organic aloe vera from Guatemala, organic cold-pressed coconut oil from Samoa, organic olive oil from Italy and wild-harvested babassu oil from Brazil. Certified ECOCERT and Leaping Bunny, the line includes facial wash, toner, day and night creams, serum, mask and eye care.

- **Kahina Giving Beauty™**, kahina-givingbeauty.com. Founder Katharine L'Heureux discovered argan oil in 2008 on the first of many journeys to Morocco. All argan oil purchased by Kahina Giving Beauty has been certified organic by ECOCERT. The brand has just added prickly pear seed oil that is 100 percent organic. Certified Leaping Bunny and Forest Stewardship Council. (The FSC label ensures that the forest products used are from responsibly harvested and verified sources). Skin care line includes oil, cleanser, mist, lotions, serums and eye treatments. Also active in body balms and soaps.

- **MÁDARA®**, madaracosmetics.com. MÁDARA Organic Skincare is a Latvian manufacturer of organic skin care products. Ingredients include biologically certified blossoms and herbal extracts from certified organic farms and approved suppliers in the Baltic region. Having conducted research with the Laboratory of Bioanalytical and Biodosimetry Methods of the University of Latvia and the Rīga Stradiņš University on the ability of biologically active substances of plants to reduce aging, its complex Galium7 is a water-free anti-aging cosmetic formula that is based on birch juice. ECOCERT and Certified B Corporation. Skin care line includes cleansers, toners, moisturizers, eye care, lip care and tinted moisturizers. Also active in hair, baby and body care, including products for cellulite and stretch marks.

- **Marie Veronique**, marieveronique.com. Marie Veronique Nadeau, who founded Marie Veronique over ten years ago, collaborates with her daughter Jay, a physicist and bio-medical engineer, on formulations to balance the skin's microbiota (microflora to help reduce the inflammation that leads to skin irritations, rashes, rosacea and other signs of distressed skin by keeping opportunistic bacteria in check). The line specializes in products that relieve problem skin conditions like aging, hyperpigmentation, rosacea and acne. Skin care line includes cleanser, mist, oils (including vegan), serum and sun protection.

- **Pratima Ayurvedic Skincare**, pratimaskincare.com. Dr. Pratima Raichur, an expert chemist, botanist and Ayurvedic physician and doctor of naturopathy, combines her traditional Ayurvedic formulations and harvests them into modern-day prescriptions that target the real reasons behind skincare issues. 100 percent organic and therapeutic-grade essential oils, cruelty-free and Sattvic — non-harming to any living being, certified lead-free and metal-free herbs. Skin care line includes cleansers, essential oils, moisturizers, masks and eye treatments. Also active in bath and body oils, hair and sun protection.

- **Tata Harper™ Skincare**, tataharperskincare.com. Tata Harper works with chemists, biologists, botanists and integrated medicine practitioners hand-crafting proprietary, natural and high-performance skin care. All of the products are 100 percent manufactured and bottled in its own facilities in Vermont. Certified Vermont Made, Leaping Bunny, ECOCERT, certified Organic by Vermont Organic Farmers, American Vegetarian Association. Skin care line includes antiaging serums, cleansers, moisturizers, toners, masks, eye cream, exfoliators. Also active in lip care, aromatherapy and body care.

Perfume, Cologne, Parfum, Fragrance

Studies show that women are swayed by scent, attaching positive emotions with certain smells. It's one reason household cleaning agents from floor wax to laundry detergents are scented — marketers try to capitalize on that. Women are also more likely to suffer from fragrance allergy than men and more likely to suffer adverse effects from exposure to fragrance chemicals,[73] partly because women use more scented products than men do. Also women generally carry a higher percentage of body fat; many of the chemicals that make up "fragrance" tend to bioaccumulate in fat tissue.

It's almost impossible to escape; almost everything we use is scented. In your morning routine, count how many products you use and how many contain fragrance:

- 96 percent of shampoos
- 98 percent of conditioners
- 97 percent of hair styling products
- 95 percent of shaving products
- 91 percent of lip moisturizers
- 91 percent of antiperspirants
- 83 percent of moisturizers
- 71 percent of lipsticks
- 63 percent of sunblocks
- 58 percent of foundations
- 33 percent of blushes and eyeliners[74]

The more products in your routine, the heavier your chemical load. Plus, no one is certain what the long-term health effects are from fragrance chemicals. This is all before you've added your "signature scent" — that spray of perfume or cologne, like the icing on our chemical cake.

The Economics of Perfume

In her book *Deluxe: How Luxury Lost Its Luster*, Dana Thomas writes, "Perfume is luxury's most accessible and powerful product. It serves as an introduction to, as well as a flag-bearer for, a brand — and it reaps great profits"[75] — to the tune of $25 billion in annual sales.[76] While we might dream that the high price we are paying is attributed to heritage ingredients of the finest quality, in reality the opposite is true. Most of it pays for the marketing campaign and exclusive distribution. An exposé in French weekly *L'Obs* revealed that for a €100 (Euro) bottle of perfume, the value of the fragrance concentrate is between €1 and €1.50 (about $2 to $3) — the rest is packaging, marketing, taxes, etc.[77]

When it comes to natural scent, it takes 150 pounds of lavender, 500 pounds of rosemary, 1,000 pounds of jasmine and over 2,000 pounds of roses to make a single pound of essential oil! The price of each essential oil is directly related to the amount of plant material needed for distillation.[78] Synthetic ingredients (and their chemical bases) are far less expensive than true essences. Real jasmine, for example, costs $2,500 per pound, whereas a synthetic jasmine scent can cost between $3 and $18 per pound.

The first synthetic was created in this industry in 1853, and by 1920 chemists had created 80 percent of the synthetics used today. Over the years, essences and essential oils distilled from natural ingredients have been replaced by cheaper synthetic materials. In Thomas's book, one industry expert estimates only 10 percent of ingredients used to create perfumes today are natural;[79] the remaining 90 percent are synthetic. Patricia Ronning, perfumer and clinical aromatherapist at Intelligent Nutrients shares, "When Chanel N°5 was created, aldehyde had just been discovered, and in fact, Chanel owes its unique smell to an overdose of aldehyde in the formulation."[80]

Synthetics play a role in every conventional perfume. There are over 300 scents in the natural world, and synthetics can increase that number to 3,000. "The synthetic process of isolating components is what makes perfumes smell the way they do," explains Ronning. "Manufacturers don't use the full essential oil, they use components."[81]

But those components are becoming more worrisome by the day. The EU is slowly banning specific ones that it suspects are linked to health hazards. One of the first, set to be banned in 2015, is a synthetic molecule called HICC, or lyral, which replicates the smell of lily of the valley. Lyral has been discovered to cause dermatitis (skin irritations or eczema) in allergy sufferers. Brands that use it and sell in the EU will have to reformulate.[82]

Although that's a step in the right direction, a 2010 report from Women's Voices for the Earth (WVE) cautioned there is concern about chronic health impacts from daily exposure to fragrance chemicals. Those of concern, such as synthetic musks and phthalates, have been linked in animal and some human studies to the disruption of estrogen, testosterone and thyroid hormones. This disruption can have significant lifelong effects on reproductive health and development, particularly when exposure occurs during pregnancy. In a study of men undergoing treatment at an infertility clinic, higher levels of MEP (a breakdown product of diethyl phthalate) were highly associated with sperm DNA damage, raising concern that diethyl phthalate exposure could affect fertility.[83]

Furthermore, body burden studies reveal these chemicals are in our blood, in breast milk and even in newborn children. Synthetic musks were present in seven out of ten newborns tested. Not only are synthetic musks persistent in the environment,[84] but a recent animal study found that low levels of nitro- and polycyclic musks interfere with the ability of structures in cell walls to keep toxic substances from entering the cell. By disturbing a cell's natural ability to fend off toxic chemicals, musks could allow poisons to build up within cells and cause damage. Human cells have the same cell wall structures as those examined in the study, indicating a cause for concern.[85]

Since fragrance is both ubiquitous and toxic, your choices for reduced exposure are varied: reduce your overall chemical load from artificial fragrances in conventional personal care products (and cleaning and laundering products), give up perfume or cologne, or switch to a non-toxic, natural perfume. The latter will require some adjusting as natural perfumes smell nothing like conventional perfumes — they are formulated with essential oils and are like walking through a field of flowers. Natural perfumes are built with chords of high, middle and low notes that provide a subtle journey as they change throughout the day.

The connection between scent and a sense of well-being for mind, body and spirit has been the basis of aromatherapy since the dawn of time. Conventional perfumes cannot be used for aromatherapy, but natural perfumes can. They can also contain a biological component that resonates with the wearer. A natural perfume smells good, can uplift, calm and heal yet contributes nothing to your body burden of toxic chemicals.

Shopping Guide

- **A Perfume Organic**, aperfumeorganic.com, founded by Amanda Walker in 2009, offers five signature scents blended from USDA-certified organic botanicals, hand-poured in Manhattan in small batches to maintain purity. The petite bottle comes in a flower seed-embedded box that can be planted and recycled as an effort to reduce wasteful packaging. Vegan and PETA Cruelty-free.

- **Buddha Nose**, buddhanose.com. Founder Amy Galper, a certified aromatherapist and Shiatsu practitioner, has always been an advocate for healthy living and smart consumption. Started in 2004, all products are still made by hand. Certified USDA organic. Sprays and balms. Also active in body scrubs and body oil.

- **Intelligent Nutrients**, intelligentnutrients.com, founded by Horst M. Rechelbacher, perhaps better known for founding Aveda Corporation in 1978 (which he later sold to Estée Lauder) uses 100 percent food-based and organic-certified ingredients. The company mission is "Everything we put in and on our bodies must be nutritious and safe." Products are USDA Organic, Soil Association Organic, Cosmos Organic, ICEA and Leaping Bunny certified. Aroma care line includes blends to provide energetic balance; essences of Jasmine, Neroli or Rose; aromatherapy remedies and aroma jewelry. Also active in hair care, skin care, body care, nutraceuticals and lip care.

- **rareEARTH Naturals**®, rareearthnaturals.com. Made in the US, rareESSENCE perfumes are made from 100 percent pure essential oils distilled from plants, seeds, roots and other botanicals around the world. Sourced close to farmers and hand-blended in small batches by master perfumers, the fragrances use rare raw materials like resins, concretes and absolutes. rareESSENCE perfumes are blended to reduce stress, enhance spiritual peace, increase mental alertness, strengthen will, inspire creativity or desire, or balance emotions. Certified Leaping Bunny and a Green America-certified business. Perfumes available in spray or roll-on. Also makes candles, diffusers and room mists.

- **VERED Organic Botanicals**, veredbotanicals.com. Creator and founder Vered Black is a New York-based esthetician and herbalist with over two decades of experience integrating phytotherapy into her practice. The line started when clients asked Black to bottle her customized facial oil blends, which many then wore as a "perfume" throughout the day. Vegan and cruelty-free. Perfumes available in three scents. Also active in skin care and body care.

Body

Now that you're armed with knowledge about "fragrance" (you probably can't name one product you use that doesn't have fragrance of some sort), there's more to discuss. As mentioned earlier, be wary of surfactants — the chemicals that make things bubble and foam. Sodium lauryl sulfate (SLS) and sodium laureth sulfate (SLES) are commonly used in shampoos but also shower gels, facial cleansers, shaving creams and toothpaste. They can cause skin irritation or trigger allergies. SLS has also been associated with eczema.[86] Depending on the manufacturing process, SLES may also be contaminated with measurable amounts of ethylene oxide and 1,4-dioxane (as previously mentioned, a carcinogen linked to organ toxicity).[87]

DEA (diethanolamine), cocamide DEA and lauramide DEA are listed in the David Suzuki Foundation "Dirty Dozen." Also used to make cosmetics creamy or sudsy or as a pH adjuster to counteract the acidity of other ingredients, they are found in soaps, cleansers and shampoos. DEA and its compounds cause mild to moderate skin and eye irritation. In laboratory experiments, exposure to high doses has been shown to cause liver cancers and precancerous changes in skin and thyroids. The EU classifies DEA as harmful on the basis of danger of serious damage to health from prolonged exposure.[88]

Shopping Guide

- **Dr. Bronner's Magic Soaps**, drbronner.com. This made-in-US brand has over 150 years of soapmaking experience. Dr. Bronner's started sourcing certified organic ingredients in 2000 but took exception to (what it perceived was) questionable pricing, wages and working conditions for farmers. Wanting to create a supply chain that offered fairness and empowerment for farmers, workers and their communities, in 2006 Dr. Bronner's committed to sourcing raw materials from certified Fair Trade and organic projects around the world that ensure fair prices, living wages and community benefits for farmers, workers and their families. USDA certified and Leaping Bunny. Body care includes castile liquid soaps, bar soaps, shaving gels, lotions, baby and sensitive skin care and body balms.

- **Dr. Hauschka**, dr.hauschka.com. Dr. Rudolf Hauschka started his company in Germany in 1935 with the goal "to support the healing of humanity and the earth." The natural skin care products are created from over 150 plants grown on its 11-acre farm or sourced from other biodynamic or organic farms. If an organic version of a raw material is not available on the global market, the Dr. Hauschka team initiates organic farming projects. NATRUE certified. Body care includes body washes, bath essences, body creams and deodorant. Also active in skin care and makeup.

- **Lavera Naturkosmetik**, truenatural.com, founded by Thomas Haase. In Latin *lavera* means "the truth." Haase, who suffered from neurodermatitis since he was a child, began cultivating plants and developing formulations for natural cosmetics that might help his skin. After more than ten years of research and cosmetic development, he launched Lavera in 1987. Certified organic, NATRUE and committed to cruelty-free, Lavera products are designed for even the most sensitive skin. Products include body wash, body creams, body oils, bath oils, sea salts, skin care for babies and children, deodorant and dental care. Also active in skin care and makeup.

- **Pangea Organics**, pangeaorganics.com, based in Boulder, Colorado, was founded in 2000 by Joshua Scott Onysko. Made in small batches, organic ingredients are sourced from international organic farmers (with fair trade certification when possible). Pangea also offers social selling — brand evangelists can become "Beauty Ecologists" and earn commission. Certified organic under USDA and NSF standards (all products contain at least 70 percent organic content). Products include hand soaps, body washes, body lotions, body oils. Also active in skin care.

Deodorants

Conventional deodorants often have aluminum, meant to "form a temporary plug within the sweat duct that stops the flow of sweat to the skin's surface,"[89] parabens and fragrance. When it comes to shaving, even the cleaner brands recommend not applying deodorant to freshly shaved areas. Common advice is: shave the night before and apply deodorant in the morning. Or, on the days you shave, go without. Here are some "cleaner" versions (for both sexes).

- **Duggan Sisters**, duggansisters.com. Unable to find a natural deodorant that worked and aware of natural products' effects on lymphatic wellness, in 2003 the Duggan sisters created Lifestinks, a natural deodorant made with three ingredients: aluminum-free sodium bicarbonate, tea tree oil and lavender oil. They've added cedarwood for a more masculine scent.

- **LOVEFRESH**, lovefresh.com. What began seven years ago as a "kitchen chemistry" experiment after Canadian Stacey Davis studied aromatherapy, has evolved into a line of body care products that includes an all-natural deodorant cream that comes in four scents. (Both sexes rave about the Lemon Verbena.)

- **Weleda**, weleda.com, created in Switzerland in 1921, was named after the Celtic goddess of wisdom and healing. It cultivates its own Biodynamic® gardens and believes natural ingredients provide what a body needs to be vibrant, beautiful and well. NATRUE certified, Weleda deodorants use essential oils and all natural ingredients to neutralize odor-causing bacteria. Also active in skin care, body care, baby and mother care products, oral and hair care.

These brands, listed in other sections, also make deodorants:

- **Dr. Hauschka**, dr.hauschka.com, makes both a roll-on and a body powder that maintains the skin's healthy pH balance and absorbs perspiration.

- **Lavera Naturkosmetik**, truenatural.com, makes a mild, all-natural roll-on deodorant.

Dental Care

I mentioned coal tar in the hair section as a carcinogen used to make pigment, but it can also show up in toothpaste as a synthetic dye — as can SLS and triclosan. The Internet abounds with homemade solutions (the simplest is baking soda, water and a drop or two of peppermint essential oil), but here are some non-toxic store-bought options.

Shopping Guide

- **The Honest Company**, honest.com. Co-founded by actress Jessica Alba, who has been actively involved with charities such as Safer Chemicals Healthy Families, ONE, Habitat for Humanity, Project

HOME and more, The Honest Company is a family brand of made-in-the-US, sustainable, eco-friendly products. Certified B Corporation and Green America, the toothpaste has no flouride, no artificial sweeteners, flavors or dyes. It makes a mouthwash and a natural strawberry toothpaste for kids. Also active in hair, body care, sun care, household cleaners and all things baby (diapers, wipes, creams, balms).

These brands, listed in other sections, also make toothpaste:

- **Weleda**, weleda.com, produces several options, including a calendula toothpaste, free of peppermint oil, making it a favorite among homeopathic practitioners, flavored with organic fennel oil and licorice. Also makes children's tooth gel and mouthwash.

- **Lavera Naturkosmetik**, truenatural.com, uses formulas with carvon oil, which is suitable for homeopathic treatment, strawberry flavour for children or fresh mint for adults. It contains sodium fluoride to harden tooth enamel and is certified vegan and organic.

- **Desert Essence**, desertessence.com, makes toothpaste with neem, an ayurvedic extract known for its dental benefits, baking soda and tea tree oil. Flavored with pure essential oil of wintergreen, it is fluoride- and gluten-free.

Men's Products

Not to be left out of the story, in 2012 Environmental Defence Canada conducted research on the contents the shaving kits of five men in four provinces in Canada. It tested ingredients in seventeen typical conventional products — Old Spice deodorant, Axe hair gel, Head and Shoulders shampoo, Gillette Shaving Cream and other aftershave, shampoo, body wash, shaving cream and deodorant brands and found the following:

- Four products contained probable human carcinogens.
- Five products contained chemicals known to harm male reproductive health.
- Ten products had artificial musks, some of which are shown to disrupt hormones in animals.[90]

With more conventional product lines dedicated specifically to men, men need to count chemicals too, especially *endocrine disruptors* that act as hormone-disruptors Hormones act as the body's internal communications system, and some common chemicals that mimic hormones include bisphenol A (BPA), polychlorinated biphenyls (PCBs), parabens, phthalates and some artificial musks found in fragrances. Men's health issues linked to hormone-disrupting chemicals include obesity, sperm damage, prostate cancer and testicular cancer.[91]

All the products and brands listed in the shopping guides in this chapter will work for everyone, plus the following non-toxic brands were created especially for men.

Shopping Guide

- **Bulldog Skincare for Men**, meetthebulldog.com, UK based, has products specifically designed and formulated by men for men, with no parabens, SLS, artificial colors or synthetic fragrances. Certified Leaping Bunny, approved by the Vegetarian society in the UK. Product line includes shave gel, body care and skin care.

- **Herban Cowboy®**, herbancowboy.com. When Luke and Lisa Vukmer launched Herban Cowboy in their log cabin in Minnesota, it was to produce organic grooming products for men, which now include cologne, aftershave, deodorant, shaving cream and soap. Vegan and PETA Cruelty-free.

- **Portland General Store**, portlandgeneralstore.com. This apothecary for men and women in Portland, Maine, offers natural, organic and vegan products made in small batches, foraged, when possible, from local ingredients. Free of parabens, sulfates and synthetic fragrance, the product line includes shaving, hair care, skin care, cologne, beard care and aromatherapy (smelling salts).

Sunscreens

While the use of sunscreen and sun protection is rising, so are cases of skin cancer.[92] One in five Americans will develop skin cancer, and one person dies of melanoma every hour.[93]

The dilemma is that we need sun for our health. Vitamin D deficiency is now recognized as a pandemic[94] and is being studied for its role in cancer, dementia, diabetes and heart disease.[95] Yet, the concern for skin cancer is so high the American Academy of Dermatology recommends wearing a minimum of SPF 30 at all times, even though wearing SPF 8 or more appears to block vitamin D absorption.[96]

Our usage of sun protection needs to be examined. Consumer offerings are advancing — it is a $600 million[97] industry in the US alone — yet the US Food and Drug Association (FDA) has not approved any new sunscreen ingredients since 1999. (Eight new ingredients are under formal review, but several of them have been in that state for over a decade.)[98] When it comes to our usage, there are three areas of concern: perceptions of SPF protection (more than 50 is unnecessary), modes of application (no more sprays) and chemical ingredients contributing to the body burden.

Whether we need a little sun or not, are vitamin D deficient or not, everyone agrees, getting a sunburn is a no-no. But our perceptions about what exactly SPF is doing might be off. It stands for "sun protection factor" but refers only to protection against UVB radiation, which burns the skin. It has little to do with protection from UVA rays, which penetrate deep into the skin, suppress the immune system, accelerate skin aging and may cause skin cancer.[99] High-SPF numbers can give a false sense of security, tempting us to stay in the sun too long, increasing UVB-related sunburns and the risk of UVA damage. In one study, beach goers spent more total time in the sun if they were given an SPF 30 sunscreen instead of an SPF 10 product.[100]

Other studies are still trying to determine why skin cancers are increasing and whether childhood sunburns play a role. Surprisingly, application, for children and adults, is still a concern. Numerous studies show that sunscreen users apply just one-fifth to a one-half the recommended quantity of sunscreen.[101] As with all products in this chapter, following the directions is key; both applying before going out in the sun then reapplying regularly are essential. Missing a spot in the application is of concern as well. This worry likely led to the creation of sunscreen sprays. Praised as a godsend by mothers of squirming children everywhere, sprays don't guarantee not missing spots. And worse, they take topical chemicals and turn them into aerosols, increasing risk by having us (inadvertently) inhaling them.

Beyond the dangers inherent in application misses or usage, the chemicals in sunscreen are worrisome. Sunscreens contain benzophenone (BP), which is persistent, bioaccumulative, a suspected carcinogen and endocrine disruptor,[102] plus a 2014 study found high exposure may impair men's ability to father children in a timely manner.[103] Benzophenone-type ultraviolet (UV) filters make up a class of about 29 chemicals commonly used in sunscreens and other products to protect skin and hair from sun damage.[104] Derivatives of benzophenones such as BP2 and oxybenzone (BP3) are used in sunscreens. Oxybenzone, an ultraviolet light absorber, can permeate the skin and accumulate in the blood, kidneys and liver; it may be toxic to liver cells.[105] These chemicals are also thought to be killing coral reefs around the world.[106]

For safer choices, opt for *broad spectrum* sunscreens (protects from UVA and UVB rays) that include "active" zinc or titanium dioxide in the ingredients. Not the chalky, white sun creams you might remember, the latest non-toxic versions are light and easy to apply. If you have to wear conventional sunscreen, here is some advice to make it safer: don't use sprays, apply liberally, reapply often and wash to remove the cream as soon as you are indoors.

Additional non-toxic sun protection advice is familiar: wear a hat, avoid the hottest part of the day and cover up when outdoors.

Shopping Guide

- **The Honest Company**, honest.com, states its sunscreens are free of oxybenzone, gluten, parabens, phthalates, fragrances, petrochemicals, dyes and synthetic chemical sunscreens. Its natural, unscented, broad-spectrum (UVA and UVB) SPF 30 mineral sunscreen is safe for babies and is non-nano, hypoallergenic, vegetarian, non-whitening, biodegradable, reef-friendly and water resistant. Also active in hair, body care, dental care, household cleaners and all things baby (diapers, wipes, creams, balms).

- **Kiss My Face**, kissmyface.com, started as an olive oil soap company created on a 200-acre farm in New York's Hudson River Valley over 30 years ago and has grown to a personal care line of over 200 bath and body products sold in over 19 countries. All Kiss My Face sunscreens are cruelty-free, paraben and oxybenzone free, including sun protection for face, body, lips and kids. Also active in hair, skin care, body care, dental care and kids.

- **Marie Veronique**, www.marieveronique.com, which app
  care offers a multi-tasking Everyday Coverage SPF 30 in tl
  extra-light, light and medium — and has zinc oxide for ful
  coverage. There is also a waterproof Kid Safe Screen SPF
  vegan and gentle enough to use around the eyes.

Makeup

Makeup is not immune to the chemical soup. How much makeu
wear and how important the "perfect face" is to you will affect how
proceed in this realm. Non-toxic makeup has come a long way in the
few years and, like other products, will require some trial and error
find what will work and which can replace your conventional favorite
Makeup artist Katey Denno shares these tips:

> When making the change to incorporating non-toxic makeup
> into their beauty routine, the biggest differences I think con-
> sumers will notice are:

> 1. If you started your day with perfectly applied makeup, you'll
>   have to touch up your face before you go out at night. This re-
>   ally doesn't differ from what takes place for the average woman
>   using mainstream brand cosmetics, but in the green beauty
>   world, since color within products tends to fade more easily,
>   and there are no -ethicone (silicone-based) ingredients to keep
>   products sitting on top of the skin, it's more apparent that skin
>   does indeed pull into it what's put on top.

> 2. The color spectrum in some lines doesn't extend to include
>   foundation and concealer for women of all colors. It's been
>   frustrating for me to see this, and I look forward to the time
>   when it's not the case. (I don't want to bash the lines for this. I
>   know a lot of it has to do with their lack of funds.)

> 3. All "green" brands are not created equal. If you've tried a
>   product from one non-toxic line and found that the texture
>   was crumbly and impossible to blend or the shimmer level
>   was not to your liking, etc., you may have had a pretty nor-
>   mal reaction and given up on non-toxic products all together.
>   However, I encourage you to keep trying the varied products

from the numerous companies now on the market. Not even conventional cosmetic companies are able to put out wonderful products across the board, and I've found that I pick and choose my favorites from across brand lines.

The last thing to note, while protecting your health and choosing non-toxic brands, is to think about the health of your products. For conventional products, standard makeup shelf life is often, as follows:

- Mascara: 3 months
- Concealer: 12–18 months
- Cream blush: 12–18 months
- Cream eye shadow: 12–18 months
- Lip gloss: 18–24 months
- Powder: 2 years
- Blush and bronzer: 2 years
- Eyeliner and lip liner: 2 years
- Lipstick: 2 years

Non-toxic product shelf life will vary depending what acts as the base: water (a bacteria magnet) or essential oils (naturally resistant to bacteria).[107] Most products should carry a "Period after Opening" (PaO) symbol: an open cosmetics pot with a number followed by the letter M (months) indicating how long the product will last after opening (see figure I).

Shopping Guide

- **Alima Pure**, alimapure.com, was created in 2004 by Kate O'Brien so that women can play with color and texture and enhance their natural beauty without worrying about any effects on their health. It offers mineral makeup products and collections, using only the purest cosmetic-grade mineral pigments. Certified B Corporation, BCIH, Leaping Bunny and PETA Cruelty-free. Line includes face, cheeks, eyes and lips, plus mineral makeup brushes.

- **Ecco Bella**, eccobella.com. Salla Malanga founded Ecco Bella in 1992 as a protest to the use of animals in cosmetic testing. She wanted to prove that natural, effective products could be created cruelty-free. (Check the FAQ page for the few items that contain carmine.) The FlowerColor cosmetics line uses flower wax to create a protective layer that keeps your natural moisture from seeping through your makeup. Line includes face, eyes and lips. Also active in hair, skin care, body care and perfume.

- **ILIA Beauty**, iliabeauty.com. ILIA launched its collection of six tinted lip conditioners in Vancouver, Canada, in 2011. Since then it has relocated to LA and become a prestige line of natural and organic beauty products. Each product contains up to 85 percent bioactive organic ingredients, sourced from organic farmers around the world and manufactured in an organic certified lab. Certified Leaping Bunny. Most of its press is about its lip line, but also active in illuminators, tinted moisturizers, concealers and mascara.

- **Kjær Weis**, kjaerweis.com, is a luxury organic cosmetic line created by Danish-born, New York-based makeup artist Kirsten Kjær Weis. Produced in Italy, almost all products are "certified organic" or "certified natural" by the Controllo e Certificazione Prodotti Biologici (CCPB is recognised by NATRUE). The cream blush, lip tint and mascara are certified organic, and eye shadows are certified natural. Also, in efforts to reduce waste, the line comes in a refillable makeup system; refills slip directly into the sleek packaging.

- **RMS Beauty**, rmsbeauty.com. Makeup artist Rose Marie Swift launched RMS Beauty in 2008 after tests revealed her blood contained toxic levels of heavy metals and high levels of pesticides and other chemicals. RMS Beauty believes the manufacturing process renders many oils — even organic ones — toxic, so it formulates the collection with raw, food-grade and organic ingredients in their natural state, allowing their living, healing attributes to penetrate and rejuvenate the skin. Line includes luminizer, "un"cover-up, lip2cheek color, lip shine, eye shadows, mascara, bronzer and balms.

- **W3LL PEOPLE**, w3llpeople.com (pronounced well people), an Austin-based toxin-free brand, is the brainchild of a makeup maven, a cosmetic dermatologist and a tree hugger. Made in the US, in small batches with natural and organic ingredients, it is PETA Cruelty-free.

Line includes powders, foundations, bronzers, blush, colorsticks, eye shadows and eye colorsticks, mascara, eyeliner, lipstick, lip colorsticks, lipgloss and brushes.

- **Zao Organic Makeup**, zaoorganicmakeup.com. An eco-luxury makeup brand made in Italy, the products are organic, chemical-free, gluten-free and vegan. Its reusable packaging and refill system is made from controlled harvested bamboo, making it stylish, elegant and durable. Certified Leaping Bunny, COSMEBIO and ECOCERT. Line includes eye shadow, pencils (eye, eyebrow and lip), liquid liner, mascara, blush, foundation concealer, bronzer, lip polish, lip balm, lip gloss, lipstick, plus brushes.

Nail Polish

Think about it — hard lacquer that can withstand hair or dish washing and doesn't come off without a chemical remover can't be that "natural" can it? Nail polish, polish removers and artificial nail products contain a host of toxic chemicals known or suspected to cause cancer, reproductive harm, asthma and other negative health effects. Nail salon workers are particularly at risk for exposure, as they work with these products all day every day, often in poorly ventilated spaces.

You might have seen brands advertised as "3-free," meaning they don't use toluene, dibutyl phthalate (DBP) or formaldehyde. These three are all on California's list of chemicals known to cause cancer and reproductive toxicity.[108] As brands start to also rid their formulas of formaldehyde resin and camphor, "5-free" is becoming a common claim.

Shopping Guide

- **Butter London**™, butterlondon.com. Founded in 2005 by British entrepreneur Sasha Muir, Butter London prides itself on creating shades for the catwalk, bringing high-fashion colour without compromise. Its formula is 3-free and free of phthalates and parabens.
- **RGB Cosmetics**, rgbcosmetics.com. Gina Carney married her background in fashion, a taste for minimalism and devotion to natural beauty when she launched RGB in 2009. RGB has been featured in national press, including *Vogue*, *W Magazine* and *Allure*. Its formula is 5-free.
- **Sheswai Lacquer**, sheswaibeauty.com. California nail stylist Debbie Leavitt created Sheswai in 2009. Products are not tested on animals and

made in the US. Sheswai donates a portion of its profits to organizations that help sustain the planet (Nature Conservancy, World Wildlife Foundation and Heal the Bay). Unique, sustainable wood caps are assembled by Willing Workers, a non-profit organization that provides job opportunities to adults with developmental disabilities. Its formula is 3-free.

- **Piggy Paint**, piggypaint.com. This brand is safe for children and pregnant women. The water-based, hypoallergenic, eco-friendly formula is "safe for use on all little piggies." Piggy Paint supports charities, especially National MS Society and Get Well Gabby Foundation (to promote childhood cancer research). Its formula is 3-free, plus free of bisphenol A, ethyl acetate and acetone. Also makes an acetone-free, biodegradable remover.

- **Priti NYC**, pritinyc.com. The concept for eco-friendly nail polish came to Kim D'Amato when she was pregnant. She launched Priti NYC in 2005. Its formula is 5-free, Certified Leaping Bunny and PETA Cruelty-free. Made in the US.

- **Zoya**, zoya.com. Parent company, Art of Beauty, was founded in1986 by Zoya and Michael Reyzis. Zoya, with her cosmetology license and Michael, an advanced chemist, shared a vision — quality, healthy, natural-ingredient products for her clients. Today, the company has grown to become a manufacturer of some innovative professional beauty products, including over 300 nail colors in 5-free formulas.

Feminine Care

You might have noticed that throughout this chapter there isn't a simple list of toxic chemicals to avoid. It would be simpler. But, as many of the watchdog reports have revealed, too many conventional products either do not list ingredients or, if there is fragrance in the product, get to hide chemicals inside the (trade secret protected) catch-all of "fragrance."

Sadly, this is also true for feminine products. In 2013, the Women's Voices for the Earth (WVE) released a report called *Chem Fatale: Potential Health Effects of Toxic Chemicals in Feminine Care Products* that highlighted the potential health concerns related to toxic and allergenic chemicals found in feminine care products.

Feminine care products are a $3 billion industry, with the most popular products being tampons and menstrual pads (used by 70 to 85 percent of US women). These are followed by personal cleansing products like douches, sprays, washes and wipes (used by approximately 10 to 40 percent).[109] "Feminine care products are not just your average cosmetics because they are used on an exceptionally sensitive and absorbent part of a woman's body," says Alexandra Scranton, WVE's Director of Science and Research, and author of the report. "Greater scrutiny, oversight and research are badly needed to assure the safety of their ingredients on women's health."[110]

In the world of the FDA, tampons and pads are "medical devices," and therefore makers are not required to list ingredients.[111] However, a sample of products examined by the WVE for its report revealed chemicals such as carcinogens, reproductive toxins, endocrine disruptors and allergens being used in some of the most popular conventional products. The report includes a "Hall of Shame" appendix highlighting examples of feminine care products that contain toxic chemicals by brand name.

The WVE cautions that not only are the tissues of both the vulva (the parts on the outside) and vagina (the internal parts leading to the cervix) structurally different than the skin of the rest of the body, they are also potentially more vulnerable to exposure to toxic chemicals and irritants. The WVE calls this a "permeable route of chemical exposure."

"The chemicals used in these products are a real concern given the inevitable exposure to sensitive and absorptive vulvar and vaginal tissue," says Dr. Ami Zota, a professor of occupational and environmental health at George Washington University. "There is a clear need for more research on the health effects of these exposures on women's health."[113]

The medical field is researching vaginal drug delivery systems because the vagina is such an effective site to transfer drugs directly into the blood without being metabolized first. Yet, when it comes to feminine care products in that region, risk factors for vaginal cancer haven't been explored, and caution about exposure of carcinogens to vaginal tissue is rarely, if ever, mentioned.

The WVE recommends:

• reduce use of feminine care products
• eliminate use of products that may be unnecessary to a healthy vagina

- choose unscented products where available (particularly tampons and pads)
- choose chlorine-free bleached or unbleached cotton tampons and pads.

Feminine Care Products of Concern

Tampons: Hazardous ingredients may include dioxins and furans (from the chlorine bleaching process), pesticide residues and unknown fragrance chemicals. Exposure concerns include cancer, reproductive harm, endocrine disruption and allergic rash.

Pads: Hazardous ingredients may include dioxins and furans, pesticide residues, unknown fragrance chemicals and adhesive chemicals such as methyldibromo glutaronitrile. Exposure concerns include cancer, reproductive harm and endocrine disruption. Studies link pad use to allergic rash.

Feminine wipes: Hazardous ingredients may include methylchloroisothiazolinone, methylisothiazolinone, parabens, quaternium-15, DMDM hydantoin, iodopropynyl butylcarbamate, Triclosan and unknown fragrance chemicals. Exposure concerns include cancer and endocrine disruption. Studies link wipe use to allergic rash.

Feminine wash: Hazardous ingredients may include unknown fragrance chemicals, parabens, methylchloroisothiazolinone, methylisothiazolinone, DMDM hydantoin, D&C Red No.33, Ext D&C Violet #2, and FD&C Yellow #5. Exposure concerns include endocrine disruption, allergic rash, and asthma.

Douche: Hazardous ingredients may include unknown fragrance chemicals and the spermicide octoxynol-9. Studies link douche use to bacterial vaginosis, pelvic inflammatory disease, cervical cancer, low-birth weight, preterm birth, HIV transmission, sexually transmitted diseases, ectopic pregnancy, chronic yeast infections and infertility.

Feminine deodorant (sprays, powders and suppositories): Hazardous ingredients may include unknown fragrance chemicals, parabens and benzethonium chloride. Exposure concerns include reproductive harm, endocrine disruption and allergic rash.

Feminine anti-itch creams: Hazardous ingredients may include unknown fragrance chemicals, parabens, methylisothiazolinone and an active ingredient, benzocaine, a mild anesthetic. Exposure concerns include endocrine disruption, allergic rash and unresolved itch.

— Women's Voices for the Earth, *Chem Fatale*, 2014 [112]

Shopping Guide

- **Luna Pads**, lunapads.com. Lunapads International is a women-owned
  and -operated social mission-based business based in Vancouver,
  Canada. Lunapads, created by fashion designer Madeleine Shaw, are
  printed cotton washable pads and underwear (lunapanties). Lunapads
  are used by thousands worldwide, diverting one million disposable
  pads and tampons from landfills every month. Certified B Corporation.
  It also sells the DivaCup: a reusable, non-absorbent menstrual cup that
  is plastic-free and BPA-free. It is made of silicone and can be worn for
  up to 12 hours at a time, making it a reliable, environmentally responsible and economically beneficial alternative.

- **Organ(y)c**, organyc-online.com, has line of feminine products made in
  the US with organic cotton. Pads, pantyliners and tampons don't contain any synthetics or wood pulp and are bleached only in hydrogen
  peroxide. Also active in nursing pads, cotton balls, makeup pads, cotton
  swabs and wipes.

- **Natracare**, natracare.com, is an award-winning, ethical company committed to offering organic and natural solutions for personal health
  care. Its pads, liners and tampons are certified organic cotton and totally chlorine free, plastic free and biodegradable. Also active in maternity
  and incontinence products.

Lunapads and Natracare are also in "No Secrets" — a list of companies compiled by WVE that disclose all ingredients and have committed
to make products without toxic chemicals. See the WVE site for more:
womensvoices.org/avoid-toxic-chemicals/no-secrets-safer-products/.

Condoms and Other Intimates

A 2012 German study found N-nitrosamine in 29 of 32 condoms it tested. Nitrosamines, mentioned in the hair section, are impurities that can
show up as a by-product in a variety of cosmetics ingredients. (Potent and
easily absorbed carcinogenics, these by-products are linked to stomach,
esophagus, liver and bladder cancer.[114]). While Germany's social ministry reassured consumers that the chemicals don't pose imminent health
risks, it advised manufacturers to seek safer alternatives.[115] But now that

you know female parts are also known as a "permeable route of chemical exposure,"[116] it makes non-toxic choices in this category imperative.

Shopping Guide

- **Glyde**, glydeamerica.com, was the first certified ethical, vegan and fair trade condom brand to be a Certified B Corporation. It is 100 percent Australian, woman-owned, with worldwide distribution, and its ingredients are sourced from worker-owned and operated producers with fair trade and labor practices. Its natural rubber is grown sustainably and within close proximity to its manufacturing facility. Flavored condoms are made with real fruit/plant extracts — no fake chemicals or sugars that could disrupt vaginal pH balance. In manufacturing, it uses oat powder instead of talc (a known carcinogen) and double washes each condom to eliminate any residue, latex taste or odor. It also offers lubricants and dams. Its lubricant is a premium medical-grade silicone formula that is paraben-free and glycerin-free.

- **Sustain Condoms**, sustaincondoms.com, is a family project created by Jeffrey Hollender (co-founder of Seventh Generation) and his daughter Meika. Its condoms, in three sizes, are fair trade-certified, organically sourced, vegan, non-toxic, non-animal-tested, GMO-free and nitrosamine-free. They also contain lower protein levels than conventional condoms, making the latex less likely to cause allergic reactions. The latex is sourced from an organic, family-owned FSC-certified rubber plantation in India that pays its workers premium wages, offers free health care at its own hospital and provides free schooling to all workers' children. The condoms are made in a family-owned, unionized condom factory, also in southern India.

- **Yes®** yesyesyes.org. Yes lubricants, started by two friends in 2003, are formulated from plant extracts, sperm friendly and created to give the most natural lubrication feeling. Organic certification from the Soil Association.

Final Notes

You can spend the approximately $2,000 for a body burden blood test and $174 to send each product to a lab for assessment, but in the end, you'll only know "which" chemicals are in you (and your products). You won't know how, or if, they'll affect you.

As you let the information from this chapter sink in, please remember that personal care products are not the only source for nasty chemicals. We live in a chemical age. Things like phthalates are in water bottles, shower curtains and the cleaners they use at the mall or at your office. There are fire retardants in sofas and on children's pajamas. My opinion, and the reason I wanted to include a beauty chapter in this book, is that just because chemicals are "everywhere" doesn't mean they also need to be rubbed into my skin or sprayed behind my ears

Please remember I am writer, not a scientist or a doctor. My research follows my passion and my desire to share the numerous studies from watchdogs. I'm fortunate to be standing on the shoulders of giants: Rachel Carson and all the writers after her who were/are concerned about and write about chemicals, so that when we choose to spend our hard-earned money on products, we know just a little more about what we are buying and whether there is a risk to our health. As a writer, I cannot endorse the safety of products listed on these pages. Rather, I salute the commitments these brands are making to creating safer products.

There are so many choices: the shopping guides reflect products I use, products that were recommended to me, reviews I've read and businesses that put their heart and soul into creating great, new non-toxic products. They are explorers and game changers, and I love the path they are walking/creating. And there are more, too many more to include. I encourage you to explore and find your own favorites.

Non-toxic products are not cheap. In fact, when compared to drugstore and conventional brands, some of them are shockingly expensive. Investing in an unknown brand can seem daunting. Luckily, many of these brands make and sell "travel kits" or sample sizes, and almost all are active on social media, where they offer deals and advertise sales.

I've listed websites in the shopping guides because e-commerce might be your only choice for some brands. Distribution is becoming more mainstream; several brands listed here are available at Target, some drug store chains and Whole Foods. Plus, new specialty shops like the Detox Market (in LA and Toronto) are popping up in cities all over the country. If you have a natural food store near you, although you may not find the exact brands listed here, you will find brands of similar quality.

Here is a list of e-commerce sites that sell a wide variety of non-toxic brands:

- Abe's Market: abesmarket.com (prices in USD)
- Beauty Habit: beautyhabit.com (prices in USD)
- Content Beauty & Wellbeing: beingcontent.com (prices in GBP)
- Fresh Faced: freshfaced.ca (prices in CAD)
- LoveLulu: lovelula.com (prices in GBP)
- NuboNau: nubonau.com (prices in USD)
- Pharmaca: pharmaca.com (prices in USD)
- Spirit Beauty Lounge: spiritbeautylounge.com (prices in USD)

For beauty advice and non-toxic makeup trends, you should also visit Katey Denno's blog: thebeautyofitis.com

Chapter 2

Clothing

"Buy less, choose well, make it last."[1]

— Vivienne Westwood,
British fashion designer

IT DOESN'T MATTER IF WE CALL IT APPAREL, fashion or "what I have to wear to work," unless we're nudists, we all wear clothing. That's why it's the world's third-largest industry, worth $1.5 trillion.[2] Fashion is also the world's second-biggest economic activity for intensity of trade[3] and is second only to agriculture as the largest polluter of clean water globally.[4]

The ills of this industry are becoming commonplace as headlines in the news. Whether it's factory worker deaths in Bangladesh, suicides of organic cotton farmers in India, toxic chemicals making rivers in China run the "it" color of the season, nylon production contributing to global warming or toxic chemicals on clothes in the store, you must have gotten a sense that something's not quite right.

Sure, most of that happens in countries far from North America; 97.5 percent of the apparel and 98 percent of the footwear sold in the United States is produced outside of the country.[5] But it's impossible to point a finger at one brand, or one country — there isn't a single troublemaker. Rather, there are many — countries with lax legislation and oversight for human and environmental welfare courting business and brands taking advantage of the economic opportunities available from working in developing countries. Plus, globalization has led to fulfillment systems and supply chains that are complex, often secretive and that jump around the globe chasing either industry expertise, cheap prices or both. Add an overarching lack of consumer expectation (we don't demand change, so they keep on), and we get the industry of today.

The change has to start with us and how and what we buy. The fashion and apparel industry includes plenty of finger pointing but not a lot of actionable change. We blame the brands; they blame us. We implore "Stop producing so many items of clothing," and they retort "Stop buying." We cry "Stop using slave labor," and they reply "Stop demanding such cheap clothing." The industry is really at a crossroads. Whether it's a simple uniform of jeans and T-shirt or an outfit straight from of one of the world's famous fashion runways, "human rights and the environment pay a heavy price — a price that people can increasingly choose to lessen with the rise of ethical fashion," says the United Nations.[6]

The good news is you probably have something ethical or eco in your closet already: an organic T-shirt, something made domestically or an item that was handed down that might be considered vintage (or maybe you've owned it so long it feels vintage). This chapter will provide some background on the issues and areas of concern when it comes to the clothing we wear, but it will also highlight some incredible game changers of the industry. Through their innovative models, we can see what is possible and what we, as consumers, can expect as ethical choices.

COTTON: The Fabric of Our Lives

Cotton is marketed as "the fabric of our lives."[7] From birth to death, we are in it. Swaddled as newborns, tucked into cotton sheets at night, handed a cotton towel as you step out of the shower. Most of our well-loved items are made with it — from T-shirts to jeans. There's no doubt, cotton is our favourite. It's also a crop that gets tagged as "the dirtiest crop on the planet."[8]

The "dirty" label shocks many, and over the years, non-governmental organization (NGO) efforts to reduce insecticide and pesticide reliance have worked, but the numbers are still a shock: cotton grows in over 80 countries, uses only 2.5 percent of arable land (imagine the size of the UK and Switzerland) but accounts for 14.1 percent of all agricultural insecticides and 6.2 percent of all pesticides[9] — not just more than for any other crop, but at numbers high enough to give concern.

When many of us think of cotton, we think of southern states like Texas and farms that are thousands of acres, with state-of-the-art technology. This is valid; cotton in Texas is a billion-dollar industry.[10] But 90 percent of cotton growers are small-scale farmers (smallholders) scattered around the globe raising cotton on less than two hectares.[11] They number between 50 and 100 million, and for them, cotton is a route out of poverty; it is a gateway to organized markets, cash and hopes for a better future.[12]

Cotton growth is often an indicator of potential for development; when farmers have enough land to grow food and a cash crop (like cotton), there is chance for economic advancement. Cotton's value as a cash crop allows farmers to invest in their children's education, in family health and in their community. But cotton growth benefits not just growers; it also provides work for 250 million people in farm labor, transport and primary processing. However, because the majority of growers are smallholders, they are also vulnerable to market shifts and climate flux. A single season can make or break a household.[13]

Who knew something as simple as a T-shirt would have worldwide implications? The kind of cotton designers choose and the kind we buy matters. Cotton comes in three forms: conventional, including genetically modified and hybrid seeds; sustainable, farmers who work with the Better Cotton Initiative (BCI) and Cotton Made in Africa (CmiA); and organic, which, like food, is GMO/pesticide free. Currently, conventional cotton represents 99 percent of all cotton.

Conventional Cotton and India's Suicide Belt

Attempts to mitigate risk in development, like cotton as a cash crop, is challenging and often involves trade-offs. In 2002, Monsanto's Bollgard (Bt) cotton became the first biotech crop technology approved for commercialization in India, and more than six million farmers adopted the technology on their farms.[14] The genetically modified (GM) seed, which produces a toxin from the bacteria *Bacillus thuringiensis* (Bt) that is deadly to the bollworm, was meant to provide a measure of stability to farmers. A bollworm infestation ruins a crop, so this seed was not only to offer better and more stable yield, it was also going to allow for the reduction in the use of insecticides.

Even though the seed was four to ten times more expensive than typical hybrid seeds,[15] Monsanto claimed Bt cotton would yield 1,500 kilograms (kg) per year. It wasn't just Monsanto making the push; the Bt seeds were heavily marketed, using film stars and even religious deities to sell the benefits. However, in reality, the Bt cotton actually required far *more* water and far *more* pesticides than hybrid or traditional cotton. In the end, Bt cotton yielded on average 300 to 400 kg per year, not the 1,500 kg expected.

The high costs and unreliable output made GM cotton a debt trap for many farmers.[16] In a report on farmer suicides and human rights, the Center for Human Rights and Global Justice (CHRGJ) summarized the problem as such:

> These farmers and their families are among the victims of India's longstanding agrarian crisis. Economic reforms and the opening of Indian agriculture to the global market over the past two decades have increased costs, while reducing yields and profits for many farmers, to the point of great financial and emotional distress. As a result, smallholder farmers are often trapped in a cycle of debt. During a bad year, money from the sale of the cotton crop might not cover even the initial cost of the inputs, let alone suffice to pay the usurious interest on loans or provide adequate food or necessities for the family. Often the only way out is to take on more loans and buy more inputs, which in turn can lead to even greater debt. Indebtedness is a major and proximate cause of farmer suicides in India. Many farmers, ironically, take their lives by ingesting the very pesticide they went into debt to purchase.[17]

This technological advance has not benefited the farmers, as intended. In fact, the opposite occurred. India's Maharashtra state, home to India's "cotton belt," has received media attention and been renamed the "suicide belt" because of the negative affect of this cycle. The same CHRGJ report shares these numbers:

> It is estimated that more than a quarter of a million Indian farmers have committed suicide in the last 16 years — the

largest wave of recorded suicides in human history. A great number of those affected are cash crop farmers, and cotton farmers in particular. In 2009 alone, the most recent year for which official figures are available, 17,638 farmers committed suicide — that's one farmer every 30 minutes.[18]

The other issue with conventional cotton and GM seeds is that many genetically engineered seeds contain "terminator technology," meaning they have been genetically modified so that the resulting crops don't produce viable seeds of their own. Therefore, new seeds must be purchased every year. Prior to the introduction of GM cotton, farmers harvested their seeds from each crop, to be planted in the next season. Cotton seeds also play part of a bigger ecosystem; beyond the fiber and the cotton, the seeds are a viable resource: used as livestock feed, to make cottonseed oil (used in margarine), even eaten in times of extreme hardship, or ground down for use as a natural fertilizer. Those options are possible only when the seed is organic.[19]

The one-dimensional aspect to GM seeds, plus their need for extra water and extra pesticide, is why many countries, including many EU members, do not allow GM cotton to be grown.

Conventional Cotton and Pesticides

In India, 54 percent of all pesticides are used on cotton, despite cotton representing only 5 percent of crops.[20] (There are other pests beside bollworm that love to feast on cotton.) Pesticides are not just a concern in India; they are a concern wherever and whenever they are used. Across all agricultural sectors, the World Health Organization estimates between one and five million cases of pesticide poisoning every year, resulting in several thousands of reported deaths, many of them children.[21]

In Egypt, over one million children between 7 and 12 help with cotton pest management, exposing them to danger. Pesticides were the leading cause of child deaths from poisonings in Iran, according to a study conducted there.[22] Even if they do not participate in spraying or cotton harvesting, children have added risks: their size, plus malnutrition and dehydration increase sensitivity to pesticides,[23] and many who live near cotton fields often play with or reuse empty pesticide containers.

Hazardous pesticides associated with global cotton production also represent a substantial threat to global freshwater resources. According to the Environmental Justice Foundation (EJF), an NGO that believes environmental security is a human right, hazardous cotton pesticides are known to contaminate rivers in the US, India, Pakistan, Uzbekistan, Brazil, Australia, Greece and West Africa.[24]

These are the worst three pesticides, commonly used on cotton, as listed by the EJF:

- **Aldicarb**, a powerful nerve agent, is one of the most toxic pesticides applied to cotton worldwide and the second-most-used pesticide in global cotton production. Just one drop of aldicarb, absorbed through the skin, is enough to kill an adult.

- **Monocrotophos**, despite being withdrawn from the US market in 1989, is still widely used in developing countries. In 1997, Paraguay's Ministry of Health and Welfare identified it as being responsible for causing paralysis in children living in cotton growing areas.

- **Deltamethrin** is a nerve agent applied in over half of the cotton-producing countries. Medical analysis in a South African village community on the edge of a major cotton production area found traces of deltamethrin in human breast milk.[25]

With consumer demand so high for cotton, your choice has the capacity to activate real change. The quality and versatility of the cotton — organic, sustainable or fair trade — will be virtually unnoticeable to you, but will positively affect the communities (and children) who grow it.

Organic and Sustainable Cotton

The largest buyers of organic cotton might surprise you: H&M, C&A (a Dutch fast-fashion retail chain with stores in 21 countries), Puma, Nike and Decathalon (a French sporting goods chain) were the top five in 2013. Target, Williams Sonoma (parent of West Elm and Pottery Barn) and Inditex (parent company of Zara) were also in the top ten.

If you think it's strange that multinational companies should be at the forefront of the organic cotton movement, then you might not have noticed how much *greening through the back door* has been going on in fashion. This is when corporations adapt green or sustainable practices, often without a marketing effort, deciding that a sustainable choice is better for their customers and for their business.[26]

Organic cotton support requires a guaranteed price set for the farmer *before* the crop is planted. Fluctuating commodity prices paired with current unstable global weather patterns make this a risky pledge, and companies with deep pockets are best suited to make those pledges. So what you see in the list of the top ten are some of the largest cotton users in apparel committed to changing systems, both at the farmer and field levels.

Big brands supporting organic cotton is the key to change for farmers and the planet. Last year, NASA released pictures of the Aral Sea that was once the fourth-largest sea on the planet but is now an arid wasteland, an ecological disaster due to cotton irrigation.[27] In Uzbekistan, almost 20,000 liters of water were withdrawn for every kilo of cotton harvested. And yet it wasn't the "thirsty crop" that was to blame but rather an aging and inefficient irrigation system. It was leaks and evaporation from the dated system, which spanned over 28,000 kilometers that was to blame. All that is left is carcinogenic dust. States the *Guardian*, "The exposure of the bottom of the lake has released salts and pesticides into the atmosphere poisoning both farm land and people alike.[28] Corporate financial support for organic cotton production is one way to avert further ecological disasters.

Another is the Better Cotton Initiative (BCI), an NGO created by the World Wildlife Foundation (WWF) and IKEA and further supported by a collective of major organizations like Adidas, Gap, H&M, Organic Exchange, Oxfam and PAN UK (more greening through the back door). BCI is the middle ground for cotton. The Initiative chooses not to engage in the GMO debate and instead refers to itself as "technology neutral." This means less focus on seed source and the opportunity for a more holistic approach to key priorities like water and integrated pest management.

BCI worked with 75,000 farmers in Pakistan who were able to reduce their water use by 39 percent while increasing their income by 11 percent. They also used 47 percent less pesticide and 39 percent less chemical fertilizer. BCI aims for positive results for farmers, which is good for other communities downstream and good for the fish, birds and other creatures that depend on rivers and wetlands.[29] Because BCI has the corporate support from companies like IKEA, it too can create a channel for sustainable sourcing in the commercial mainstream.

With BCI and organic cotton movements underway, past numbers cited for pesticide and insecticide use are dated and don't reflect the changing landscape. In some communities, cotton is no longer the "dirtiest" nor the "thirstiest" crop. With sustainable efforts in place to grow cotton with people and planet in mind, when talking about cotton "any claims about water use, pollution or poverty are meaningless unless applied to a specific context."[30]

The amount of cotton grown globally each year is enough to provide each person on the planet with 18 T-shirts[31] and of that, 99 percent is conventional cotton.[32] There is plenty of room for improvement.

Beyond Cotton

It's not just cotton we love; 80 percent of us say that our favorite fibers to wear are either all-natural or all-natural blends.[33] Natural fibers come from seeds (cotton, linen) or animals (silk, wool, alpaca) instead of laboratories (where synthetics likes nylon and polyester were created). Not only do we think they feel better, natural fibers are unparalleled in their inherent qualities: hemp has antibacterial properties, linen is the most hygienic textile for hospital bed sheets, wool acts as an insulator against both cold and heat, and coconut is used in mattresses because it has a natural resistance to fungus and mites.[34]

There are also social reasons to seek out ethically produced, natural fibers. As with cotton, natural fibers are tied to the livelihoods and food security of millions of small-scale farmers and processors. These include four million small-scale jute farmers in Bangladesh and India, one million silk industry workers in China and 120,000 alpaca-herding families in the Andes. Choosing natural fibers, where you know the source, boosts contributions to global economic growth and can directly help fight rural poverty and hunger.[35]

Natural fibers are also a renewable resource. Growing one ton of jute fibre requires less than 10 percent of the energy used to produce polyester. Natural fibers are carbon neutral; processing can lead to high levels of water pollutants, but they consist mostly of biodegradable compounds. This is in contrast to the persistent chemicals, including heavy metals, released in the effluent (the liquid waste discharge) from synthetic fiber processing. Plus, at the end of their life cycle, natural fibers are 100 percent biodegradable.[36]

Other Natural Fibers

Hemp: It grows easily without agrochemicals, can be grown in cool climates and yields two- to four-meter plants that are higher than any other fiber. (You can get more from less.) It is also an environmentally positive plant that can improve both the structure of soils and capture large quantities of carbon. Production is still restricted in some countries, where the plant is confused with marijuana. It's common to find hemp blended with cotton, linen, silk or wool to give it a softer feel.

Linen (Flax): Used for fiber production since prehistoric times, flax grows best in northern temperate latitudes, but is used mostly in the south for clothes and home linens because it absorbs and releases water quickly. This makes linen comfortable to wear in hot weather.

Other natural fibers will be covered in future chapters (silk, in Special Occasions and cashmere in Outerwear, etc.). Once you've chosen a natural fiber, you want to check how it was dyed and processed (often a chemically intensive process). Additionally, avoid textiles labeled permanent press, no-iron, crease-resistant, shrink-proof, stretch-proof, water repellent, or water-proofed. These finishes are based on perfluorinated chemicals (PFCs), a known carcinogen, and you might not want them next to your skin[37]. Plus, they may off-gas formaldehyde.[38]

Bring in the Synthetics

If we're not wearing natural fibers, then we are wearing synthetics: polyester, nylon, Spandex, Lycra, etc. These easy-care fibers are becoming the textile industry's miracle solution; however, their manufacture creates pollution and afterlife issues. (Nylon takes 30 to 40 years to decompose.)[39] Nylon and polyester, the most common synthetic fabrics, are cheap to make and usually cheap to buy. The bad news: both are made from petrochemicals and are non-biodegradable. Even worse, manufacturing nylon releases nitrous oxide, a greenhouse gas that is significantly stronger than carbon dioxide and causes global warming. The good news: polyester, also known as PET (polyethylene terephthalate), can be recycled.

Polyester made its debut in the US in 1951 and quickly became the country's fastest-growing fiber.[40] Easy care of the permanent press fabric made polyester double-knits extremely popular in the 1960s, but then the fiber fell out of fashion until polar fleece debuted in the '80s. Then, in the '90s, people realized polar fleece could be recycled. Honed by the Japanese firm Teijin Limited, its closed-loop, chemical recycling process, ECO CIRCLE®, is revolutionary because polyester fabric can be broken down at the molecular level and reprocessed into highly pure raw materials over and over. The resulting materials do not drop in quality or degrade, even after repeated processing. Compared to making new polyester materials from petroleum, the process is touted to reduce energy consumption and CO_2 emissions by about 80 percent.[41]

This polyester recycling system is so efficient that when Patagonia did its own life-cycle assessment, it decided even "when the transportation from Patagonia Customer in the US to Japan is factored into the ECO CIRCLE® recycling system, manufacturing polyester fiber from recycled materials results in 76 percent less energy usage and 71 percent less CO_2 emissions than producing polyester from virgin materials."[42]

It's easy to feel like polyester is an ecologically sound choice, especially if it's part of the ECO CIRCLE® chain or part of the latest trend: recycling plastic water bottles (PET) into fabric. This is common in performance sports apparel, and the tag often boasts how many bottles the item has "rescued." Seems like such a wonderful concept: to take the deluge of empty soda and water bottles and upcycle them into clothing. Especially since every few months the media highlights how big the Pacific Gyre is getting. Also known as "the world's biggest landfill in the Pacific Ocean," this gyre is a collection of marine debris particles, mostly plastic, in the central North Pacific. An estimated 11 million tons of floating plastic cover an area of nearly five million square miles.[43]

It's natural to want to be part of the solution, and clothes containing recycled PET bottles feel like it should be one of those solutions. But as William McDonaugh and Michael Braungart state in their seminal book *Cradle to Cradle*, "people may feel they are making an ecologically sound choice by buying and wearing clothing made from fibers from recycled plastic bottles. But the fibers from plastic bottles contain toxins such as antimony, catalytic residues, ultraviolet stabilizers, plasticizers, and antioxidants, which were never designed to lie next to human skin."[44]

If you are still thinking about all the chemicals in your personal care routine, the thought of adding more in your clothing might not seem like such a great idea. However, synthetic fibers are not going away: they are affordable, they possess great performance qualities, and most are recyclable. They can be a great choice, perhaps just not next to your skin. Plus, the environmental reality is, "The natural material to meet the needs of our current population does not and cannot exist. If several billion people want natural-fiber blue jeans dyed with natural dyes, humanity will have to dedicate millions of acres to the cultivation of indigo and cotton plants just to satisfy the demand."[45] There's not enough land to eat and dress too.

Dyes and Production

Choosing an environmentally friendly fiber is just the first stage of apparel choice. There are still several steps toward a finished garment. Let's go back to cotton, after the fiber is harvested there are preparation processes such as cleaning and combing to turn raw fiber into yarn; then there's spinning and weaving; finally finishing processes like dyeing, bleaching, scouring and printing before the fabric goes off to be cut and sewn.[46] If thinking about conventional cotton, the environmental assault doesn't end in the field; the production process required to turn plants into clothing also adds to environmental pollution: petroleum scours, softeners, heavy metals, flame and soil retardants, ammonia and formaldehyde — just to name a few. In many cases, the process results in large amounts of wastewater putting the residues from chemical cleaning, dyeing and finishing into local waterways.

In China, where apparel exports account for 30 percent of the global market, the apparel-related wastewater discharge is roughly 2.5 billion tons per year,[47] of which, dyeing and finishing account for 80 percent.[48] Greenpeace was curious about the quality of that wastewater, so in 2010, it began a year-long investigation on wastewater discharges from two facilities in China. Greenpeace revealed,

> The scientific analysis of the samples found that both manufacturing facilities were discharging a range of hazardous

chemicals into the Yangtze and Pearl River deltas. Significantly, hazardous and persistent chemicals with hormone-disrupting properties were found in the samples. Alkylphenols (including nonylphenol) were found in wastewater samples from both facilities, and perfluorinated chemicals (PFCs), in particular perfluorooctanoic acid (PFOA) and perfluorooctane sulphonate (PFOS), were present in the wastewater from the Youngor Textile Complex. This was despite the presence of a modern wastewater treatment plant at the Youngor facility. The alkylphenols and PFCs found in the samples are a cause for serious concern, as these chemicals are known hormone disruptors and can be hazardous even at very low levels. Many of the substances within these groups are regulated in the Global North, for example by the EU or by international conventions.[49]

Titled *Dirty Laundry: Unravelling the Corporate Connections to Toxic Water Pollution in China,* the report had two immediate effects. The first was to raise the flag that all was not clean in fiber production (more hormone-disrupting chemicals?!). The second was to illuminate the lack of supply chain transparency. Even though Greenpeace could link multinational companies to the facilities, they couldn't establish *which* companies were using toxic chemicals in production. Set to resolve this convenient lack of transparency, Greenpeace proceeded to conduct further research.

Since it knew which brands were coming out of the facilities, like the beauty watchdogs, Greenpeace bought clothing from those brands and sent them off to test clothing samples for the chemicals in the effluent. The 41 samples were purchased in 29 countries and regions, all from authorized retailers. The clothes were in the stores, on the racks.

The results were shocking. In the follow-up report, *Toxic Threads: the Big Fashion Stitch Up*, Greenpeace revealed that the surfactant nonylphenol ethoxylates (NPEs) was in 89 articles of clothing (63 percent of all items). NPE, which is toxic to fish and other water-dwelling organisms, is considered an endocrine disruptor.[50] The investigation also revealed high levels of toxic phthalates in four of the samples and cancer-causing amines from the use of azo dyes in two samples.

Shocked? So were other consumers who read the report or saw the information in the ensuing Greenpeace "Detox" campaign. The study was a wake-up call, testing the clothing and revealing the industrial use of NPEs, which have been restricted in many regions for nearly two decades, affecting the rivers in China, plus the fact that the chemicals remained on the clothes meant they were next to consumer's skin. To top it off, once consumers washed the items, the NPE residues and other hazardous chemicals would be released into domestic wastewater and affect local waterways too.[51]

Greenpeace released the names of the brands with the highest chemicals and through its highly publicized "Detox" campaign was able to get many brands to commit to phasing out hazardous chemicals across their entire supply chains by 2020. So, you need to worry about toxic chemicals on your clothes for a few more years.

Luckily, there are international certifying bodies that support safe chemical processing and dying: Global Organic Textile Standard (GOTS), OEKO-TEX®, bluesign®, plus several independent, natural dye houses.

Know Your Labels

GOTS, recognized as the world's leading processing standard for textiles made from organic fibers, was the first label to certify a product from a life-cycle perspective. The certification covers every stage of the production process from raw material through the manufacturing processes, including cleaning, spinning, weaving, dying, finishing and sewing. Each stage must be environmentally and socially responsible. The label is a white shirt in a green circle (figure II).

In order to be GOTS certified, textiles must be made from at least 70 percent certified organic natural fibers, or to carry the GOTS "organic" label, there must be a minimum of 95 percent certified organic fibers. At all stages of processing, organic fiber products must be separated from conventional fiber products and be free of restricted and banned chemicals, including bleach, azo dyes and NPEs. In addition, manufacturers must have an environmental policy that covers production factors such as fair labor practices (including no child labor), water consumption and wastewater treatment. In 2013, the top ten countries with the most GOTS-certified facilities were India, Turkey, Germany, China, South Korea, Italy, Pakistan, Bangladesh, Japan and Portugal.

UK/Japan-based brand People Tree was the first to develop a fully integrated supply chain for organic cotton from farm to final product plus the first organization to achieve GOTS certification on a supply chain entirely in the developing world.

The OEKO-TEX Standard 100 is not an organic certification. Rather, it was developed through the collaborative efforts of two labs (in Austria and Germany) to identify textile materials that are harmless to health. The label is a daisy with a long green stem on a white rectangle. Tested textiles

Figure II

1. The Soil Association Organic Standard 2. OEKO-Tex 3. GOTS 4. Fair Trade USA 5. World Fair Trade Organization 6. Fair Trade International 7. FWF 8. Fair Trade Federation 9. WRAP 10. Certified B Corporation 11. The Forest Stewardship Council 12. 1% For The Planet 13. Made-By 14. C2C 15. Positive Luxury

are awarded one of four OEKO-TEX product classes based on their intended end use; the more closely a product comes into contact with the skin and the more delicate the skin of the user, the stricter the human ecological requirements. For example, Class 1 is the most stringent and is for baby products. (The most delicate skin gets the most rigorous testing.) Class 4 is for decorative products such as tablecloths and curtains.

They test for substances including those that are prohibited or regulated by law, such as

- carcinogenic dye stuffs
- chemicals that are known to be harmful to health, such as formaldehyde and heavy metals
- substances that according to current knowledge are harmful to health, but are not yet regulated or prohibited by law, such as pesticides, allergy-inducing dye stuffs or tin-organic compounds
- precautionary parameters that safeguard health, such as colorfastness or skin-friendly pH value

German-based underwear and pajama brand Calida carries the OekoTex label on its products.

Brands like Patagonia, G-Star RAW and EILEEN FISHER use bluesign, a certification process based on a systems approach. Rather than focusing on finished product testing, all input streams — from raw materials, to chemical components, to water and energy resources — are analyzed at the beginning.

Natural Dyes

Are natural dyes the answer? Although natural dyes offer what we perceive as "cleaner" options, they have their own complications. Natural dyes require (mostly) plants and arable land, in some cases, large amounts of arable land. About 25 years ago, it was estimated that to dye all fiber with natural dyes would require around one third of the world's agricultural land.[52]

Natural dyes are becoming more popular, especially for using clothing as medicine. Ayurvastra is an ancient technique of dyeing textiles using medicinal herbs. Literally translated to herb clothing, the concept was practiced in India before the industrialization of the textile industry.[53]

This has been used purposefully (putting eczema medication in clothing) and is starting to make its way into fashion. New York-based designer Anjelika Krishna has been a modern conduit for this ancient art to North America through her label a.d.o. clothing. With her desire to help revive the ancient tradition, she sources dyers in Kerala and has been offering a small line of contemporary styles dyed using natural Ayurvedic ingredients such as turmeric, lemon and pomegranate since 2008.

Supply Chains and Workers

Less than three percent of our clothes are made domestically. That means they come from "there," but what does that even mean? Is one place better than the next? Should we be boycotting certain countries that pop up in the news? Would that help?

Making a garment can be a long and complex process. The advances in technology and modern logistics mean that a single piece of clothing can start as a seed in one country, be woven in another, and cut and sewn in yet another. From farmer to fiber, to weaver to sewer, the list is long and often a tangled web. Would we even be boycotting the right place, for the right reasons?

The Greenpeace "Detox" reports served as a warning to companies and brands that had complex and tangled offshore supply chains: develop transparency, know where and how your garments are made. This was further echoed after the Rana Plaza tragedy, which saw brands scrambling to explain why their labels were found in the rubble when they, according to their own records, hadn't contracted factories in the building.[54]

On April 24, 2013, the Rana Plaza, an eight-story building in Bangladesh that housed five garment factories supplying major Western brands including Benetton, Joe Fresh and Mango, collapsed in one of the deadliest industrial accidents in garment industry history.[55] Sadly, it was not the only industrial accident in the region; the previous year, the Tazreen factory fire claimed at least 117 lives. Similar accidents occurred around the same time in Karachi and Lahore in Pakistan.[56]

The Rana Plaza, which was not designed for industrial use and had three illegally added levels, collapsed, killing over 1,100 workers and injuring another 2,500. Some brands involved quickly acknowledged their links to the tragedy, while others denied they had authorized work at factories in the building, even when their garment labels were found in the rubble.[57] This went on to expose a complicated web of contractors and sub-contractors that criss-crossed countries and highlighted that supply chain transparency, with some brands, was nonexistent.

Rana Plaza remained in the news for so long because many brands denied responsibility and several refused to offer compensation to the almost 4,000 families that were affected by the tragedy. This had many activists calling for a boycott of anything made in Bangladesh.

Bangladesh is one of the biggest exporters of clothes to the United States and Europe because of its low wages.[58] Over the past decade, major fashion brands flocked to Bangladesh, where a minimum wage of about $38 a month helped increase corporate profits, while providing employment to several million people.[59] This is key. Boycotting a country of production because of bureaucratic decisions and loopholes really hurts only the workers.

International production moving into a developing country can be a gift and a curse. A 2008 World Bank report revealed 70 percent of apparel exports came from developing countries, making the sector a critical engine of growth. Like the transformative role of cotton, the apparel industry often provides entry into formal employment for the unskilled, the poor and women because of the relatively low technology and labor-intensive nature of the work.[60]

Sweatshop, or Relief from the Sun

In 2009, human rights advocate Nicholas Kristof wrote a *New York Times* article called "Where Sweatshops Are a Dream." He had interviewed women in Phnom Penh, Cambodia, who live on a landfill site and scrape together an existence by scavenging for recyclable materials from the mountain of festering refuse. In the article, one mother said she dreamt of a job in a factory because at least she would have shade. Another stated she would love her ten-year-old son to get a factory job because many children are run over by garbage trucks and a sweatshop job would be safer. The article presented a controversial point: "Sweatshops are only a symptom of poverty, not a cause." Kristof stated, "The best way to help people in the poorest countries isn't to campaign against sweatshops but to promote manufacturing there."[61]

This point is also echoed in "Fashionable Dilemmas." Author Austin Williams points out that "the greatest number of humans ever have been lifted out of poverty in the last decade or so without the use of Fair Trade, with 300 million Chinese now officially earning above poverty wages. In India, 100 million have been lifted out of extreme poverty over the past ten years."[62]

Factory work can contribute to national prosperity. Workers do not need to be put in perilous situations, but neither do specific countries or regions need to be "boycotted" when accidents happen. The International Labor Organization (ILO) states:

> Let's not forget the story of Bangladesh, beyond the head-lines of industrial disasters. This is a country that has made enormous progress in terms of economic and social development. For example, the share of the population living under the upper poverty line as defined nationally declined from 56.7 per cent in 1991–92 to 31.5 per cent in 2010. That is a remarkable achievement.
>
> Also, Bangladeshi women have been an integral part of Bangladesh's shift towards manufacturing and industrialization. They have helped to enhance agricultural productivity, been central to the emergence of the RMG [ready made garment] sector and participated in poverty reduction efforts through microfinance and social programmes.
>
> In the agricultural sector, 65 per cent of workers are women and in RMG over 80 per cent of workers are women. This comes on the heels of the progress Bangladesh has made in bridging the gender gap across several areas such as health, education and political participation.[63]

The ILO has been overseeing labor standards around the globe since 1919. Created shortly after World War I to "reflect the belief that universal and lasting peace can be accomplished only if it is based on social justice,"[64] the ILO works on tripartite cooperation between governments and employers' and workers' organizations in fostering social and economic progress.

The apparel industry has been grappling with worker health and safety since the ILO began. The Tazreen disaster, a 2012 garment factory fire where 177 died, mirrored a similar tragedy 101 years earlier in New York City. The Triangle Shirtwaist Factory fire claimed 146 lives, as many young women could not escape because the bosses had locked the doors.[65] There have been some advancements in the past century, but in the arena of worker health and safety, not as much as there should; the ILO estimates that 2.34 million workers die each year from work-related accidents and diseases.

Improving Working Conditions in Developing Nations

While there have been advances in worker rights and worker safety, global progress remains elusive for a variety of reasons including the following:

- Even though established labour laws exist in garment-producing countries, law enforcement might be inadequate.
- For many workers, the garment industry is their first step in formal employment, so often they do not understand their rights under the law. Employers themselves often have limited training.
- Factory compliance auditing can be a flawed system, with factories fabricating compliance rather than improving working conditions.
- The varied and complex nature of global supply chains has created a lack of accountability and ownership for improving compliance and has weakened direct oversight.
- International buyers have to set up parallel monitoring systems to fill gaps, resulting in a failure to focus on building the long-term capacity of government, employers or trade unions and also leading to fragmentation and duplication of efforts.[66]

To the last point, with so many buyers (retailers) doing their own monitoring, it was hard to create a cohesive plan for mass improvement. To fill this need, in 2007, the ILO partnered with the International Finance Corporation (IFC) to create "Better Work," a program that supports garment sector improvements, particularly in factories across Cambodia, Haiti, Indonesia, Jordan, Lesotho, Nicaragua and Vietnam. This means more partnerships, and you can expect to see more garments on the market from these countries. It's not a perfect evolution. The ILO doesn't just move into countries that could benefit from production jobs and everyone lives happily ever after, but it's a beginning.

The ILO can't oversee everything. For this reason, brands enlist external auditors like BSCI (Business Social Compliance Initiative), ETI (Ethical Trade Initiative) and SA8000 to help institute audits and change that are progressive and fair.

Let's be clear, not every garment or apparel company cares about worker health and safety. But those that do usually use external auditors, set benchmarks for improvements and share their efforts on their websites, in their corporate communications and annual reports. Sadly, there is no label, stamp or hangtag identifier that says "I'm a brand that cares." The onus is on consumers to delve into a brand's philosophy on workers and seek the evidence of their efforts.

One brand that has been making efforts to show how much it cares, from seed to shelf, is New York-based womenswear company EILEEN FISHER. It shares the story of its yoga tank, to show how complex all of these elements are and what steps a "brand that cares" goes through to bring ethical clothing to fruition.

The label says Made in USA, but EILEEN FISHER's organic cotton yoga tank is a global citizen. It travels to three countries and two continents, logging 17,000 miles before it reaches the company's New Jersey warehouse.

1. A seed is planted in Arizona

In April, it is planted in the warm Arizona sun. It is a seed to an extra-long-staple cotton plant, unaltered by genetic modification. It sprouts, leafs and grows, nurtured by compost. Workers roam the rows, hoeing weeds by hand, a labor-intensive alternative to chemical herbicides. To deter bugs, they spray essential oils — cedar, citrus and neem —and set out pheromone traps, low-tech contraptions that lure bugs with sex hormones.

Seven months later, the field bursts with ivory-colored cotton. It's October, time for the harvest. But first the cotton plants need to shed their leaves. On a conventional farm, chemical defoliants clear away the leaves. On an organic ☞

farm, nature does the work. "I wait for the frost," says the Arizona farmer who grows this crop.

When the leaves have fallen, huge mechanical harvesters roar through the fields, stripping the plants and picking the fields clean. The cotton is then ginned, baled, packed in forty-foot containers and trucked to the Port of Long Beach in California.

Time lapse: 11 months

2. Across the Atlantic to a Swiss river town

Yarn spinners with the expertise to work with organic extra-long-staple fiber are a rare breed. None exist in the United States. And in Europe, there is just one: Hermann Bühler, located in Sennhof, Switzerland, where the River Töss has contributed hydro power since 1858.

Bühler spins yarn at the rate of a million kilometers — per day. But 95 percent of its yarn is conventional. "Organic is a niche market," says Martin Kägi, Bühler's CEO.

A time-intensive niche market. For an organic cotton run, production must be halted while key machines — the cotton mixer, the carder, the comber — are cleaned to ensure that no conventional fiber contaminates the organic cotton yarn. To achieve certification from the Global Organic Textile Standard (GOTS), Bühler must meet a strict set of rules that cover everything from cotton warehousing (separate quarters only) to machine lubricants.

The end result: fine yarn that is wound on cones the size of an ice cream bucket. The yarn is visually and chemically indistinguishable from its conventional counterpart. Only a Bühler label and a GOTS certificate set it apart.

Time lapse: 1 to 2 months travel, 1 month spinning

3. Four thousand miles to Montreal

The EILEEN FISHER portion of the farmer's harvest — a twenty-foot container with six tons of ivory-colored yarn — travels by ship from Rotterdam to Montreal. There it is trucked a short distance to Tricots Liesse. The mill takes the undyed yarn — greige in industry parlance — and knits it with spandex on a machine that produces very little waste. The yardage is then carted to a separate wing to be dyed.

Time lapse: 1 month travel, 2 weeks knitting, 2 weeks dyeing ☞

4. **By truck to Long Island City, Queens**

   After an overnight trip from Montreal, huge bolts of Organic Cotton Stretch Jersey arrive at Apex Cloth Cutting, where they are unrolled on banquet-sized tables for cutting. The yoga tank's four pieces — the scoop-neck front, the racer-back and the front and back self-bras — are puzzled together on a computer-generated pattern called a marker. Wearing protective gloves, workers guide precision cutters along the marker's blueprint lines. A day or two later, the yoga tank pieces are bagged and ready to be trucked to Eternal Fashion in Manhattan's garment district.

   Time lapse: 1 day travel, 2 days to cut and truck

5. **A Manhattan moment**

   On Eighth Avenue and 38th Street, at a factory called Eternal, a loft is filled with dozens of sewing machines, steamers, pressers and the tools of the textile trade. Chatter, mostly in Chinese, criss-crosses the room. At the front door, a shrine to the Chinese god of prosperity keeps watch. Eternal's workers are immigrants, largely from Asia and Latin America. Here, with a few simple seams, the farmer's organic cotton undergoes its final metamorphosis: a yoga tank with a Made in USA label. Once folded and packed, it is sent by truck through the Lincoln Tunnel to New Jersey.

   Time lapse: 5 to 6 weeks

6. **Across the Hudson to Secaucus, NJ**

   EILEEN FISHER's distribution center is on Enterprise Avenue, a street of look-alike warehouses. The warehouse roof is covered in solar panels that generate 60 percent of its electricity usage. Trucks pull up regularly, bearing clothes from all over the world.

   Time lapse: A half hour, depending on traffic

7. **Next step: your closet**

   Once unloaded in Secaucus, yoga tanks in all sizes are logged and shipped to EILEEN FISHER's stores — the closest is 8.7 miles away in Manhattan, the farthest is 3,458 miles away in London.

Fair Trade in Fashion

Another way for a brand to signal that it is committed to worker well-being is to seek a fair trade certification. While we might be familiar with fair trade from foodstuffs like chocolate, coffee and bananas, not all of us know what it really means. Fair trade principles are easy to get behind; they almost seem like human principles:

Ten Principles of Fair Trade:

1. **Creating opportunities for economically disadvantaged producers** — poverty reduction through trade forms a key part of the organization's aims. The organization supports marginalized small producers, whether these are independent family businesses, or grouped in associations or cooperatives.

2. **Transparency and accountability** — the organization finds appropriate, participatory ways to involve employees, members and producers in its decision-making processes.

3. **Fair trading practices** — the organization trades with concern for the social, economic and environmental well-being of marginalized small producers and does not maximize profit at their expense.

4. **Payment of a fair price** — a fair price is one that has been mutually agreed by all through dialogue and participation, which provides fair pay to the producers and can also be sustained by the market.

5. **Ensuring no child labor and forced labor** — the organization adheres to the UN Convention on the Rights of the Child and national/local law on the employment of children. The organization ensures that there is no forced labor in its workforce and/or members or homeworkers.

6. **Commitment to non-discrimination, gender equity and women's economic empowerment, and freedom of association** — the organization does not discriminate in hiring, remuneration, access to training, promotion, termination or retirement based on race, caste, national origin, religion, disability, gender, sexual orientation, union membership, political affiliation, HIV/Aids status or age.

7. **Ensuring good working conditions** — the organization provides a safe and healthy working environment for employees and/or members. It complies, ☞

at a minimum, with national and local laws and ILO conventions on health and safety. Working hours and conditions for employees and/or members (and any homeworkers) comply with conditions established by national and local laws and ILO conventions.

8. **Providing capacity building** — the organization seeks to increase positive developmental impacts for small, marginalized producers through fair trade.

9. **Promoting fair trade** — the organization raises awareness of the aim of fair trade and of the need for greater justice in world trade through fair trade.

10. **Respect for the environment** — organizations which produce fair trade products maximize the use of raw materials from sustainably managed sources in their ranges, buying locally when possible. They use production technologies that seek to reduce energy consumption and where possible use renewable energy technologies that minimize greenhouse gas emissions. They seek to minimize the impact of their waste stream on the environment. Fair trade agricultural commodity producers minimize their environmental impacts by using organic or low-pesticide-use production methods wherever possible.[67]

In 2013, the World Fair Trade Organization (WFTO) launched a Product Label that is awarded only to companies who are 100 percent fair trade, dedicated to a transparent and accountable supply chain. This new label (figure II) guarantees that practices across the supply chain are checked against the WFTO Fair Trade Standards, a set of compliance criteria based on the 10 Principles of Fair Trade. UK-based brands Pachacuti and People Tree are the two pioneering companies to hold the label.

People Tree founder Safia Minney, who has been a fair trade pioneer for over two decades, started her UK/Japan-based brand with workers' skills and capacities at the forefront. For People Tree, fair trade works in symbiosis along the entire supply chain, from farm to fashion. Minney Shares, "Fair Trade takes a long term view, working in partnership with producers and enabling communities to 'invest' in environmental and social development initiatives. It recognizes that, if farmers are given the chance, they will protect the environment."[68]

The WFTO is not the only group certifying fashion. Also in 2013, the factory owned by Canadian shoe brand Oliberté, in Addis Ababa, Ethiopia, became the world's first Fair Trade Certified™ footwear manufacturing factory (by Fair Trade USA). Then in May 2014, Patagonia® began selling select women's sportswear styles that were Fair Trade Certified™ (also with Fair Trade USA).

While certification is ideal and convenient for consumers to know that the claim is being verified by a certifying body, many smaller labels and designers work to fair trade principles without a certificate, either because they aren't able to afford it or they've postponed the certification. If someone claims to be fair trade, it doesn't hurt to ask them how.

With such divergent approaches to production — chemically laden cotton versus EILEEN FISHER's source who sets out pheromone traps as a pest management strategy, from toxic dyes to Ayurvedic dyes that could heal while you wear them, to workers in unsafe conditions versus workers in fair trade cooperatives and many who work from home — the variance may make buying better seem daunting. Don't worry, there are so many great brands ahead of this curve that you'll be able to keep wearing the clothes and styles you love, easily.

Shopping for V.A.L.U.E.

As with beauty products, I wanted to devise a way for you to be able to evaluate brands and items of clothing on your own, not get bogged down in trying to remember what to avoid. Rather, a simple guide to lead you to brands that care, to products that match your ethics, in order for you move to beyond the shopping guides included with each chapter and discover your own favorite brands. The secret — shop for value.

This should be easy to remember because most of us, at our core, are "value" conscious. Fast-fashion chains who offer really cheap clothes say their "bottom line price" policy is because we (the customers) are price-conscious and demand low prices. True, we do want lower prices, but the trade-off is when we pay less, we also get less: less transparency, less accountability, fewer ethics and lower quality. We want low prices, but not at all costs. What we are really seeking is value. V.A.L.U.E.

Each letter correlates to an ethic that both helps decrease some of the burden on the industry and help you buy better. When it comes time to shop, the questions to ask are: Does it already exist (Vintage)? Does it support craft, empower women or alleviate poverty (Artisan)? Does it serve my community (Local)? Does it save something from the landfill (Upcycled)? Lastly, is it Ethical?

Let's take a look at the V.A.L.U.E. categories a little more closely. Chances are you won't ever check off every box with a single purchase, but as you read the book, and think about what's in your closet or which brands you love or aspire to own, you can think of this list.

Vintage

If you've felt the weight of a cotton T-shirt or jeans lately and found yourself remarking, "They don't make these like they used to," you are not wrong. Global warming and drought have affected cotton crops year after year. The cost of cotton has increased at the same time our demand for pricing has decreased, leaving manufacturers scrambling to either blend fibers or to simply use less; as a result, many garments don't have the same grade of fiber, weight or durability they used to have.

That's why a second-life garment, maybe one from an era when they made things better, might be a more suitable choice. Not only will it be less expensive than a newer, lighter-weight version, it will probably last longer too. **Vintage** officially refers to items that are at least 20 years old. In this book, "vintage" also means thrift, resale, second-hand, handed down and other second-life garments.

Vintage works especially well for on-trend pieces. The adage "everything old is new again" fits for fashion. Trends reappear often. The moto jacket, the plaid shirt, the fringe leather purse, the cowboy boots — they've all had their day in the fashion limelight, and it will come again. There are over 25,000 resale, consignment and vintage shops in the US alone, with more and more popping up online, and the reason is simple: vintage offers good, quality, unique pieces at affordable prices. Plus, it isn't contributing to any carbon footprint because they've already been produced.

Artisan

Artisan can mean handcrafted, handmade, collectable, one of a kind, made to order and/or fair trade. "Crafts," which the United Nations identifies as handmade goods, make up a large portion of work and profit for the developing world, especially for women. Supporting artisan products usually means you are also supporting female makers, women-led organizations and communities of people who create and make things.

Creative communities around the world are facing extinction. Textile arts, natural dying and weaving techniques are being lost. Yet, consumers have the power to halt that. More and more artisan groups are bridging the divide from their communities to Western markets with the help of designers, NGOs, the United Nations, the Smithsonian and more.

When you see the word "artisan," you should also clearly see the path to the maker. Or be able to count the steps between you and the maker. This is particularly key as often, these days, fast fashion appropriates craft and artisanal products for trend. For example, in 2012, the Navajo tribe launched a suit against Urban Outfitters for trademark violations and violations of the federal Indian Arts and Crafts Act, which makes it illegal to sell arts or crafts in a way to suggest items are made by American Indians when they're not. Urban Outfitters was selling something that looked and said it was Navajo, but wasn't.

The Navajo have about ten registered trademarks that cover clothing, footwear, online retail sales, household products and textiles.[69] They want consumers to feel confident that when they buy something that says "Navajo," they are supporting the community.

Sadly, not every artisan community has the resources for litigation or are aware of when they are being copied. But if consumers question, the truth is usually revealed. Most of the (A) listed options in the book are designers who work directly with artisans or an NGO that collaborates with artisan cooperatives. If you're not sure whether something qualifies as artisan, ask the seller if they know the maker or how the maker is getting compensated. It's common to see wording like "a portion of sales goes to...," and many retailers and websites share links, QR codes or show biographies of the makers or artisans so consumers can feel more confident about who their purchase is supporting.

Local

You don't have to support artisan communities half-way around the world; you can look for the same traits in your own backyard. Urban centers like Austin, Nashville, Los Angeles, New York, Toronto and Vancouver are full of local designers, makers and craftspeople. Local summer markets, holiday fairs, even Etsy.com show that there are makers everywhere.

Movements like Small Business Saturdays are drawing attention to small businesses and shops, local craftspeople or designers right in the neighborhood. The more general "Made in —" (insert your country here) movement is trying to raise support for homegrown manufacturing to make a resurgence.

A few words of advice here: often, when V.A.L.U.E. shopping, many want to check off **local** with other aspects. They want local and, for example, ethical, but that's not always possible. H&M has organic T-shirts, so it's easy to assume local maker-sellers should too. But H&M has a supply chain that gives them access to organic cotton, where a small business or local maker may not. So the maker may decide to use conventional cotton to make the item more affordable. Or some consumers want *all* aspects of a garment to be local when the reality is, with the offshoring of manufacturing years ago, many things, like zippers and buttons, just aren't made here anymore.

Upcycled

Upcycling is usually a feat of design genius, for example, the book shelf made of books, the door mat made of wine corks, changing our perceptions about materials and creating something new out of what might have been waste. **Upcycled** has become a trend of its own, in fashion especially.

When we are done with an item, there are really only three directions for it to go: downcycle, recycle or upcycle. Downcycle is when the item can't be reused. Maybe we can break up parts of it for other things, for example, old clothes that can't have a second life because they are too worn or stained can be downcycled into stuffing for upholstery or insulation in homes. Recycle, you recall from your 3R training (reduce, reuse and recycle), is when an object goes back into the cycle to be used again. Upcycling takes a waste that is headed downstream (often towards a landfill) and adds design or innovation to make it come back "up"-stream as an item of value.

One example is the handcrafted shoe brand Brother Vellies' Tyre Sandal, which uses tires for soles. Three million tons of tires are sent to landfills or burned in Kenya each year. Brother Vellies uses this waste product in of one of its high-end sandals. Another, the Swiss brand FREITAG (freitag.ch) takes truck tarps and remakes them into messenger and courier bags. Plastic also fits into this category. Bionic Yarn (bionicyarn.com), with Pharrell Williams (yes, that Pharell) as their creative director, makes fabrics primarily from recycled plastic bottles.

Upcycling makes a perfect addition to the ethical wardrobe: the items are almost always unique and showpieces, they are usually handmade, and you've saved something from being downcycled.

Ethical

Over a third of global consumers view style, status and sustainability as intertwined, according to a recent study. (That number jumps to 40 percent when looking specifically at millennials.)[70] Soon responsible consumption will be the norm. Words like sustainable, environmentally friendly, organic, recyclable, recycled, low impact, cruelty-free, fair trade, fair made and others related to ethical fashion may seem confusing, or hard to differentiate, but consumers are seeking them out more and more.

Ethical fashion, in my definition, encompasses cruelty-free treatment of animals, ethical and fair labor practices and/or positive environmental practices — a lot of "ethics" in one category (care of animals, people and planet), and they are not always inclusive of each other. It is possible to find companies and designers who focus on only one of these aspects. That's not so surprising — if you had a dinner party and asked friends around the table what's more important — protecting the planet, the animals, or the people — you would likely have a lively debate. Let's take a look at these three components separately.

CRUELTY-FREE (VEGAN)

Many people can't speak about ethics without discussing the ethical treatment of animals, especially in fashion. With the global increase of veganism, some consumers want to avoid animal products altogether, while others want to know how the animals were treated in the making of their products, including leather, angora, cashmere, wool and fur.

This has created a huge niche for animal- and cruelty-free designers. Stella McCartney is probably the most well-known, but the options have increased to include globally known brands like vegan designer Vaute Couture (outerwear), Cri de Coeur (shoes), Olsen Haus (shoes) and Matt & Nat (bags).

If your ethics include veganism, it is possible to dress head to toe without a single animal product. If you're not vegan, but care about the ethical treatment of animals, upcoming chapters also deal with specific animal materials and how to shop for ethical versions.

Fair Labor Practices

An earlier section covered this quite extensively. Worker treatment and worker rights are an aspect of consideration for many buyers. If we can buy eggs based on the treatment of the chickens — were they fed vegetarian feed or hormones? were they enclosed in cages or allowed to run outside and be free-range? — surely we should be able to know the conditions in which our garments are made. The myriad fair trade labels are starting to make this easier to know.

Positive Environmental Practices

Choosing environmentally friendly practices is essential to the future of the fashion industry. Pesticide and water usage to grow fibers, water usage to dye and wash the garments (presale), the energy to both manufacture and ship — it's clear fashion needs to clean up its act. The good news is that the industry has started, in some ways that are transparent to consumers and in others that are completely hidden (greening through the back door.)

Brands like Levi's and H&M make very public claims about the efforts they are making, sharing these in their marketing plans. You might have seen the Water<Less™ labels on Levi jeans, indicating their efforts to reduce water usage. Or the Conscious Collection at H&M, a seasonal effort to produce garments using sustainable fabrics.

There are real efforts going on behind the scenes as well. In 2009, Walmart and Patagonia sent out a letter to some of the largest clothing companies, inviting them to participate in a coalition to measure sustainability. Many responded, and now brands, manufacturers and retailers that represent 40 percent of the global market dollars for apparel and footwear work together to share ideas and best practices in the Sustainable Apparel Coalition. Brands including Adidas, Asics, Brooks, Burberry and Columbia and retailers Gap, J.C. Penney and Macy's are working to build standardized tools to measure sustainability. Called the Higg Index, this new global sustainability tool measures and scores products, factories and companies and aims to set a universal standard for sustainability and how to communicate it to consumers. When the Higg Index launched in 2012, it measured only environmental stewardship. It relaunched a 2.0 version in 2013 that now also includes measurements for social and labor standards.

While the Higg Index is an industry-specific tool, a new certification that communicates care for people and planet is Certified B Corporation. B Corps, as they are often called, or benefit corporations, started in 2007 as a way for companies to state that their corporate focus would put as much emphasis on doing good as on making money. Patagonia, Indigenous Designs, Ben & Jerry's, Method Products and an additional 1,047 companies across 34 countries and in 60 industries have amended their legal corporate framework to declare they're both a "for profit" and a "for good" company. They pledge to meet standards in three silos: how they impact the environment, treat employees and benefit the community. This means that companies have clarified with shareholders (if they have them) and stakeholders that corporate decisions must meet the triple bottom line: benefit people, planet and profits. You can look for companies with these declared values by seeking the B in a circle icon on their products or hangtags.

Now that you're armed with the principles and background of the Magnifeco V.A.L.U.E. checklist and you know whether to look for something **vintage, artisan, local, upcycled** or **ethical**, let's dive a little deeper into some industry game changers and brands to shop.

Game Changers
PEOPLE TREE

People Tree, the first fashion brand to be certified by the WFTO, was also the first to be certified by the Soil Association, a British organic certification primarily for food, showing the products met organic standards from field through manufacturing. Like some American beauty brands gravitating towards USDA Organic certification, for People Tree it was important to align with a certification that consumers associated with safe farming as the People Tree collection is primarily organic cotton.

The company's tagline is "For every beautiful garment People Tree makes, there is an equally beautiful change happening somewhere in the world." People Tree Japan and UK work with over 150 fair trade groups in 12 countries, creating a livelihood for over 4,000 farmers and artisans. Over 20 years ago, People Tree began as a global fair trade campaigning organization in Japan and has never lost that sense of protecting the planet and the workers. The leader in the organic cotton fashion movement, it developed the first integrated supply chain for organic cotton from farm to final product, and was the first to achieve Global Organic Textile Standard (GOTS) certification on a supply chain entirely in the developing world.

Factory work is beneficial to raising standards of living, but often requires migration and separation of families. One of the key issues for People Tree is supporting hand skills. Says Minney:

> Hand skills such as weaving and embroidery promote livelihoods and good incomes in rural areas for artisans and sustenance farmers all over the developing world. There are ten million living by hand weaving in India and Bangladesh alone. The production of fabric using hand loom rather than a machine saves one ton of CO_2 per year. Which means that if we Western consumers switched to buying fair trade, millions of families would be lifted out of poverty and we would be reducing global warming.[71]

People Tree has garnered the support of Emma Watson and Alexa Chung and collaborated with designers like Boru Aska, Orla Kiely and Vivienne Westwood.

Nicole Bridger Designs

Canadian designer Nicole Bridger interned at Vivienne Westwood, then worked with Lululemon developing a sustainable line called Oqoqo before designing her first line and launching her eponymous label, Nicole Bridger Designs, in 2008.

Bridging the gap between cool, comfortable clothing and sustainable design matched Bridger's West Coast sensibility. When she opened her first flagship in Vancouver in 2011, she felt on her way to her goal of international expansion. Then she got a call: the owners of her Mount Pleasant factory were going to retire. Bridger scrambled to secure financing so that the 15 employees wouldn't lose their jobs and she wouldn't lose her access to local manufacturing. Successful, she now owns her own factory, which is less than five miles from her boutique. In addition to her own line, she's also able to provide small-run production for other local designers.

Study NY

In reaction to overconsumption and mass merchandising, some designers are stepping away from the traditional fashion calendar (which can see them designing up to 12 collections a year). One of the first to step away from this mode of business was Montreal-born, New York-based designer Tara St. James and her label Study NY. The motto at Study is "Making fashion without making waste." In 2013, tired of producing an endless cycle of "change" and creating new pieces to feed a never-ending fashion cycle, Study launched seasonless capsule collections.

Capsule collections are made up of essential pieces that are not trend driven and are not meant to go out of fashion, what St. James calls a "timeless uniform." She designs three to six pieces, usually stemming from her search for the "perfect" piece, for example, a good sweater, made by a women's cooperative in Peru, and releases them monthly or bi-monthly.

This is not the first time St. James has broken the traditional designer mold; she named her label "Study NY" because she wanted the flexibility to "study" fashion and its possibilities and potential to be different. Since it launched in 2009, Study NY has been at the forefront of ethical fashion design in New York, including collections produced entirely from environmentally friendly fabrics, collections using zero waste methodology and most recently cross-cultural collaborations with cooperatives and artisan groups.

There are so many more entrepreneurs, designers and companies who are getting it right; the following shopping guide is but a small segment in an ever-growing sector of ethical fashion.

Shopping Guide
Womenswear Canada

- Nicole Bridger, nicolebridger.com. Nicole Bridger Design is a fashion line for the effortlessly chic and environmentally conscious woman. Also has a maternity-friendly line. V.A.L.U.E. — (A) A small portion of each collection is made overseas, including fair trade artisans in Nepal. (L) 90 percent of the Nicole Bridger line is manufactured at her own factory in Vancouver. (E) Uses environmentally friendly fibers, low-impact dyes and ethically made fabrics, such as linen and Tencel®, plus many fabric suppliers are Global Organic Textile Standards (GOTS) certified. Also uses buttons made of tagua nuts, shells or reclaimed materials. See also pages 84–85. Shop at Nicole Bridger boutique in Vancouver, Canada, available at independent retailers in Canada and the US or online with international shipping.

- Thieves, thievesboutique.com, a contemporary brand by Sonja den Elzen is dedicated to slow fashion. Its signature Metamorph dress can be worn over 20 ways. V.A.L.U.E. — (L) Designs and manufactures in Canada. (E) Uses fabrics such as organic wool, organic cotton, peace silk, Tencel®, bamboo and hemp. Online with international shipping.

- Zen Nomad, zennomad.ca, also by Sonja den Elzen (Thieves, above), is a yoga lifestyle collection that honors the non-harmfulness element of yoga in its sustainable production methods. V.A.L.U.E. — (E) Many of the pieces are made from locally knitted, organic, closed loop bamboo/spandex jersey. Available in select boutiques and yoga studios and online with international shipping.

Womenswear US

- a.d.o., adoclothing.com, stands for Anjelika Dreams Organic and integrates the ancient Indian tradition of Ayurvedic herb dye with a fluid and feminine design aesthetic. V.A.L.U.E. — (L) Produced in the New York garment district (E) Most a.d.o clothing is 100 percent certified organic fabric, dyed using natural Ayurvedic ingredients such as indigo, turmeric, lemon and pomegranate to give them beneficial properties. Available at independent retailers in Canada and the US and online with international shipping.

- Alabama Chanin, alabamachanin.com, offers heirloom pieces sewn by hand, each made to order. V.A.L.U.E. — (A) The homegrown group of artisans use straight stitch, appliqué, reverse appliqué, embroidery and beading to embellish garments. (L) Everything is made in Alabama, even the organic cotton is from the US. (E) Company is rooted in slow design movement, and creates all products in socially and environmentally responsible ways. Online store with international shipping, offers studio style do-it-yourself workshops and sells sewing guides and patterns.

- Alternative Apparel, alternativeapparel.com, is focused on fabric innovation and creating womenswear and menswear, casual and activewear grounded in social responsibility. V.A.L.U.E. — (E) Sustainable fabrics make up 65 percent of the collections, use low-impact dyes on all sustainable fibers. Committed to worker rights in all countries and supporting the right to fair and safe workplace conditions, factories are under the Fair Labor Association, and some certified by WRAP. Brand boutiques in the US. Online US only.

- Amour Vert, amourvert.com. Casual womenswear where "Paris chic meets Cali cool." V.A.L.U.E. — (L) All clothing designed and sewn in San Francisco, CA. (E) Works with a zero-waste design philosophy and uses only organic and sustainable fabrics along with low-impact dyes. Also partners with American Forests and plants a tree for every T-shirt bought, planning to plant 100,000 trees by the end of 2015. Amor Vert boutique in San Francisco, online store with international shipping.

- Bhoomki, bhoomki.com, designs and manufactures ethically produced womenswear collections. V.A.L.U.E. — (L) Produces much of its collection in New York City. (E) Uses fabrics committed to environmental and social responsibility like US-grown organic cotton and handwoven, fair wage artisan fabrics. Shop at Bhoomki Boutiques in Brooklyn and online.

- Datura, datura.com, is an elegant, slow fashion brand redefining the basics, both formal and informal. Designed and made in New York and in the designer's native Spain. V.A.L.U.E. — (E) Uses natural fabrics such as organic cotton, silk, linen and cashmere. Online only with international shipping.

- ecoSkin Collections, ecoskincollections.com, a California brand, offers easy-wear, contemporary womenswear that is good for the planet. V.A.L.U.E. — (E) Uses only environmentally sustainable luxury fabrics woven, dyed and sewn in the USA. Available at independent retailers in the US and Canada and online with international shipping.

- EILEEN FISHER, eileenfisher.com, a New York fashion brand, is known for simple clothes in fabrics, shapes and proportions that work together effortlessly, is a socially responsible company, committed to sustainability, human rights and global initiatives that empower women and girls. V.A.L.U.E. — (U) GREEN EILEEN program: recycles EILEEN FISHER clothes for resale, keeping clothing out of landfills while raising money. In the first four years, sales from this program totalled $2.2 million, all of which went to non-profit groups that work to empower women and girls. (E) 20 percent made in US. Committed to sustainable fibers and production. See also sidebar on pages 72–74. Stores in US, Canada and UK. Online store with international shipping.

- Feral Childe, feralchilde.com, offers seasonal collections, elegantly tailored featuring original prints; pieces are wearable silhouettes for forward-thinking women. V.A.L.U.E. — (L) Produced in the New York garment district. (U) Often uses upcycled fabrics or mill-end/reclaimed/vintage/deadstock fabric. (E) Uses natural fibers such as organic cotton, hemp, Tencel®, Cupro, linen and silk; conscientious application of printing and dyeing (less water-intensive digital printing for the silks, water-based silk screening, low-impact dyes); uses domestic printers and dye houses. Available at independent retailers in the US and abroad, and online with international shipping.

- Groceries Apparel, groceriesapparel.com, offers men's and women's basics with all the right ingredients. V.A.L.U.E. — (L) Vertically integrated garment manufacturer based in the L.A., all the manufacturing, sourcing and creative aspects of the business support the local economy (U) Many fibers are recycled; including recycled polyester and recycled cotton. (E) Traces all fabrics from farm to factory and use organic cotton from India and CA. Available at independent retailers in the US and abroad, and online with international shipping.

- Indigenous, indigenous.com, creates clothing that is versatile and elegant. V.A.L.U.E. — (A) The brand works with fair trade artisan partners in Peru. (E) Clothes are made with organic and natural fibers, such as cotton, alpaca, merino wool and Tencel®. Uses low-impact dyes. Committed to full transparency. Certified B Corporation. At select retailers, and online US only.

- Organic by John Patrick, organicbyjohnpatrick.com. CFDA (Council of Fashion Designers of America) member John Patrick launched Organic in 2004 as a line of contemporary, conscious apparel that prioritizes organic materials, fair labor practices and ecological awareness. V.A.L.U.E. — (E) He was one of the first designers to develop a direct relationship with organic farm collectives in Peru and has helped to innovate the use of botanical dyes, digital print techniques, recycled fabrics and organic wool yarns. Uses organic cotton and other OEKO-TEX certified fabrics. Available at select retailers and online with international shipping.

- Loomstate, loomstate.org, is a casual basics line with a focus on supply chain transparency. V.A.L.U.E. — (L) Active in sustainable fashion initiatives and often hosts environmental events around New York. (E) Works with sustainable farming communities around the world to design 100 percent organic cotton apparel and only with factories that accept its strict vendor compliance agreement and restricted substances list. Online store with international shipping.

- Osei Duro, oseiduro.com, produces textiles and garments in Ghana, applying traditional techniques such as hand dyeing and weaving. Ethical clothing rooted in traditional textiles. Active in womenswear, jewelry and bags. V.A.L.U.E. — (A) Produces fabric and garments in Ghana, working with local artisans on traditional weaving and dyeing. Available at select retailers in Canada and US and online store with international shipping.

- Raleigh Denim, raleighworkshop.com, is a "Made in the USA" denim line founded in North Carolina in 2007. V.A.L.U.E. — (L) The Raleigh store also contains the workshop. (A) It crafts denim the old-school way, by hand and in small batches. Hand-stamped leather patches show that they're one of a limited run. Stores in Raleigh and New York plus select global retailers and online store with international shipping.

- Simply Natural Clothing, simplynaturalclothing.com, is a sustainable fashion brand of luxury apparel and accessories designed by Holly Henderson NY. V.A.L.U.E. — (L) This knitwear brand is manufactured in the US using US-sourced alpaca. (E) Cruelty-free: alpaca is harmlessly sheared from the animal, the fleece is then spun into yarn. Alpaca is chemical free, and biodegradable. At select retailers and online store with international shipping.

- Study NY, studyny.squarespace.com, is an ethical contemporary womenswear company that believes clothes should be well-made using quality materials, and the hands that manipulate those materials should be respected and cared for. V.A.L.U.E. — (L) Manufactures in New York and is sold in many local boutiques. (U) Has collaborated with other ethical designers on an exclusive line of quilts utilizing off-cut scraps. (E) Offers full transparency on its website, uses environmentally friendly fibers and low-impact dyes. See also page 85. Available at independent retailers in the US and abroad, and online with international shipping.

WOMENSWEAR INTERNATIONAL

- Bibico, bibico.co, a British brand, has been focusing on simple, ethical clothing and offering great knits since 2007. V.A.L.U.E. — (E) Collections are stitched, woven and knitted from high-quality natural materials in fair trade cooperatives. Much of the knitwear is made by hand. Online store with international shipping.

- Christopher Raeburn, christopherraeburn.co.uk. British fashion designer Ræburn creates menswear, womenswear and accessory collections, known for bringing sustainable design to the mainstream through collaborations with brands like Victorinox, MONCLER and Fred Perry. V.A.L.U.E. — (U) His RE-MADE ethos results in many upcycled offerings like jackets made from parachutes and dresses made from 1950s Royal Air Force silk escape maps. Over 60 stockists worldwide plus online store with international shipping.

- From Somewhere, fromsomewhere.co.uk, has been upcycling since 1997. Rather than a traditional fashion collection, From Somewhere operates as an idea factory, combining sustainable thinking with fashion-forward design. The brand has brought upcycling to the mainstream through wholesale and collaborations. (Past collections have appeared in Topshop.) V.A.L.U.E. — (U) Works primarily with pre-consumer surplus from the manufacturing houses and textile mills of the luxury fashion industry. Online store with international shipping.

- Good One, goodone.co.uk, is a British brand who believes that design should not only satisfy a hunger for new and constantly evolving concepts in style, but should also address the environmental impact of the fashion industry. V.A.L.U.E. — (U) Specializes in upcycling, Good One has developed a design method that uses recycled fabrics in its color-blocked styles. (E) With its "One Good Factory" in Bulgaria, it facilitates sustainable manufacturing and support to other brands and retailers to work with pre- and post-consumer waste textiles. Available at independent retailers in the US and abroad, and online with international shipping.

- Kuyichi, kuyichi.com, is a Dutch brand started in 2000 when the founders, NGO Solidaridad, wanted to secure big brands for its organic cotton but couldn't find any interest. V.A.L.U.E. — (E) Uses recycled cotton and PET bottles, as well as other sustainable materials with a low ecological footprint like Tencel®. Works with textile dye houses, laundries and mills with advanced water recycling and cleaning processes in place, where water is recycled and reused. Also uses natural indigo dye. Works with MADE BY and Fair Wear Foundation. Available at independent retailers in the EU, Switzerland and Singapore and online with international shipping.

- Monkee Genes, monkeegenes.com. The tagline from this British denim brand is "Organic Jeans Made by People Who Care." V.A.L.U.E. — (E) The first jeans label to have accreditations from the Soil Association, the Global Organic Textile Standards (GOTS) and PETA certified. Online store with international shipping.

- Nurmi, nurmiclothing.com, is a sustainable clothing label from Lahti, Finland, that creates casual and classic menswear and womenswear and accessories in the Nordic tradition of minimalism and long-lasting design. V.A.L.U.E. — (E) Organic cotton, hemp, recycled fabrics and leftover materials are always used, not thrown away. Available at independent retailers in Finland and the EU and online with international shipping.

- People Tree, peopletree.co.uk, offers casual and comfortable menswear and womenswear. V.A.L.U.E. — (E) Certified fair trade, certified GOTS. (A) WFTO certified for its fair trade work with artisans in developing countries. (E) Uses 100 percent organic cotton, low-impact dyes, as much handmade as possible. Certified by the Soil Association and many items are GOTS certified. See also pages 83–84. Online store with international shipping.

- Skunkfunk, skunkfunk.com, an international fashion brand from Spain, believes a sustainable fashion industry is vital. V.A.L.U.E. — (E) 41 percent of the collection is made from sustainable fabrics, such as organic cotton, linen, recycled polyester and Tencel®. GOTS certified, the percentage increases each year. GOTS certified, the percentage increases each year. Application for OEKO-TEX standard 100 is in process, plus all new Skunkfunk suppliers are requested to have a social certification (BSCI, SA8000, ETI, FLA, FWF or WRAP). Skunkfunk stores in Paris, Berlin, San Francisco, Bilbao, Dublin, Santiago de Chile and Barcelona; select retailers and online store exclusively for US and Canada.

MENSWEAR CANADA

- Zen Nomad, zennomad.ca. See page 86.

MENSWEAR US

- Alternative Apparel, alternativeapparel.com. See page 87.
- Groceries Apparel, groceriesapparel.com. See page 88.
- Indigenous, indigenous.com. See page 89.
- Loomstate, loomstate.org. What started as the idea to make a totally transparent T-shirt has evolved into a relaxed basics line with plans to add organic denim in 2015. See page 89.
- Raleigh Denim, raleighworkshop.com. See page 89.
- Simply Natural Clothing, simplynaturalclothing.com. See page 90.

MENSWEAR INTERNATIONAL

- Christopher Raeburn, christopherraeburn.co.uk. See page 90.
- Kuyichi, kuyichi.com. See page 91.
- Monkee Genes, monkeegenes.com. See page 91.

- Nudie Jeans, nudiejeans.com, is a Swedish brand that has been selling denim products since 1999. In addition to jeans, it offers selvage denim, khakis, jackets, sweaters, shirts and T-shirts. V.A.L.U.E. — (E) It has a transparency map that highlights where each piece in the collection is produced. Uses organic cotton. Certified Fair Wear Foundation, OEKO-Tex 100 and Global Organic Textile Standards (GOTS). Nudie also wants you to keep your jeans as long as possible, and has repair shops in Sweden, Germany and the UK. Available at independent retailers in Finland and online with international shipping.
- Nurmi, nurmiclothing.com. See page 91.
- People Tree, peopletree.co.uk. See page 92.

UNIFORMS AND BLANKS

- Alta Gracia Apparel, altagraciaapparel.com, is a socially responsible producer of collegiate licensed apparel. Parent company Knights Apparel has strategic licensing arrangements with the NHL and the majority of colleges and universities in the US. V.A.L.U.E. — (E) It owns the factory and offers living wages, benefits and education for workers and families in the Dominican Republic, producing collegiate wear that is "sweatshop-free."
- Loomstate, loomstate.org. Aside from seasonal collections, Loomstate also designs and produces custom private label uniforms, crew uniforms and corporate wear, including Chipotle Mexican Grill. It also sells wholesale blanks in 100 percent organic cotton and produces promotional gear. See also pages 89, 92.
- TS Designs, tsdesigns.com, is a full-service apparel manufacturing and screen printing company in Burlington, NC. V.A.L.U.E. — (L) Cotton of the Carolinas products offers "dirt to shirt in 700 miles." (E) It offers the most sustainable T-shirts and options including its patented water-based print/dye system, REHANCE.

Thrift Shops

Lastly, don't forget all of your local thrift, charity and second-hand shops. Also consider raiding the closets of those sartorially blessed in your circles or family, jumping into local clothing swaps or organizing your own. The

E-commerce Sites

You can also try these multi-brand e-commerce sites who specialize in ethical fashion offerings.

Canada

- Body Politic: shopbodypolitic.ca
- GreyRock Clothing: greyrockclothingco.com
- New Classics: newclassics.ca

US

- Beklina: beklina.com
- Helpsy: shophelpsy.com
- Kaight: kaightshop.com
- Of A Kind: ofakind.com
- The Pure Thread: thepurethread.com
- Shop Ethica: shopethica.com
- Zady: zady.com

International

- ASOS (Green Room): asos.com/Women/Green-Room
- A Boy Named Sue: aboynamedsue.co
- Gather and See: gatherandsee.com
- Master Muse: masterandmuse.com
- NOT JUST A LABEL (NJAL): notjustalabel.com

options abound! Plus, online is also an option. Beyond eBay (still a great source), there's a new generation of online thrift and consignment shops:

- Bib + Tuck: bibandtuck.com
- Poshmark: poshmark.com
- Threadflip: threadflip.com
- thredUP Consignment: thredup.com
- The RealReal: therealreal.com

Final Notes

Where things are made, by whom and how, are key to ethical fashion, but our role in this cycle and ethical consumption cannot be overlooked. Several years ago, before this book was even a wisp of an idea, I created a pamphlet called the *Guide to the Conscious Wardrobe*. There have been a few versions, but each one starts with the same point: *buy less.*

The industry is producing 90 billion garments per year.[72] And we are buying them at an unprecedented (and unsustainable) rate: an average of 62 items per year.[73] And we are paying less per item than ever before: on average $19 per piece.[74] Shockingly, 18 of those garments never get worn[75] — that's almost 1.7 billion unworn items.[76]

The issue of sustainability is central to this book, but consumption rates cannot be overlooked. Nor can our quest for the lowest price. When I speak at events or even with friends, the topic of pricing always comes up. Many balk at the thought of "ethical fashion" because of preconceived notions of higher prices. This is not entirely unfounded; careful fashion takes time (recall EILEEN FISHER's journey of a yoga top), and that costs money.

We didn't arrive at our desire for the lowest price overnight; mass manufacturing uncoupled consumption from production long ago. We no longer think about *who* made what we buy or *how* they made it.[77] In her book *Cheap*, Ellen Ruppell Shell suggests, "Cheap objects resist involvement. We tend to invest less in their purchase, care and maintenance and that's part of what makes them so attractive.... We have grown to expect and even relish the easy birth and early death of objects."[78] Maybe that's why fast fashion seems like a habit hard to break: it's a quick, pull-off-the-rack purchase that requires so little thought due to the low price point that it feels like a stress-free purchase.

Commitment to change and towards a more sustainable wardrobe requires rewriting this expectation. It requires a new commitment to "V.A.L.U.E." My hope is, with this acronym, we can limit waste by appreciating the quality and resources that have already been expended in vintage and second-life garments. Saving money on those purchases so we can invest a little more in the garments being made by the game changers, and other ethical designers and retailers, will slowly start to change the system.

Chapter 3

Special Occasions

"If you don't have transparency everything else is
just words and heritage, which has become a legacy
disconnected from the product."[1]

— Bruno Pieters,
Founder and CEO, Honest By

IN OTHER BOOKS, this chapter might be called "luxury," referring to
high-end items made with exquisite attention to detail. However, in
the context of ethical fashion, luxury and its associated meaning are
being re-examined. Our perception of luxury, and the brands traditionally associated with that term, is becoming dated and jaded. For most of
the 20th century, paying more money equated to buying a product that
was truly exceptional: luggage from Louis Vuitton, gowns from Christian
Dior — the prestige of these items, with their superior craftsmanship
and design, defined luxury. Sadly, times have changed. Heritage brands
are still garnering high prices (Louis Vuitton, Hermès, Gucci, Prada and
Rolex were the top five luxury brands in 2014[2]) but consumers are not
always getting the craftsmanship of days gone by. Luxury is now a vehicle
for big business — sector sales are set to reach US $405 billion by 2019.[3]

In 2007, Dana Thomas, a cultural and fashion writer for *Newsweek*, in
Paris, wrote an exposé titled *Deluxe: How Luxury Lost Its Luster*, revealing
that, like contemporary and fast fashion, luxury brands had moved to less
expensive offshore production. However, the high ticket prices associated

with those brands remained as if they were still being produced in the "atelier." Then in 2012, the *Financial Times* reported, "It is the worst-kept secret in the retail industry that many luxury brands have outsourced to China."[4] The general feeling is that offshoring is not a subject that a brand should discuss in public because it could undermine brand value, but it has been whispered about, for years.

This is not the section where I bash China. Finger pointing at a country doesn't account for the complexity of production in developing countries that can serve as a bridge to prosperity (not always a smooth, direct bridge, but a bridge nonetheless). Nor does it acknowledge that every country has an artisan sector. Modern China is synonymous with mass production, yes. But it is also home to some of the first recorded textile artisans and the creation of silk. So to speak negatively about something *made in China* is throwing the artisans out with the mass-market bathwater.

The bigger issue is buyers of modern heritage luxury thinking they are getting the work of domestic artisans (French seamstresses, Italian tailors, etc.) when that may not be the case. It is becoming more probable that domestic artisans are not being replaced by equally skilled counterparts from other regions, but rather the kind of cost cutting that is normally reserved for mass production. To repeat Thomas, luxury has lost its luster.

Common cost cutting strategies in the sector don't just include offshoring production and using cheaper materials but also employ tactics such as cutting sleeves a half an inch shorter, replacing finished seams with raw edges and eliminating linings on the grounds that "women didn't really need" them.[5] All to increase shareholder bottom line. Replacing skilled artisans with machines and outsourcing labor to less expensive markets offers the same cost savings to luxury brands that it does to contemporary and fast-fashion brands, which is increasingly a requirement of the corporate conglomerates who have been acquiring luxury brands since the eighties. To date, 40 of the top fashion brands belong to six conglomerates.[6]

With these conglomerates shifting luxury to meet corporate objectives, the question remains: What, exactly are consumers paying for by purchasing "heritage luxury" on the basis of ancient craftsmanship? Lack

Who owns who in fashion

LVMH Moët Hennessy —
Louis Vuitton:
A world leader in
high-quality products

Over 60 prestigious brands

Total 2013 revenue:
€29,149 million

Louis Vuitton, Fendi,
Donna Karan, Loewe,
Marc Jacobs, Céline, Kenzo,
Givenchy, Thomas Pink,
Pucci, Berluti and
Rossimoda and more

Kering (formerly PPR):
A world leader in apparel
and accessories

Total 2013 revenue:
€9.7 billion

Gucci, Bottega Veneta,
Saint Laurent,
Alexander McQueen,
McQ, Balenciaga, Brioni,
Christopher Kane,
Stella McCartney,
Sergio Rossi, Boucheron,
Girard-Perregaux,
JeanRichard, Qeelin,
Pomellato, Dodo, Puma,
Volcom, Cobra, Electric
and Tretorn

PUIG: A third-generation
family-owned fashion
and fragrance business
based in Barcelona

Total 2013 revenues:
€1,499 million

Carolina Herrera,
Nina Ricci, Paco Rabanne
and Jean Paul Gaultier

Richemont SA:
The owner of some of the
world's most prestigious
luxury goods Maisons

Total 2013 revenue:
€10 649 million

Alfred Dunhill,
Azzedine Alaïa, Chloé,
Lancel as well as
Net-A-Porter

OTB: The holding company
of some of the most
iconic fashion brands

Diesel, Maison Margiela,
Marni, Viktor & Rolf

JAB Holdings:
A Luxembourg-based
and privately held
group

Jimmy Choo, Bally,
Belstaff and Zagliani

*Source: corporate annual reports and websites

of transparency in this sector has created an opportunity for a new, ethical, transparent luxury. One that focuses again on craftsmanship and on artisan talent rather than brand name or geographical locale. One that focuses on the luxury of hand-loomed silks from Kanchipuram, gilded brocades from Benares, batik from Indonesia, even kimonos from Kyoto. New luxury supports some of the world's most beautiful and endangered craft communities in remote locations to ensure that the time-honored secrets held in the families of ancient craftsmen once used to adorn nobles and kings are not lost. These items might be purchased only for special occasions or when worn, might lift every occasion to be special.

Silk

Nothing epitomizes luxury garments like silk. When silk was first discovered in China (some samples date back to 4000 BCE[7]), it was reserved exclusively for the use of the ruling classes. The lustrous material changed the way people dressed, influenced the way luxury was perceived and paved the way for linking artisan cultures from China to Europe.

After China revealed its discovery (sometime in the first millennium BCE), the fabric solidified trade routes between China and India in the East and Europe and Persia in the West. Silk was so highly desirable that it was often used as a currency with equal value to gold, silver and precious stones.

A variety of indigenous wild silk moths are found around the globe, and sericulture industries (the business of silk production) have developed in more than 20 countries. China produces about 70 percent of the world's silk, followed by Brazil, India, Thailand and Vietnam. Sericulture is labor intensive and provides incomes for about 1 million workers in China, 700,000 households in India and 20,000 weaving families in Thailand.

Domesticated or cultivated sericulture involves two factors: perfecting the diet on which the silkworms feed and preventing the moth from hatching. A key reason why silk is expensive and often finds its home in the luxury category is that this process is lengthy and requires constant attention. The Silkroad Foundation shares the steps:

- After they hatch, baby silkworms feed every half-hour on fresh hand-picked and chopped mulberry leaves until they are very fat. The newly hatched silkworm multiplies its weight 10,000 times within a month, changing color and shedding its whitish-gray skin several times.

- The silkworms feed until they have stored up enough energy to enter the cocoon stage. While growing, they have to be protected from loud noises, drafts, strong smells, even the odor of sweat. When it is time to build their cocoons, the worms produce a jellylike substance in their silk glands, which hardens when it comes into contact with air. Silkworms spend three or four days spinning a cocoon around themselves until they look like puffy white balls.
- After eight or nine days in a warm, dry place, the cocoons are ready to be unwound. First they are steamed or baked to kill the worms or pupas. The cocoons are then dipped into hot water to loosen the tightly woven filaments. These filaments are unwound onto a spool. Each cocoon is made up of a filament between 600 and 900 meters (almost a mile) long. Between five and eight of these super-fine filaments are twisted together to make one thread.[8]

The undamaged cocoon is key to silk production and is often why vegans and animal rights activists take exception to this. But there are more natural options. Rather than spinning silk from domesticated worms, natural silk — sometimes called "wild silks" or "peace silks" — can be created by allowing the silkworms to complete metamorphosis and emerge from their cocoons. Broken cocoons are then collected and, because the cocoon is "damaged," the silk is often spun as a fiber rather than reeled as a thread. This produces a different fabric and often costs more due to the added time required to salvage and spin the abandoned cocoons.

Perhaps the most well-known peace silk is the Ahimsa Silk Project, a process patented by Kusuma Rajaiah in Hyderabad, India. Ahimsa is a Sanskirt word for "non-violence," and Rajaiah's vision was to promote non-violence through fabric. The Ahimsa Silk Project works to develop the peace silk industry in India, to train local artisans in the manufacturing of wild mulberry ahimsa silk and to raise global awareness for these silks.

Ahimsa silk can be purchased dyed with Ayurvastra, the ancient method of using Ayurvedic methodology and medicinal plants for dyes mentioned in chapter two. Wild and peace silks can also come raw, natural undyed or, in the case of Muga silk, in its natural golden-hued state.

It's common to find Ahimsa and peace silks used by vegan and ethical designers who are not deterred by the price tag associated with the rarity and effort of creation.

Artisans Around the World

Behind agriculture, artisan activity is the second-largest employer in the developing world.[9] According to the Alliance for Artisan Enterprise, "hundreds of thousands of people in the developing world, largely women, participate in the artisan sector. For many, their livelihood depends on income earned from their artisan activities."[10]

The last chapter revealed that 70 percent of worldwide apparel exports come from developing countries, highlighting how apparel often provides entry into formal employment for the unskilled, the poor and women.[11] Formal employment is one way to enhance poverty eradication; support of artisan sectors is another.

In Cambodia, for example, poor farmers and producers living in rural areas make up 85 percent of the population; however, there are also an estimated 20,000 silk weavers. The government of Cambodia has identified the silk industry as a strategic area for poverty reduction that can directly contribute to job creation, particularly in rural communities.[12]

Similarly, in India, Varanasi silk has been produced for so long that common folklore holds that the Buddha was laid to rest in a veil made from the famous handwoven brocade.[13] Until a decade ago, the Varanasi region was flourishing with over 100,000 handloom weavers; however, current estimates see those numbers dwindling to around 40,000.[14] As artisan skills and handcrafted talents compete with modernization and the power sector (in this case, power looms), artisan communities are coming under pressure. Typically, artisan skills and knowledge are passed down through the generations; however, the current generation sees more value in migrating to an urban locale and falling into the formal employment sector rather than carrying on traditions. Varanasi silk, like many other renowned skills, is considered an *endangered craft*.

The economics in the artisan sector is upside down: working on an electric loom pays weavers more than the more laborious (and also delicate, unique and handcrafted) handlooming. Handloom artisans in Varanasi earn around 200 rupees a day (about $3.10 US), while their counterparts in factories earn 500 (about $7.90). Both are paid, in part, on how much cloth they produce: one meter of cloth can be produced per day on a handloom, compared to ten meters on an electric loom.[15] A backward aspect of the fashion industry at large: quantity has more value than quality.

While the financial pull of mass production is a strain on artisan communities, so are consumer choices. Consumers who would normally pay a higher price for intricate items, like a sari of Varanasi silk, find themselves drawn to lower cost items. Removed from fashion production and source and without the context of artisan skill to associate with the price tag, we are often choosing price over provenance or quality, leaving many artisan groups competing with low-cost, mass-produced imitations.

That's why groups like the United Nations, the Smithsonian, UNESCO, Ethical Fashion Initiative and NGOs like Build a Nest are getting involved. If Greenpeace and the WWF have been striving to save species from extinction, the collective effort of these groups is striving to save ancient artisan skills from extinction.

If you are a modernist, you might be wondering — why? Why not move forward with time and technology, and embrace the machine (or power loom) and let it go? For many communities, textiles are a form of communication and a fabric of history, not to mention that urban migration is not going to suit all seven billion of us. The Alliance for Artisan Enterprise puts it this way:

> The depth and scope of economic development impact of artisan enterprises is often not fully appreciated. They generate income, create jobs, foster economic communities, sustain ancient techniques, and preserve culture and meaning that is an essential component of healthy and sustainable development—development that is grounded in the uniqueness of people and place. And in conflict regions, economic community through artisan work can promote reconciliation, healing, and empowerment.[16]

It begs the questions: If we can romanticize Florentine leather workers, can't we also do the same for Kenyan beaders? If the artisans of Western Europe could live solidly middle-class lives, why can't those in

Africa and Southeast Asia? Several groups and designers are aiming to ensure that happens. Maiyet, a new luxury brand that celebrates rare artisanal skills from unexpected places, is attempting to make Varanasi silk the new "it" textile, not just for its beauty, but because its use in high-end fashion is part of a bigger mission, consumer purchases making a direct impact on artisan livelihood.

As the appeal of exquisite, artisan craft grows, fashion companies, accustomed to the reliability of factory-made goods, are struggling with the unique challenges of manufacturing in a community setting. Factors like weather, access to materials and catering to Western tastes are some of the challenges facing artisan groups, and where NGOs like Nest (a New York-based non-profit that partners with artisans to build sustainable businesses) come in. In addition to Maiyet, a strategic partner of Nest, other brands like TSE cashmere, Valentino, Celine, the Elder Statesman and ABC Carpet & Home have benefitted from Nest's artisan business and leadership training and design mentorship, plus assistance in construction of new facilities for artisans.

Nest has created a model that estimates the value of individual artisan work on the greater community. It estimates 20 lives are touched for every one Nest artisan employed in its six existing project sites in India, Kenya, Swaziland, Bali, West Java and Mexico. That means artisan work and access to Western markets can transform entire communities through alleviation of poverty. Plus, in many cases, supporting artisan products also empowers women.

While the brands and designers of this modern luxury may be new, the price tag isn't. This is luxury as it was in heritage days—craftsmanship, attention to detail, top textiles and fabrics—with the prices to match.

Shopping for V.A.L.U.E.

Let's get back to the idea of Special Occasion wear. If you are on a reduced budget, or don't see yourself finding much use beyond the single wear, then perhaps renting will suit you. Once an option reserved exclusively for men (and tuxedos), this category has seen incredible growth in the last few years. Whether it's cocktail dresses or full evening gowns, bridesmaids dresses or wedding dresses, the borrowing economy has started to take hold — and yes, men are still covered.

Keeping with the digital age, many rental websites offer solutions that include sending several dresses to try on at home, well in advance of the event, and then reserving your chosen dress for the future date; or choosing a style and receiving two sizes, so that there are no surprises on the big day.

Popular Rental Options:

- Borrowing Magnolia, borrowingmagnolia.com. Rental options for modern brides: borrow or buy with in-home-try-on program. Plus takes submissions and offers to rent or sell dresses for past brides.
- The Black Tux, theblacktux.com. Based in LA, tuxedos and suits for every body type and occasion. Also offers shirts, vests, neckwear, suspenders, belts, shoes and even cufflinks and studs.
- Little Borrowed Dress, littleborroweddress.com. The solution for bridesmaids: dresses come in 12 styles and 18 colors. All dresses are made in New York and are designed to flatter all body types. Prices start at only $50.
- Rent frock Repeat, rentfrockrepeat.com. Canada's option to rent designer dresses. Offers private fittings by phone or Skype with an RfR stylist.
- Rent the Runway, renttherunway.com. High-end designer dresses and accessories for rent. Specializing in formal, cocktail, night out, daytime and wedding dresses. (The Las Vegas shop is dedicated to bridal gown rentals.) Has iPhone app and offers personal styling appointments at retail locations (NY, DC).
- Vow to be Chic, vowtobechic.com. With a tagline "being a bridesmaid is an expensive honor," it offers designer bridesmaid dress rentals starting at $50. Offers complimentary consultations with a bridal stylist.

If renting isn't for you, another way to get into the spirit of a seldom-worn garment is to seek vintage. Hollywood sirens are commonly seen on the red carpet in archive and vintage designer wear these days; why not you? The resale market is booming, especially for well-made fancy items. If you are inexperienced or nervous about what to look for and how to buy a good piece, New York vintage maven and thrift hunter Ariana Boussard-Reifel shares her wisdom on what to look for and how to ramp up your vintage knowledge before starting the search.

How to Buy Vintage

Vintage clothing, as a rule, was made at least 20 years ago. It is very common to walk into a garage sale or thrift store and find true vintage from the 70s, 80s and 90s. Earlier clothing is less common, but also still present

Buying used clothing can be tricky. How do you discern the difference between a rare designer 1980s blazer — say, Moschino — and something from the DressBarn three seasons ago with an equally wacky pattern? When you are buying a piece that is being sold as vintage, how do you know it is worth the asking price? How do you even identify vintage in the first place? Here are a few tips.

Why Is Vintage Sometimes Quite Expensive?

A lot goes into that vintage dress, but you wonder if you should spend $60 on it.

First it has to bear the test of time. Someone loved it, saved it and cared for it so that you could find it. This is a great testament to the quality of the piece and should add to its value in your mind.

It was chosen by a vintage clothing dealer, likely cleaned, repaired, stored, researched, steamed, maybe even photographed, styled, uploaded, measured, described, packaged and shipped. So you are paying not just for the special piece but for someone's time and taste to bring it to you. The markup on vintage is far less than the markup your typical fast-fashion chain is getting and you're supporting a charity or small business!

Ways to Spot Quality Vintage

1. Look for Flaws — Know When to Hold It, Know When to Fold It

- It is rare to find something flawless, be sure to check the piece out well.

- Look for stains in the underarms, collar and inseam. These usually won't come out; nearly everything else can be removed with care and patience.

- Check for holes. Knits especially get holes from moths. The easiest way to check is to put your head inside it and look out. Where you see pinpricks of light, there are holes.

- Check the seams. Often a seam or hem will open up. This is an easy and inexpensive fix, so if you love the piece, don't let this stop you from buying it! ☞

- Check the closures. Zip and unzip everything, clasp and unclasp everything. These parts have a tendency to break and can be pricey or impossible to fix.
- Pay attention to the quality of the fabric. Some vintage pieces have become brittle or delicate with age, so if you are planning on wearing it, look carefully and see that the material isn't starting to be threadbare or cracked.

It is tempting to buy things that just need a little work if they are a good deal. Know yourself and decide whether you really will do the repair or cleaning. If not, save on all those $15 pieces that are almost perfect and buy something lovely for a little more money that you will cherish.

2 Look at the Fabrication — The Truth Is in the Making

Good, quality manufacturing was common practice 50 years ago. You can expect that a casual vintage piece is made as well as a contemporary designer piece and a designer vintage piece is made as well as couture is today.

- Something that actually has some age will be made differently and likely be of a natural material, silk, wool or cotton, not polyester (unless you're hunting 70s bell-bottoms). You'll see acetate too, especially in 40s and 50s gowns.
- Skirts and dresses will be lined, maybe even with silk.
- Zippers will be metal pre-1960s.
- The label will look old, be stitched, not glued on. It will probably be made in the US (there might even be a union label), Italy, France, India, Hong Kong or Taiwan, but probably not China. Chinese manufacturing boomed in the 1970s.
- Handmade garments will have stitching that looks slightly irregular. A beautiful dress from pre-1970 would likely have been finished by hand, so that is a great way to determine quality.

3. Authenticity — Don't Fake It Till You Make It

- Authenticity can be hard to determine as labels and fabrications styles change season to season for many fashion houses. Look to see that it meets all the fabrication guidelines for great quality set out above; if so, the Internet is an incredible resource. Spend a little time on your smartphone Googling pictures of labels. ☞

- It's probably real. Unless is it Louis Vuitton, Fendi, Chanel, Hermes, Louboutin or Pucci (popular brands for fakes). Some really popular items (like the Alexander McQueen skull scarf or a Coach purse) get knocked off as well. But if you're looking at a designer piece that hasn't been blogged about, it probably wasn't worth it for the criminals to fake and is thus likely to be real.

- If it is a very expensive item, think about it and walk away, talk to an independent dealer about it, do some research and then come back. Vintage people usually love to help bring awareness and you'll find a wealth of information can be yours with a smile and a few kind questions.

- Most importantly, trust your gut. Once you've seen a handful of vintage, you'll sense what is nice and what isn't. Trust that.

Buying Online

It is hard to buy on auction sites. Blurry pictures, dealers you don't know, incomplete descriptions... I would suggest only buying items that are cheap enough that if you lost out, you would feel all right.

Instead, buy from independent online boutiques where the love of vintage is apparent. Buy from dealers that have long-lasting reputations and have return policies. Again, educate yourself over time, and then you'll feel confident to move into the pricier items.

All in all, vintage has irregularities and inconsistencies; it is unusual and might surprise you. That is what makes it wonderful. Don't go in looking for perfection; look for something that makes your heart beat a little faster. Buy something that makes you feel pretty or speaks to you. It is all about the love of the item, the life it has lived and the life you can bring back to it. Buy what you love, regardless if you feel that it is valuable. Valuing pieces is the job of the dealer; loving it is what we hope a customer will do.

The joy of a great vintage piece lies in the pleasure it gives you, plus depending on the care you give it, you can probably recoup some of the investment in resale (if you choose to put in back into the resale cycle after your use).

— Ariana Boussard-Reifel, Founder of Mode Marteau

If you're not interested in rental or vintage and have committed that this special occasion deserves the splurge, here are some brands that most certainly will be future vintage.

Game Changers
LEILA HAFZI

Leila Hafzi defines luxury as "something rare that has taken considerable time to make." Her hand-draped collection of formal dresses and bridal gowns fit that description. When traveling in Kathmandu, she found herself inspired to start a fashion company that met several purposes: to help shift the impression of Nepal and raise awareness of artisan communities there; to employ women and teach them highly specialized skills (like draping); and to build a sustainable, ethical business that would grab consumers' attention and imagination before they even knew the label's backstory. When launched in 1997, the brand was heralded as the first high-end ethical and eco-conscious fashion brand to empower women in developing countries while inspiring the fashion industry into a global shift.

Her work has been featured in numerous European magazines, and LEILA HAFZI was the first non-Italian brand to win the prestigious prize at Sposa Italia in 2012. Although she regularly has new bridal and red carpet collections, she is also available for custom orders.

Honest By

Belgian-born Bruno Pieters has a storied background that rivals most luxury designers: he attended the Royal Academy of Fine Arts in Antwerp; upon graduation worked with Martin Margiela, Christian Lacroix and others before becoming creative director for Belgian luxury leather brand Delvaux; and then was art director for Hugo Boss. At the same time, he had his own label of ready-to-wear collections for men and women that received accolades for its craftsmanship and sharp tailoring.

Then, in 2010, Pieters stepped back. Burned out and needing a break, he found himself in India, pondering his future and wondering if fashion, as he knew it, would be in his future. During this two-year sabbatical, he became increasingly aware of and concerned for the environment, animal welfare and children's causes, and drew on these new passions to craft a fashion company that respects the environment, eschews animal products in production and finds ways to add value throughout the supply chain.

Launched in 2012, his brand Honest By became a pioneer by featuring designer products with complete transparency in price and manufacturing. By offering full transparency on cost, source, supply chain and markup, Pieters created a new paradigm in fashion. This figured into the brand name: *honest*, refers to the way in which the Honest By company operates, with 100 percent transparency and traceability.

Home to Pieters' own limited-edition pieces for men and women, the Honest By website also provides a platform for other designers and brands who share the transparency vision. This is not the only step forward for Pieters; he plans to create the first 3-D printable collection of shoes and accessories, which will eliminate labor issues and allow consumers to choose their own recyclable (hopefully) materials.

Maiyet

To hear Maiyet's co-founder Paul Van Zyl speak requires a little pinch; he is not a typical fashionista, but then again, Maiyet is not a typical fashion company. Created as a vehicle to lift artisans in developing economies and to help alleviate poverty, promote peace and empower women, Maiyet has a backstory that is anything but typical.

Brainstorming in Davos, as Van Zyl and social entrepreneur Daniel Lubetszy (of KIND Healthy Snacks) tried to think of a vehicle to create the greatest social change, they kept circling back to fashion as the industry that could create the greatest results and meet the goal. Linking the influence and affluence of some of the world's most beautifully dressed with some of the world's most under-recognized artisans, Maiyet has fast-tracked its way to the top of the "new luxury" category.

Following the conventional luxury brand playbook, Maiyet recruited a veteran fashion executive (co-founder Kristy Caylor), named a top model as the face of the brand (Daria Werbowy, also spokesperson for Lancôme), presented at Paris Fashion Week and is now featured regularly in international publications of *Vogue, Elle, The New York Times* and *Harper's Bazaar*.

Named after the Egyptian goddess of truth and harmony (Ma'at), Maiyet recognized that superb artistry could be saved and new life could be breathed into ancient techniques like Varanasi silk, knitwear from Peru and Bolivia, and jewelry from Jaipur. The hangtags on items in its SoHo flagship store read,

> Maiyet is pioneering a new luxury by celebrating the rare and unexpected. Rooted in craftsmanship, Maiyet is cultivating the next generation of global artisans from Kenya to Indonesia, Colombia to India, Peru to Italy. Due to the handcrafted nature of our products, certain irregularities should be expected.

Pioneers in this arena, Maiyet has also crafted a new business model that includes a strategic partnership with Nest, the non-profit organization dedicated to training and developing artisan businesses to promote entrepreneurship, prosperity and dignity. This partnership allows Maiyet to forge ahead with the goals and benchmarks of a typical luxury fashion brand and leaves artisan needs assessments, customized training/development programs and overseeing goals to alleviate poverty, empower women and promote peace to Nest.

Shopping Guide

- Brave GentleMan, bravegentleman.com, offers classic menswear tailoring and ready-to-wear suits, shirting and accessories in premium ethical fibers. V.A.L.U.E. — (L) Made in US. (E) PETA vegan fashion award winner; uses luxurious, recycled or organic textiles free of animal fibers. In addition to high-end menswear, also active in shoes made from Italian-milled future-leather and outerwear featuring Japanese-made future-suede, made from 80 percent recycled polyester, as well as hats featuring future-wool from a US-based mill that turns polyester from mechanically recycled soda and water bottles into felt. Online store with international shipping.

- David Peck USA, davidpeckusa.com, is a full-scale American fashion house, specializing in ready-to-wear, custom evening and bridal wear. V.A.L.U.E. — (L) All designs and manufacturing in his own factory in Houston, TX. (E) Socially responsible company, dedicated to employees and community. Available at select boutiques in the US.

- Deborah Lindquist Eco Couture, deborahlindquist.com, is one of LA's top environmentally conscious designers. Deborah Lindquist specializes in bespoke and limited-edition red carpet special-occasion dresses, skirts, bustiers and corsets, plus wedding garments. V.A.L.U.E. — (L) Made in LA. (U) Makes unique pieces with upcycled parachutes and Sonic Fabric, an audible textile developed by artist Alyce Santoro and created from recycled recorded audio cassette tape. Also has a line of reincarnated cashmere items. (E) Uses peace silk, organic cotton and organic linen grown from non-genetically modified plants and Tencel®. Available at select boutiques, special order and online with international shipping.

- Eden Diodati, edendiodati.com, is an ethical luxury line committed to social justice, founded by Jennifer Ewah. V.A.L.U.E. — (E) High-end formal gowns are ethically produced in Italy, providing sustainable employment for formerly marginalized women. Uses GOTS-certified organic silk, plus 10 percent of dividends are donated to Médecins Sans Frontières International. Online store with international shipping.

- Honest By, honestby.com, founded by Belgian designer Bruno Pieters. Honest By's position is that fashion is about beauty and that the story behind fashion can be equally beautiful. V.A.L.U.E. — (E) Extensive research is conducted on organic and sustainable fabrics and their suppliers. Website lists production information from yarn and button origin to fabric and manufacturing details. Suppliers are vetted to ensure every component in every product has the smallest impact on our health and environment. Honest By is a hub for designers who share Pieters' philosophy and also want to feature full transparency. Online store with international shipping. See also pages 109–110.

- LEILA HAFZI, leilahafzi.com, has been heralded as the first high-end, ethical and eco-conscious fashion brand to empower women in developing countries while inspiring the fashion industry into a global shift. V.A.L.U.E. — (A) All dresses are hand-draped and handmade by skilled artisans in small production units based in Kathmandu, Nepal. (E) Materials include organic cotton and silk loomed in Nepal with organic silk yarn and natural dyes. A member of the Ethical Trading Initiative, Norway (IEH), a multi-stakeholder initiative involving companies, employers, organizations, trade unions and NGOs. Available at select boutiques in France, Spain, Italy and the US, with plans for a flagship boutique in Hafzi's native Oslo. Also does trunk shows, various fashion weeks and may be contacted directly for special orders. See also page 109.

- LINDEE DANIEL, lindeedaniel.com, has carved a unique niche within the world of handmade and hand-draped wedding dresses. V.A.L.U.E. — (L) Gowns are created locally in LA. (E) Uses only sustainable fabrics like wild and peace silks, organic cottons and other natural fabrics, in the fiber's natural color or with a natural dyeing process. Signature indigo is sourced from a women's co-op in Central America. Available through select bridal boutiques or contact directly for custom orders.

- Minna, minna.co.uk, was launched by Finnish-born, UK-based designer Minna Hepburn in 2008. The line includes vintage-inspired bridal dresses and accessories and also features womenswear and a range of children's clothing inspired by Hepburn's daughter's love for pretty and playful dresses. Her children's wear label, launched in 2009, is made entirely from leftover and end-of-roll textiles. V.A.L.U.E. — (L) Dedicated to local manufacturing. (E) Each dress is hand embellished and made from sustainable, organic, recycled and locally produced textiles. Available at the London boutique, online with international shipping and for custom orders.

- Maiyet, maiyet.com, is pioneering a new luxury by creating a fashion brand that celebrates rare artisanal skills from unexpected places. V.A.L.U.E. — (A) Revives ancient artisan techniques in places such as India, Indonesia, Italy, Kenya, Mongolia and Peru. (E) Interested in building capacity, with Nest, creating customized training programs that assist artisan partners in creating higher-quality, exceptional products and promoting stability and prosperity in their communities. Available at its flagship SoHo boutique, through Barneys, Net-a-Porter, Moda Operandi and at select boutiques worldwide. See also pages 110–111.

- MAYER, Peace Collection, mayer-berlin.com. German designer Christine Mayer uses materials as a source of creativity. Renowned for her Peace Collection made from recycled pillowcases, Russian army backpacks, men's vests, French army jackets, etc. V.A.L.U.E.—(L) Pieces are handmade in the studio attached to her Berlin Atelier. (U) Exquisite antique materials are reborn into unique, one-of-a-kind pieces. (E) Charity work is an essential element of the business; a portion of the income, as well as the complete profits of the charity shirts, is given to various charity and children projects. In 2012, launched a new Spirit & Soul Line made from Seacell, 100 percent seaweed jersey. Available at the Berlin Atelier or online with international shipping.

- Obakki, obakki.com, is a Vancouver-based luxury label that offers timeless staples based on a model of "fashion with a purpose." The brand uses fashion as a fundraising vehicle to bring water and education to people in Africa. Obakki covers 100 percent of the administrative costs for the Obakki Foundation, allowing every donated dollar to go directly to humanitarian projects. The Foundation is currently focused on providing access to water and education in Cameroon and South Sudan. V.A.L.U.E. — (L) Manufactured locally in Vancouver, BC, whenever possible. (E) The Obakki Foundation has built 15 schools in Cameroon, provides ongoing support to three orphanages and has built more than 700 water wells in South Sudan. Available at select boutiques and online with international shipping.

- OSKLEN, osklen.com, is one of Brazil's leading luxury designers. Oskar Metsavaht created OSKLEN to represent the lifestyle of contemporary women and men in a world where urban and nature, global and local, organic and technological live together. V.A.L.U.E. — (E) Considered both ethically minded and eco-friendly, Metsavaht also founded E Institute (Instituto e), a non-profit organization dedicated to the promotion of sustainable human development, which develops the e-fabrics project that, in partnership with companies, institutions and research centers, identifies fabrics and materials developed from social and environmental criteria. Available at 77 OSKLEN stores in Brazil, New York and Miami and in select department stores worldwide.

- Prophetik, prophetik.com. Tennessee-born designer Jeff Garner creates unique luxury sustainable designs that showcase better sartorial options than traditional luxury. He has dressed ethically minded celebrities like Gisele Bundchen, Esperanza Spalding and Kings of Leon. V.A.L.U.E. —

(L) 90 percent of designs are created in his Tennessee studio. (E) Uses sustainable fabrics like hemp, silks and blends of natural fabrics. Available at high-end boutiques across the US and for custom orders.

- Stella Jean, stellajean.it. The Rome-based fashion label of Haitian-born Stella Jean blends old-continent cultures with the verve of the new continent in her women's and menswear collections. V.A.L.U.E. — (E) Collaborating with the International Trade Center (ITC), a joint agency of the World Trade Organization and the United Nations, the ITC Ethical Fashion Initiative is about creating beautiful luxury handwork produced 100 percent ethically by disadvantaged communities in Africa. Sold in select boutiques across Italy and available on Moda Operandi.

- Titania Inglis, titaniainglis.com. Each season, designer Titania Inglis chooses a unique, sustainable element to incorporate into her minimalist line of dresses, jackets and separates. Past collections have included responsibly sourced fur, natural dyes, Japanese denim and laser-cutting. V.A.L.U.E. — (L) Each garment is sewn in a small factory in New York. (E) Collections are made from high-quality sustainable fabrics including organic wool, Japanese organic cotton, dead stock from the local garment industry and ethical fur. Plus chooses low-impact dyes and non-toxic silkscreen inks. Available at select boutiques, online with international shipping and for custom and bridal orders.

Final Notes

Dr. Kate Fletcher, an academic and leading voice in ethical fashion (she literally wrote the textbook), has a side project called Local Wisdom. This five-year project collected stories and "examples of garments that are used in ways that save resources and give us satisfaction" — stories about the connections that people make to their clothes and how they think and feel when they wear certain clothes. Participants are invited to bring cherished items, be photographed in them and share their stories. My favorite, from an event in Devon in 2009, is a woman photographed in a beautiful gown, who shares,

> At the moment I just wear [this dress] for special occasions, but I once met a woman who was in her 80s and who wore

evening wear all the time. She'd made a decision years before not to buy any new clothes and to wear everything until it wore out. She'd worn her way through her wardrobe and had got to her evening wear. So when I'm in my 80s, it's going to be this dress.[17]

That encapsulates my hope and dream for "special occasion" wear — that this chapter provides a roadmap to finding special pieces that give you delight and meaning. Pieces that you can (and will) wear often. Or at least every day in your 80s.

Chapter 4:

Jewelry

> When we buy things in one place, it has repercussions
> some place else.... When we put our credit card down
> we endorse a corporation and their practices and
> what it takes, and how it affects thousands, if not
> millions of lives.[1]
>
> — Edward Zwick,
> director of the Hollywood movie, *Blood Diamond*

AS WITH BEAUTY AND FASHION, the ethical element of jewelry is dependant on source and supply chain. While arguably the brightest and possibly most expensive items in our wardrobe, the glitter of jewelry can mask the deplorable conditions that are rampant in this industry: civil war, human atrocities, child and forced labor, and environmental catastrophes. The list is as shocking as it is long. While the first three chapters covered chemicals, reducing our toxic load and recognizing artisan value, this chapter is about human rights violations and environmental degradation.

Driven by the demand for natural resources, conflict is mounting across the globe. We are familiar with conflicts over oil and petroleum, but they are also being waged for water, timber and minerals such as cobalt, tungsten, copper, gold and diamonds. Sadly, jewelry consumers are complicit in supporting the nefarious side of this industry, lured by marketing and hampered by lack of transparency.

Wearing jewelry and adorning ourselves are as old as time. A piece of jewelry can be a promise, a repository of memories or a statement of our individuality and generally falls under three categories: fine, bridge and costume. *Fine* jewelry includes items that use gold and other precious metals in addition to precious stones like diamonds, sapphires, emerald or rubies. *Bridge* describes the pieces that bridge between fine and costume, often using gold filled, silver or vermeil (gold plating over silver) as the metal and then semi-precious stones such as amethyst, citrine, jade, garnet or freshwater pearls. *Costume* uses base metals, glass, plastic, wood and other materials. Price points are dictated as much by craftsmanship and artistry as materials.

Gold

This bright, lustrous metal, used over the ages to express wealth and love, has a dark side. In addition to funding current conflicts in the Democratic Republic of the Congo, Sudan and the Central Africa Republic, "blood gold" or "conflict gold" is often mined through forced and slave labour. In South Africa alone, an estimated $2 billion worth of illicit gold is brought to market by criminal syndicates that, in looting the country's gold mines, force miners to stay below ground so long their skin turns gray — giving them the nickname "ghost miners."[2]

Mining, like cotton, involves both large-scale industrial and small independent miners, often called "artisanal miners" (a term used in tandem with "small-scale mining" and referred to as ASM).[3] The terms "artisanal miner" and "artisanal mining" are misleading. "Artisanal" is generally understood to mean independent, creative enterprise; however, in the case of mining, it is a warning sign that the mining is unregulated, done informally and, in many cases, illegally. It is estimated that the livelihoods of more than 150 million people, mainly in developing countries, rely on ASM.[4] But coerced and forced labour aren't the only concern; child labor is rampant in ASM.

The International Labor Organization (ILO) reports,

> Gold mining is extremely dangerous work for children. Yet still today, tens of thousands are found in the small-scale gold mines of Africa, Asia and South America. Children

work both above and underground. In the tunnels and
mineshafts they risk death from explosions, rock falls, and
tunnel collapse.[5]

Human Rights Watch estimates more than 20,000 children work in
gold mining in Mali,[6] and the ILO estimates as many as 50,000 children
work in Peru.[7] A joint report by the ILO and the International Programme
on the Elimination of Child Labour, titled *Child Labour in Gold Mining:
The Problem*, describes the dangers:

> In the tunnels... they breathe air filled with dust and some-
> times toxic gases. Above ground, children dig, crush, mill,
> and haul ore — often in the hot sun. Some stand for hours in
> water, digging sand or silt from riverbeds and then carrying
> bags of mud on their heads or backs to sieving and washing
> sites. In all mining sites, there is risk of falling down open
> shafts or into pits that are scattered around the areas.[8]

Then, there's the environmental impact of mining, which includes
contamination of soil, groundwater and surface water by chemicals.
According to Earthworks, producing gold for one wedding ring generates 20 million tons of waste (a mass larger than the pyramids), often
leaving the surrounding water and land polluted with mercury and cya-
nide.[9] Mining chemicals are persistent and can stay toxic for centuries.[10]

Ethical Choices

To help consumers find ethical alternatives, Fairtrade International
launched a certification for gold and silver in 2013. Based on a new set
of standards and premiums for gold, silver and other precious metals,
the certification is meant to help grow the market for small-scale miners
worldwide and deliver an ethical and responsible source of gold for the
jewelry trade.[11] Although they are new to the market, you should now be
able to find certified fair trade gold and silver. Other metals are expected
to follow.

On the broader environmental side, "No Dirty Gold" is a campaign
launched by the NGO Earthworks to drive consensus in the industry
(miners and retailers) to commit to environmental pledges. This also

led to the creation of the Initiative for Responsible Mining Assurance (IRMA), a voluntary, multi-sector collaboration of industry, retail, labor and civil society groups to set and independently verify best-practices standards for mining companies. Like other "greening through the back door" initiatives, IRMA should help bring change to the large-scale mining side of the business.

Thanks to these initiatives, ethically sourced, traceable gold is now available. Since the demand for jewelry consumes 80 percent of the world's gold,[12] this means we (and our consumer dollars) have a lot of sway in creating change in this industry. And thinking of V.A.L.U.E. — many smaller jewelry designers are now working exclusively with recycled metals, using the 157,000 tons of gold that have already been mined.[13]

Diamonds and Other Precious Stones

Everyone knows that "a diamond is forever," but what most of us don't know is that statement, and everything we believe about the romanticism of the diamond engagement ring, was all part of a marketing plan launched by N.W. Ayer & Son, the advertising agency for De Beers Consolidated Mines in the 1930s. The romanticizing of diamonds was an advertising ploy to create an endless market for De Beers.

To create a market for a product that people neither wanted nor needed, N.W. Ayer focused on the one ritual that would never go out of fashion — the engagement — and placed the engagement ring, in our minds, as the ideal medium for the transaction. In this way, for as long as people got engaged, De Beers would have a steady stream of customers.

In further marketing genius, in order to ensure that consumers didn't sense they were being marketed to, or at the risk of having the campaign come across as a "marketing" scheme, the agency enlisted Hollywood starlets and socialites to help make diamonds an aspirational item. Newspapers were fed pictures of celebrities displaying the stone as a symbol of romantic commitment, and soon every girl wanted one. Thus, the concept of the diamond engagement ring as the eternal symbol of love for both starlets and the girl next door was born.[14] The campaign was successful not just in America; De Beers also successfully created engagement ring markets in Japan and Germany.

Advertising executives the world over have being trying to emulate the complete market creation and success of the N.W. Ayer/De Beers team. *Advertising Age*, the magazine for the industry says,

> Before the De Beers mining syndicate informed us "A Diamond is Forever," associating itself with eternal romance, the diamond solitaire as the standard token of betrothal did not exist. Now, thanks to the simple audacity of the advertising proposition, the diamond engagement ring is de rigueur virtually worldwide, and the diamond by far the precious gemstone of choice.[15]

In 1999, *Advertising Age* cited the slogan as the most memorable of the 20th century.[16]

But the sparkle of the industry had a sudden crisis in late 2006 with the opening of the film *Blood Diamond*, which told the story of the illicit diamond trade and its funding of the bloody civil war in Sierra Leone. For the first time, in harsh Hollywood style, consumers got a peek at the nefarious side of the diamond trade. The movie had an immediate effect: at the 2007 Academy Awards (the film was nominated for five), the red carpet was nearly devoid of any diamonds. For the first time since N.W. Ayer had made the red carpet synonymous with the brilliant stones, movie stars wanted to distance themselves from the jewels and any presumed support of the conflict mineral business.

Since *Blood Diamond*, most conversation and exploration of supply chain has focused mainly on "conflict" diamonds. Some in the industry have even quipped that it's not the 4Cs of diamonds — a reference to the diamond quality rating system devised by N.W. Ayer and De Beers — it's the 5Cs: cut, color, clarity, carat and *conflict*. Diamonds have fueled civil conflicts in Sierra Leone, Angola, Liberia, Ivory Coast and the Democratic Republic of Congo, resulting in the displacement of millions and the deaths of millions more.[17] Allegedly, they also have a place in conflicts closer to home in funding Bin Laden and al-Qaeda.[18]

To try and stem diamonds' role in conflict, the Kimberley Process Certification Scheme (KPCS) was established in 2003. It started as a working group to monitor the industry, when 83 countries joined together to (try to) ensure that any diamond originating from their country did not finance a rebel group or other entity seeking to overthrow a UN-recognized government. The participating countries also agreed that no diamond would be imported from, or exported to, a non-member of the scheme.

However, this last part has proven problematic. Allegations that diamonds are secretly moving from countries not participating in the KPCS through countries that are participating has cast a shadow on the program as a whole, and as a result, several NGOs have pulled their support for the KPCS, including UK-based Global Witness, the group that initiated it. In 2009, Global Witness stated, "Despite having all tools in place, the Scheme was failing effectively to address issues of non-compliance, smuggling, money laundering and human rights abuses in the world's alluvial diamond fields."[19]

Edward Zwick, director of *Blood Diamond*, has joined Global Witness in its efforts to separate diamonds from conflict. Says Zwick, "Unfortunately, the Kimberley Process's refusal to address the clear links between diamonds, violence and tyranny has rendered it hopelessly ineffectual. In effect, it has become an accomplice to diamond laundering — as well as the corruption and depredations that inevitably follow — by offering the illusion of institutional cover to endemic and escalating corruption."[20]

One industry specialist told me that "the KPCS should be respected as the first attempt. The process is not perfect, but it has raised awareness and shone a light on a problem that might never be solved." Unfortunately, diamonds are not alone in the conflict stone arena; there are rubies from Burma, sapphires from Sri Lanka, emeralds from Columbia; the list goes on. Conflict stones are difficult to avoid.

New York-based jewelry designer, lapidarist, gemologist and past president of the American Society of Jewelry Historians Reema Keswani has direct experience with the issues surrounding gemstone mining. She shares that, from a jeweler's perspective, it is almost impossible to honestly guarantee that every stone is 100 percent clean. She states, "Precious or semi-precious stones move through a complex supply chain. Even if you are being as careful as possible, you can't have eyes everywhere. Transparency is not possible yet but we are making our way surely, if slowly."[21]

Mining is just one part in the supply chain. After they are mined, rough gems are consigned to a broker, who sells to jewelers and wholesalers.

The gems still need to be cut. Here too, issues arise. If the gems are cut abroad, often in Southeast Asia, there is a high risk of child labor; small fingers and acute eyesight make children the ideal candidates for this job. In 2013, World Vision Australia came out with a report titled *Behind the Bling* that focused on the use of child labor in the entire jewelry supply chain. According to its research, in addition to mining and gem work, children in India can be found flattening pieces of silver with hammers to be adorned with gems, cutting links of silver and hooking them together into chains, welding on adornments or fasteners, or cutting and polishing gemstones.[22]

Just as in fast fashion, the jewelry industry runs on a business model that is supported by the interwoven dependency of mass production and mass consumption. If you see commercials or advertisements for what seem to be exceptionally low-priced gems, they are most likely part of a system that funnels gems, blind to provenance, through sweatshop factories in Thailand, India and China, so that chain stores can sell their jewelry at artificially low prices. If buying gemstones, it is wise to ask not only where the stone came from but also where it was cut.

Lab-grown Diamonds

Want to be 100 percent certain that a diamond isn't involved in conflict? Choose one of the new crop of *lab-grown* or *cultured* diamonds. Technology can grow a diamond with the same quality and purity as a mined diamond without any of the associated issues.

Valuable for their unparalleled hardness, diamonds are often used in industrial settings for cutting and grinding and are even found in automobiles — there is over one carat of industrial diamond used in the production of every car made in the US.[23] Eighty percent of all mined diamonds end up in industrial use, so eventually technology was going to be tasked to mirror geology and fuse carbon. However, in the last few years, the laboratory quality has been high enough to duplicate the physical characteristics of gem diamonds, to the point that appraisers often cannot tell the difference.

Critics of lab-grown diamonds still fall back on the De Beers marketing doctrine, claiming that mined diamonds are rare, precious and valuable, and make a wiser investment. Not true, revealed Edward Epstein, in his exposé "Have You Ever Tried to Sell a Diamond?": "Those who attempt to sell diamonds often experience disappointment at the low price they are offered."[24] Diamonds, shares Epstein, are neither rare nor valuable.

Ethical Options

If you have your heart set on diamonds or other precious stones — you can shop with V.A.L.U.E. Some jewellers sell antique and vintage stones. You can enjoy the vintage setting or reset the stones in a contemporary setting. Add recycled or fair trade certified metals and you are set.

Jewelry comes in so many other materials beyond the traditional metal and gem combinations, especially as we delve into artisan offerings from around the globe. Let's take a look at the good: sustainable, natural and upcycled materials; the bad: wildlife and endangered materials; and the ugly: heavy metals and toxins.

The Good — Sustainable Pearls

Pearls were once considered the "Queen of the Gems." At the height of the Roman Empire, natural pearls were so rare that a necklace, made up of about 50 perfectly matched spheres, was considered the most expensive jewelry in the world.[25] But by the early 1900s, several Japanese entrepreneurs, mostly notably Makimoto, shifted the industry as they developed techniques to get oysters to produce pearls on demand and unlocked the secret to "farming" oysters.

Cultured pearls are now available from many countries and can be grown in both fresh and salt water. Zhejiang province in China has become the new epicenter of the world's freshwater pearl market. With a comparably high quality, these Ming pearls are grown in mussels instead of oysters and appear on the global market at a fraction of the price of their international counterparts[26] — the "fast fashion" of pearl farming.

An alternative to cheap, mass-produced pearls are *sustainable pearls*, a label that is being used by ethical pearl farms in Fiji, French Polynesia, Mexico, Micronesia and the United Arab Emirates. Sustainable pearls focus on economic, environmental and social sustainability.[27] When consumers seek out brands using this term, they supporting pearl farms that are committed to

• protection of the biosphere

- sustainable use of natural resources
- production transparency and product disclosure
- developing and operating farms in a socially and culturally responsible manner
- management commitment and local law compliance[28]

Sustainable pearl farms are often located in zones with sensitive coral reef ecosystems, so the pearl farmers are also guardians of the reef. This is the case for Kamoka, a small sustainable pearl farm on a Pacific Ocean atoll that has been pioneering environmentally friendly farming techniques since 1992.

Other Natural and Sustainable Materials

Horn and bone often play a role in artisan jewelry. The types of horn and bone depend on geography, as the source is usually the meat industry. Artisans then upcycle the by-products into stunning pieces. Some horn can look like lacquer or tortoiseshell (the trade of tortoiseshell has been banned since 1973), and some bone, when polished, resembles ivory (also banned).

Nuts and seeds can also resemble precious materials. Tagua, often called vegetable ivory, grows south from Panama along the Andes to Ecuador, Bolivia, Columbia, northwestern Brazil and Peru. The nuts are harvested after falling to the ground and dried out before several artisan groups craft them into rings, necklaces, bracelets, etc. Other common seeds include Job's tears, sourced from wild grass native to Southeast Asia but also prominent throughout the Western Hemisphere. When dried, the seeds are oval and pearly white (often used to make rosaries). Coral seeds, bright red and resembling red coral, come from shade trees on coffee and cacao plantations of Central and South America. They are also used for necklaces.

Golden grass is a plant that grows in Brazil. It shines and, when woven into necklaces, bangles and earrings, is often mistaken for gold. Golden grass is protected by Brazilian laws in order to preserve the environment and social and economic balance for the community and artisans that depend on it. True golden grass cannot be sold unprocessed outside the artisan region of Jalapão.[29]

Upcycling

Magazine pages rolled into paper beads, bicycle inner tubes laser cut to look like intricate lace, sea glass handcrafted into pendants — upcycling can be found in all price ranges, adding value through creativity and design. Fonderie 47 makes high-end luxury jewelry, including watches, out of guns and weapons confiscated in African conflict zones.

Brass

With its gold-like appearance, but without any of the mining issues (or price tag) of gold, brass isn't just for musical instruments. A common material in artisan jewelry, brass is an alloy of copper and zinc (the latter added to lighten the color). Wearing copper is considered to have healing properties, although it can sometimes cause green discoloration of the skin. A layer of enamel will often prevent that, as New York designer Natalie Frigo explains:

> I began enameling brass jewelry because I wanted to add more color and texture to my work. I love the smooth quality of the painting strokes and how durable the enamel is. Then it occurred to me that if I enameled the inside of a brass ring, it might prevent discoloration on the wearer's skin. In addition to having this utilitarian quality for brass rings, it gives the wearer a little secret about their jewelry.[30]

Beyond rings, brass is common in cuffs, bracelets and necklaces.

The Bad — Wildlife Jewelry

On the bad list are items made from animals listed as endangered or threatened. The Convention on International Trade in Endangered Species (CITES) has banned the use of ivory, rhinoceros bone and any products made from them or other endangered or threatened species. The US has also banned sale of products made from migratory birds (duck or geese feathers) and marine animals (this includes whale bone or teeth).[31] But that doesn't mean items on the banned list aren't still available, especially when shopping abroad. Products that have caused or are causing harm include

• Ivory — found in carved hair clips and ornaments

- Turtle shells — made into jewelry, hair combs and sunglass frames
- Reptile skins — used in watch straps
- Seashells — especially Queen conch and giant clams, carved into pearls[32]

The same is true for coral: many of the world's coral species have experienced population décline, yet the use of coral in jewelry is ongoing. Tiffany + Co. took the lead in advocating against the use of coral in jewelry, and many other jewellers have joined and signed the "Too Precious to Wear" pledge, committing to never use coral in their collections.[33] Environmentalists are working to have coral added to the CITES list of endangered species in an effort to save it from being harvested into extinction.[34]

The Ugly — Heavy Metals

In 2012, the Michigan Network for Children's Environmental Health and the Ecology Center, a Michigan-based non-profit organization, wanted to see what was in low-cost children's and adult jewelry. Concerned that the Consumer Product Safety Commission (CPSC) was not safeguarding consumer safety, they purchased 99 pieces of jewelry from 14 different retailers — Claire's, Forever21 and Walmart among the list — to test for toxic chemicals. Researchers tested for chemicals including lead, cadmium, arsenic, mercury, bromine and chlorine (PVC), which have been linked in animal and some human studies to acute allergies and to long-term health impacts, such as birth defects, impaired learning, liver toxicity and cancer. The results:

> Over half (59 percent) of the products tested had a "high" level of concern due to the presence of one or more hazardous chemicals detected at high levels. Four products contained over ten percent cadmium, a known carcinogen. Fifty percent contained lead, with over half (27 percent) of these containing more than 100 ppm of lead in one or more components, exceeding the CPSC limit of lead in children's products.[35]

Later that same year, California officials cracked down and filed a lawsuit against 16 downtown Los Angeles jewelry stores and distributors, accusing them of selling items with toxic levels of lead.[36] Not all low-cost and costume jewellery is toxic, but you might want to limit wearing pieces of unknown origin, choose to wear costume pieces on top of clothing and most certainly keep them out of the mouths of children.

Game Changers
By/Natalie Frigo

New York-based designer Natalie Frigo creates timeless bridge pieces that are meant to be worn and cherished for generations to come. A self-proclaimed "sustainable jeweler," Frigo keeps a close eye on her supply chain. She sources only from suppliers who track their materials and sell stones that come from mines that pay a living wage, have high environmental standards and are far from conflict regions.

Out of a deep worry about environmental degradation of mineral mining, each piece is cast by a certified green caster who uses only recycled metals. Creating a community of suppliers is important to Frigo, and all aspects of production from mold maker to gem dealer to stone setter are done in New York. Her collection of rings, necklaces and bracelets have graced the pages of *Nylon, Elle, Vogue* and *Harper's Bazaar* and been worn by celebrities like Rachel Ray, Jennifer Lawrence and Emma Stone. Particularly popular are pieces inspired by her own cats and the felines of ancient Egyptian and Etruscan art (like the recycled brass Cat Cuff with white sapphire eyes). She also designs a unique line of engagement and commitment rings.

Dirty Librarian Chains

Jewelry is the ideal category for vintage and upcycled, and Dirty Librarian Chains (DLC) combines both. Designer Susan Domelsmith has been creating sustainable jewelry made from repurposed vintage materials since 2004. Inspired by the belief that avant-garde fashion can be ethical, the DLC collection is founded on a zero-waste design model, which finds Domelsmith scouring flea markets around the country and old jewelry factories in Rhode Island for vintage and remnant supplies. The resulting pieces combine materials dating from the '60s through the '80s and offer a distinct, eye-catching appeal.

The DLC collection has been seen many times on the runway during New York Fashion Week, as well as featured in *British Vogue, Elle, WWD* and *Teen Vogue* and has gained many celebrity followers. Her pieces have been worn by Jessica Alba, Anne Hathaway, Debbie Harry and Gwyneth Paltrow, to name a few.

In keeping with the name, DLC's charitable work supports libraries and literacy (including Literacy for Incarcerated Teens) locally and throughout the US. DLC displays and packaging are also tailored to the theme by repurposing vintage encyclopaedias.

GOLCONDA

Luxury, ethical, high-end pieces can be found at New York's GOLCONDA, which specializes in fine and unusual gems and jewels. Founder and principal Reema Keswani is an expert gemologist, jewelry historian and designer trained by A.V. Shinde. (Unknown outside the jewelry world, Shinde was the chief designer at Harry Winston for over 40 years and credited with creating the iconic Winston aesthetic.) Disappointed that the jewelry industry was a zero-sum game, Keswani set out to establish a business model that did not sacrifice ethical sourcing and manufacturing for profit, and launched GOLCONDA. Specializing in luxury and bridal jewelry, the jeweler also manufactures gold and platinum jewelry and sells loose gemstones.

Armed with the belief that jewelry is a repository of energy, akin to talismans and amulets, Keswani travels the world to hunt down exceptional gemstones or pearls that are rare but ethically sourced. On a recent trip, she spent an entire day mining in Kenya for her favorite, garnets, to see how the mine was run and how rare the stones are. She also avoids conflict diamonds and is often quoted, "There should be a fifth C on the list for diamonds — *a clear conscience.*"

Shopping Guide

- Adèle Dejak, adeledejak.com, creates handmade luxury fashion accessories inspired by African shapes, textures and traditional techniques. Creates rings, necklaces, earrings and bracelets. V.A.L.U.E. — (A) Employs artisans in the East African region. (U) Uses recycled Ankole cow horn, a by-product of the meat industry. (E) Uses local materials such as recycled metals. Available at stores in Nairobi, Capetown and Johannesburg, plus online with international shipping.

- Alexandra Hart Jewelry, alexandrahart.com, has been making socially responsible jewelry since 1995. Designs wedding rings, rings for men and women, necklaces, earrings, bracelets and pins. V.A.L.U.E .— (L) Everything made in the US. (E) Uses and promotes responsibly researched and sourced precious metals and gemstones. Member of the Board of Directors of Ethical Metalsmiths. Available at select boutiques in the US.

- Brilliant Earth, brilliantearth.com, is aiming to be the global leader in ethically sourced wedding and engagement rings. V.A.L.U.E. — (V) Has an extensive catalog of vintage and estate rings. (E) Diamonds are ethically sourced from mines that adhere to strict labor, trade and environmental standards. Uses recycled gold and platinum. Donates 5 percent of profits to help communities harmed by the jewelry industry build a brighter future. Online with international shipping.

- By/Natalie Frigo, bynataliefrigo.com. Each unique, handcrafted piece is created in Natalie's Lower Manhattan studio using the ancient practices of metalsmithing and "cire perdue" (also known as lost-wax casting). Creates rings, necklaces, bracelets, wedding and commitment rings. V.A.L.U.E. — (L) Beyond design, pieces are finished in New York City. (E) Uses recycled metals with personally selected, ethically sourced gemstones. Available at select boutiques and online. Available at select boutiques and online. See also page 128.

- CRED Jewellery, credjewellery.com, launched in 1996, is a leader in fair trade jewelry and was the first to pay social premiums for ecological gold. Creates wedding and engagement rings, necklaces, earrings, bracelets and more for women and men. V.A.L.U.E. — (E) CRED has helped develop fair trade practices for mining gold and silver, uses certified fair trade gold, fair trade silver, recycled platinum. Supports the Kimberley Process but also works with the Alliance for Responsible Mining and other international partners to make the dream of a fair trade diamond a reality. Founding member of the Alliance for Responsible Mining, British Jewellery Association and, through CRED Foundation, provides developmental support for Fair Jewelry Action, a Human Rights and Environmental Justice Network within the industry. Available at its studio in London, store in Chichester or online with international shipping.

• Dirty Librarian Chains (DLC), dirtylibrarianchains.com, offers unique jewelry from upcycled and vintage materials. DLC creates necklaces, earrings, bracelets, rings, brooches, eyeglass chains, guitar straps and hair accessories. V.A.L.U.E. — (V) Sources vintage pieces from clients and flea markets around the country to incorporate into her designs. (L) Handmade in Brooklyn. (U) Sources remnant and excess pieces from dormant factories in Rhode Island. (E) Additional ethical elements include offering community classes to teach jewelry making to the New York community and supporting libraries and literacy throughout the US. Available at select boutiques and online with international shipping. See also pages 128–129.

• Eco Lustre, ecolustre.com, was founded by sisters Luda and Natalia, who curate a unique selection of eco-friendly, artisan and handcrafted jewelry. Offers necklaces, earrings, bracelets and rings. V.A.L.U.E. — (L) All artisans are based in the US. (U) Many pieces are made from upcycled materials (vinyl, flatware, antique watch faces, etc.) (E) Partners with artisans who are environmentally proactive. Supports organizations that are working to improve mining practices and regulations, like Ethical Metalsmiths. Available online.

• Fonderie 47, fonderie47.com, founded in 2011, creates handcrafted, high-end jewelry and watches made from AK-47s confiscated in African conflict zones. V.A.L.U.E. — (L) In 2013, it launched sister brand Liberty United to address gun violence in the US; all products in this line are made in the US. (E) Sales from the brands go directly to programs working to reduce gun violence, including the collection and destruction of illegal guns and bullets, which it then transforms into fine jewelry and art to complete a virtuous cycle. Available at trunk shows and through private inquiry.

• GOLCONDA, golcondajewelry.com, sets new benchmarks for integrity not just in design, quality of gemstones and craftsmanship, but also in sourcing. This luxury brand offers unique custom pieces as well as bridal (including LGBTQ) jewelry. V.A.L.U.E. — (L) Aware of the issues in the supply chain, everything is manufactured in a midtown Manhattan workshop near its sales showroom. (E) All stones and gems are ethically sourced and conflict-free; all metals are 100 percent recycled. Sustainability is only one piece of their commitment to social responsibility. GOLCONDA works as close to mine sources as possible in order to assess labor conditions, to find mines and workshops that support and promote women and by supporting minority-owned businesses wherever they can. Available in Manhattan showroom. See also page 129.

- K/LLER COLLECTION, kllercollection.com. This Brooklyn-based label won the CFDA Eco-fashion Challenge in 2014. Creates necklaces, earrings, bracelets, rings and nail shields. V.A.L.U.E. — (L) Everything is handmade in the US. (E) Majority of the jewelry is cast of 100 percent recycled metal and any porcupine quills or horn used are by-products of the farming industry. Available at select boutiques worldwide and online with international shipping.

- Kirsten Muenster Jewelry, kirstenmuensterjewelry.com, uses unusual materials and ancient artifacts to create bold jewelry that is about finding beauty in the unexpected. Creates rings, necklaces, bracelets, wedding rings and cuff links. V.A.L.U.E. — (V) Uses vintage materials like naturally unearthed fossilized walrus and mammoth tusks. (L) Everything is handmade in the US. (E) Values are based on sustainability and ethical practices. Member of Ethical Metalsmiths. Available online with international shipping.

- Kamoka Pearls, kamokapearls.com, offers sustainable pearls from a small Tahitian pearl farm on the French Polynesian atoll of Ahe. Necklaces, rings, pendants and bracelets. V.A.L.U.E. — (E) Recycles local mother of pearl as nuclei in the pearl grafting process; oysters are cleaned by the lagoon's fish population. Energy needs come almost entirely from wind and solar power. Select distributors (ask for them by name) or online.

- Mikuti, mikuti.com, based in New York, aims to invoke change and touch artisan communities through bold pieces that complement the wearer's individuality. Creates rings, bangles, necklaces and collars. V.A.L.U.E. — (A) Produces collections with artisans in East Africa. (E) Committed to developing a sustainable, supportive supply chain in Sub-Sahara Africa. Available at select boutiques in the US and online with international shipping.

- Mode Marteau, modemarteau.com, sells unique vintage and antique jewelry curated by Ariana Boussard-Reifel (our vintage expert from chapter 3). An eclectic collection of jewelry ranges from Victorian mourning rings to Berber necklaces, with a focus on the rare and remarkable. V.A.L.U.E. — (V) Sells second-hand and vintage designer, tribal and antique jewelry. Available by appointment and online.

- MONIQUE PÉAN, moniquepean.com, launched her environmentally friendly line of fine jewelry in New York in 2006. As a member of the Council of Fashion Designers of America (CFDA), this brand aims to raise awareness about global environmental issues through design. Creates one-of-a-kind, avant-garde rings, bracelets, necklaces and earrings. V.A.L.U.E. — (A) Partners with artisans in areas including the Arctic Circle, Colombia, French Polynesia, Guatemala, Peru and the Philippines to support traditional craftsmanship and cultural heritage. (E) Proceeds from sales contribute to global philanthropic organizations, which provide clean drinking water and basic sanitation to people in developing nations. Member of the No Dirty Gold campaign and supports Too Precious to Wear. Available at select boutiques and online with international shipping.

- Pure Grown Diamonds, puregrowndiamonds.com, grows diamonds that are 100 percent conflict-free. Offers colored and colorless diamonds in pendants, earrings and rings. V.A.L.U.E. — (E) Advanced technology allows for the creation of these diamonds without any societal or environmental impact. Available at authorized retailers and online.

- SOKO, shopsoko.com, created by women for women to help "fashion a better world," uses technology to connect online consumers directly to African artisans. Makers and artisans become entrepreneurs through mobile technology, bridging handcrafted jewelry from the developing world to Web consumers worldwide. Sells necklaces, bracelets, earrings and rings. V.A.L.U.E. — (A) Built on a peer-to-peer model. Each piece is created and sold directly by the artisan. (E) By leveraging mobile technology, SOKO is able to generate more revenue for the artisan while offering value for consumers (no middleman). Artisans use natural and upcycled materials. Available online with international shipping.

• Urban Lace, urbanlacejewelry.com, launched in Portland in 2006, makes a unique line of upcycled, eco-friendly jewelry from inner tubes or Ultrasuede®. It creates bracelets, earrings, chokers and masks. V.A.L.U.E. — (U) All jewelry is made from either recycled bicycle inner tubes collected from local bike shops or recycled ultra-microfiber from post-industrial fabric waste. (E) Three percent of each purchase is donated to an environmental education group. Also supports Breast Cancer Awareness, Bicycle Transit Alliance, Sisters of the Road, Seeds of Opportunity, Education for Equality International and Global Green. Available at select boutiques and online.

Final Notes

As mentioned earlier, this chapter could warrant a whole book and so could the shopping guide, which offers just a small sample. Given the widespread access to recycled, artisan and upcycled materials, there are tons of great ethical jewelry makers. This sector might have some of the darkest shadows, but it also has some of the brightest lights — working in all price ranges and all styles.

As in previous chapters, source matters. If you agree with Reema Keswani of GOLCONDA — that "jewelry is a repository of energy" — then it shouldn't be one filled with guilt or doubt; choose pieces that speak to you, from makers who share your values.

Chapter 5

Outerwear

My wardrobe — like those of many fashionistas —
is full of contradictions, much like
sustainable fashion itself.[1]

— Hilary Alexander,
Fashion correspondent, *Daily Telegraph*

WHEN THINKING ABOUT THE ORGANIZATION OF THIS BOOK, I
thought this chapter would be the perfect place to explore the
ethical use of animals in fashion. Not just fur coats, but the ethical options of alpaca, cashmere, down and wool. For as long as I've been writing
about ethical fashion, I've highlighted both vegan fashion options and
ethically sourced animal fiber and hide products. The Magnifeco blog
supports people who are trying to dress with their values and avoid animal products (vegans) but also communities and families who make
their livelihood from animal products.

The issues of animal rights and anti-cruelty are complex and receive a
lot of press thanks to groups like Greenpeace and People for the Ethical
Treatment of Animals (PETA). Occasionally, what gets lost in the mes-
sage are the people (and ways of life) behind the animals. A good example
is the international pressure to ban the seal hunt. Although chiefly target-
ed at commercial hunters, the campaigns brought hardship to Aboriginal
communities across the North who had supplemented their incomes
with the pelts of seals (by-products of their sustenance hunt). Unable

to differentiate between ethical and commercial fur, countries and consumers turned their backs on seal fur and on those communities. The hardship was so extreme that in 2014 Greenpeace apologised to indigenous hunters for the damage "Save the Harp Seal" campaigns did to their communities.[2] Whichever side of the issue you are on, it's getting easier to navigate fashion with your values intact.

Wearing Animals

We've come so far with technological advances you may be wondering why we even need to wear animal fibers. It's true, it is entirely possible to be dry and warm without using animal skins and if your beliefs preclude you wearing anything of animal origin, rest assured, you have options. Outdoor apparel companies have developed performance wear that protects against almost every element without any need for animal fibers. However, those options are usually synthetic, leaving the choice between petroleum-based or natural fibers. Not only are animal fibers natural, but they are also renewable, often biodegradable and provide livelihoods for the people who care for them.

Historically, we hunted for meat and then found uses for every single part of the animal, including the pelts and hides. Several communities have continued in those traditions, whether because they are geographically predisposed, living in the North like Inuit and Sami; their culture has continued its nomadic ways, like Kazakh or Mongolian herders; or it's the family business, like many mink or fox farms that are second-, third- or fourth-generation.

If your beliefs preclude wearing animal products, then feel free to skip ahead (to Defending the Ethical Price tag).

Ethical Animal Husbandry

Ask anyone who works and lives with animals and they'll say, "Raising animals simply requires common sense." To put the common sense principles on paper, in 1965 the UK government drafted a code of conduct that has become universal, whether raising, herding, tending or farming. Refined by the Farm Animal Welfare Council, it assumes that the welfare of an animal includes its physical and mental state and "good animal welfare" implies both fitness and a sense of well-being. Put another way, any animal kept by humans, must be protected from unnecessary suffering. Referred to as the Five Freedoms, they assume that every animal, whether on the farm, in transit or at slaughter, should have the following freedoms:

1. Freedom from Hunger and Thirst — by ready access to fresh water and a diet to maintain full health and vigor

2. Freedom from Discomfort — by providing an appropriate environment including shelter and a comfortable resting area

3. Freedom from Pain, Injury or Disease — by prevention or rapid diagnosis and treatment

4. Freedom to Express Normal Behavior — by providing sufficient space, proper facilities and company of the animal's own kind

5. Freedom from Fear and Distress — by ensuring conditions and treatment that avoid mental suffering

Ethical animal products come from people who treat animals in the manner outlined in the Five Freedoms, not the kind of treatment seen in a PETA video. There is much debate about how and where PETA gets its animal cruelty videos (the ones that show pulling rabbit hair out by the roots or skinning an animal alive); they are atrocious, stomach-turning and sensational. They raise attention (and money), but almost no one can bear to watch them. And everyone — vegans, animal caregivers and I agree — the images are unfathomable.

Animal fibers and hides are luxury items. Not merely because designers wish to price them out of reach, but because of the time, care and effort it takes to properly raise and nurture an animal under the Five Freedoms. When animal fibers (especially fur) are offered at fast-fashion prices, it is one of the worst effects of *masstige* (a portmanteau of the words *mass* and *prestige*), also referred to as "prestige for the masses."[3] And should raise doubt about whether the Five Freedoms could have been provided for a product priced so inexpensively.

Alpaca, Angora, Cashmere and Wool

Alpacas are the main source of income and subsistence for an estimated 120,000 families in the highlands of Peru, Bolivia and Chile. Usually in herds of less than 50, alpacas can play a vital role in the local fair trade supply chains in those countries, where most alpaca products are also made. There is limited scope to expand production in the Andes, due to lack of grazing land. However, herds in North America and Australasia are expanding by almost 20 percent a year and could soon become significant world suppliers.[4] An example of ethically priced alpaca, New York-based Simply Natural Clothing, sources alpaca fiber from farms across the US; their scarves range in price from $140 to $175.

Angora, from rabbits, is ideal for thermal clothing and for people suffering from wool allergies or arthritis. Until the 1960s, France was the leading producer of angora wool. Since then, almost 90 percent of all angora comes from China. Other producers include Argentina, Chile, Czech Republic and Hungary.[5] A 2013 PETA video revealed rabbits being abused in the shearing process and resulted in many fast-fashion brands pledging to boycott angora, which is good news because angora does not belong in the fast-fashion cycle. The unfortunate downside of boycott actions is that they force an immediate glut in the market, causing animal lovers to question what happens to all of those rabbits. The other problem with boycott actions is they don't account for ethical alternatives. For example, New York farmer Ambika Conroy raises and shears her own angora rabbits. All of her Ambika products are hand-spun and hand-crocheted. Headbands and hats range in price from $95 to $260.

True **cashmere** comes from the kashmir goat. For centuries, Mongolia's nomadic herders dominated this market. China is now the world's leading cashmere producer, although experts still say Mongolia produces the finest fiber. Other smaller producers include Australia, India, Iran, Pakistan, New Zealand, Turkey and the US. The interest of fast fashion in selling cashmere products has led to volatile prices, causing herders to increase their herds. The concern about cashmere starts with the planet. From 1990 to 2009, the Mongolian goat population grew from 5 million to 20 million, a rapid growth suspected to be directly responsible for the desertification of the Gobi desert.[6] Unfortunately, this growth hasn't led to better revenue for herders; in 2011–2012, raw cashmere prices fell by 35 percent.[7] Traditionally cashmere was combed, but often goats are now shorn, which mixes coarser hair with the soft combed hair. Ethical, undyed, Mongolian cashmere is sourced by EILEEN FISHER, and sweaters range in price from $348 to $438.

Wool, the world's leading animal fiber, is produced in about 100 countries, on 500,000 farms and comes from about one billion sheep in 200 breeds. Major producers are Australia, Argentina, China, the Islamic Republic of Iran, New Zealand, Russia, the United Kingdom and Uruguay. Depending on the country and region, wool producers range from small farmers to large-scale commercial grazing operations.[8] Recent attention to wool has focused on *mulesing*, the practice of removing strips of skin from the buttocks of sheep. Australian merino sheep are at risk for *flystrike*, an infestation of blowflies that lay eggs in the damp wool. The eggs hatch into flesh-eating maggots that lead to blood loss and possibly death. The preventative solution removes skin around the tail area to reduce the chance of infestation.[9] This practice caught the attention of PETA and has led to a call for boycott of mulesed wool. The good news: there has been notable improvement. According to the Australian Wool Exchange, annual production from non-mulesed animals rose by 15 per cent in 2009–2010, then by 40 per cent in 2010–2011.[10]

New Zealand, not so stricken with flystrike, not only has been able to produce unmulesed merino, but has established an independent accreditation program that ensures environmental, social and economic sustainability of wool growers, animal welfare (non-mulesed) and traceability of the product back to the source. Called Zque, the label has been adopted by a number of premium brands such as SmartWool, Ibex, Aquascutum and Icebreaker.[11]

There are other sheep-positive brands like Britain's Izzy Lane. Putting an ethical face on the British and Scottish wool industries, North Yorkshire designer Isobel Davies has rescued 500 rare-breed sheep, mostly Wensleydale and Shetland, by taking them to her farm sanctuary. She has their wool locally processed and creates collections that have shown at London and New York Fashion weeks.

Down

It came as a surprise to outdoor brands when they learned that there might be a problem with down, as feathers and down were assumed to be a cruelty-free by-product of the meat industry. However, in the last few years, it was discovered that ducks bred for foie gras may be force-fed (especially in Hungary and France) and that down might be retrieved via live plucking. In 2014, steps were made towards regulating supply chains and halting animal mistreatment.

Patagonia launched their own Traceable Down Standard, while most other brands are following the Responsible Down Standard (RSD) in partnership with the Textile Exchange (a global non-profit dedicated to sustainability in the textile industry). North Face, which led in the creation of the RSD, expects that this standard will create improved animal welfare conditions and better traceability in the down supply chain. Brands like H&M, Eddie Bauer, Mammut, Helly Hansen and Fjällräven have also signed on.

There are advantages to choosing (traceable or responsible) down: it offers lighter insulation than synthetics; it has a higher warmth-to-weight ratio than synthetics; and it is more durable, offering products that can last a lifetime.[12] With growing awareness in this sector, all ethical down products should soon be accompanied by some wording or promise on the hangtags about the ethical treatment of geese.

Fur

Fur in fashion is a hot topic and probably touches more nerves than any other subject in this book. But fur can be ethical — whether reused and upcycled, sourced from indigenous and other trappers, or from monitored, family-run farms.

Let's start with fur farms. According to the *Economist*, Denmark is the hub of the global fur-farming industry, home to 1,500 mink farmers who rear about 17.2 million a year, about one-fifth of the world's supply.[13] Denmark has built a circular economy around the industry, where mink, as carnivores that require a high-protein diet, are fed abattoir or fish-packing waste. They eat the leftover fish heads, tails and other waste at farms close to the sea, or lungs, hearts and other offal at farms inland. The fur farms then deliver manure as fertilizer for agricultural partners. Even the carcasses (mink are typically euthanized by CO_2 gas) can be composted or repurposed as biofuel, creating a sustainable ecosystem.

A similar system operates in North America, where breeding mink began in 1860. There are about 400, mostly small, family-run farms in

Canada and the US. The proper nutrition, housing, health and well-being of farmed mink is assured in the US with certification by Fur Commission USA, and in Canada with codes of practice developed by the National Farm Animal Care Council.

Figures reported by the International Fur Federation show that sales of all fur products are estimated at $35.8 billion, with farmed furs accounting for about $7.8 billion.[14] The rest is accounted for by retail sales, processing and the money earned by trappers. Canada and the US are the world's main suppliers of wild fur.

Fur trapping is woven into the economic histories of both Canada and the US and, even today, continues to be an important source of income in many communities. In a story about the resurgence of the fur industry, the *National Post* newspaper stated it eloquently, "Before we were anything we were trappers; a nation built on pelts."[15] To ensure hundreds of years of tradition stay current, the North American fur industry has strict standards and oversight, including scientific protocols for international humane standards with state and provincial regulations and licensing for trappers.

For the past 20 years, the US and Canadian governments have invested more than $20 million in trap research.[16] This work provided the scientific basis for the Agreement on International Humane Trapping Standards, which was also signed in 1997 by Russia and the European Union.

The state and provincial wildlife departments require that traps comply with the standards and set hunting seasons in each region to ensure that furbearer populations are not endangered by trapping. Even if we didn't use fur, many wildlife populations would need to be managed to prevent the spread of disease (for example, rabies among raccoons and foxes) or to protect property and habitat (for example, from the flooding caused by beaver dams). According to the Fur Council of Canada, "There are about 70,000 licensed trappers in Canada and more than 200,000 across the US; trappers are 'our eyes and ears on the land,' monitoring the habitat conditions and wildlife populations in every region of the continent."[17]

In many cases, trapping and hunting are tied to cultural heritage — not the pictures of trophy hunters smiling in social media photographs, but real families who hunt for food and sell the skins. Alan Herscovici, author and current executive director of the Fur Council of Canada, says this of community based trapping and hunting:

> The death of animals is not treated lightly, nor are their "gifts" abused, as animal rights groups would have us believe. On the contrary, the experience, skills and traditions of cultures as diverse as those of Cree hunters and Kastorian furriers came together to produce, with these furs, some of the most meticulous craftsmanship to be found in clothing today.[18]

The Fur Information Council of America reports, "Nearly 500 designers presented fur in their collections for fall 2014,"[19] making finding fur easy. However, finding ethical fur might not be. One way to ensure that it is ethical is to look for the "Origin Assured" tag, launched in 2006. Only fur from approved (not endangered) species, sourced from approved countries and sold through certified auction houses can carry the OA™ mark.

Another option for ethical fur is to buy direct from local producers. The NaturaL Boutique in St. John's (Canada) is run by husband and wife Jennifer and Kerry Shears, both Newfoundland Mi'kmaq, and sells handcrafted (fur) products that are sourced and produced by Aboriginal communities in Newfoundland, Labrador, northern Quebec, Nunavut and Greenland. The boutique's goals are tied to sustainability and supporting small-town business and Aboriginal enterprise.

Another example is Nunavik Creations who, with an in-house design team, employs Inuit women from various communities in Nunavik (Canada) to create products that reflect the traditions of Inuit handcrafted (fur) clothing and accessories.

When shopping with V.A.L.U.E., fur is also ethical when it's vintage or second-life. Fur is an incredibly durable product; raccoon, otter and beaver fur can last up to 100 years. And when fur is crafted properly, it is made to be remade and refashioned. This means that fur, whether it's vintage, thrift-shop or hand-me-down, can be taken to a furrier and given a new life.

Defending the Ethical Price Tag

Aside from the idea that many items, like fur coats, are durable and long-lasting, another reason why I sought an acronym that put the letter

V first was to help defend cost. Ethical clothing, the kind with effort and attention to supply chain all the way through, made in the manner of slow fashion often costs more.

We've seen it so far in every chapter. The economies of scale have distorted our perception of cost versus value, so when we see a low price in a mainstream, department or fast-fashion store, we assume that to be the true cost of a product. For example, when we see a $5 T-shirt at a fast-fashion shop, we internalize that low price as the "real" price. However, in reality, that is the price...

- if the person who cultivates or harvests the natural fiber gets paid the lowest market value
- if production happens in countries with the lowest cost of living
- if quantities are so large that the cost per item, through mass repetition, can be reduced
- if the seller pays their employees the lowest possible wage
- if enough sells to offset any losses, then the ticket price to the consumer can be held artificially low

However, the ethical reality and the core behind ethical fashion is that everyone along the supply chain should be paid fairly. And when items are handcrafted, they are not cheap. One choice to be ethical and stay within the fast-fashion price range is to buy vintage or second-life. Another option is to budget for higher-priced items over the duration or lifespan of the item. For example, if a higher-priced item is something that will be worn as often as outerwear (every day during the winter season) and can be worn over several seasons, then when buying better, estimate the *cost-per-wear*. Cost-per-wear evaluates the ticket price against the estimated longevity of an item. This differentiates low-cost, poor-quality items that may last for only a few wears against higher-cost items that will be staples in your wardrobe for the long term.

To estimate the cost-per-wear, divide the sticker amount by the number of times you think you will wear the item. This can be done up or down the chain; a cashmere sweater that might cost a whole paycheck but last a lifetime or a flimsy, fast-fashion item that might not last through its first wash.

As an example, let's take a sweater. Earlier, we mentioned a cashmere sweater from EILEEN FISHER that costs $400. A comparable fast-fashion sweater might cost $60. Given your experience with clothes in your closet (we've all had cheap sweaters that lose their shape halfway through a season) plus that of others you know (my mother has a cashmere sweater she has had for 20 years), work with those numbers:

Example:

Sweater	Price	Life expectancy	Times/year	Cost-per-wear
E.F.	$400	10 year	20*	$2.00
Generic	$60	1 year	20	$3.00

*Let's assume the sweater is worn once a week from November–March.

Even though the outlay for the cashmere sweater is initially more expensive, the quality and longevity make it both the better ethical choice and better value for money.

Let's do another example: a winter coat made with sustainable down and recycled materials by Patagonia might be double (or even triple) the price of a fast-fashion store coat.

Example:

Coat	Price	Life expectancy	Cost per season
Patagonia	$400	10 year	$40.00
Generic	$150	2 year	$75.00

Again, the longevity makes the Patagonia coat a better, less expensive purchase over time. The longevity makes it also more likely to (eventually) be found at a second-hand shop, or online.

Game Changers
Harricana by Mariouche

Every hangtag on a Harricana item says "made from your mother's old coat." The Montreal-based luxury brand has made a name and created a niche out of recycling and recrafting fur. In a manner reminiscent of but predating *Project Runway*, in 1993 fashion student Mariouche Gagné was competing in the Fur Council of Canada's Fur Design Student Contest and realized she lacked some required materials for her entry: a reversible ski suit. Realizing her mother's old fur coat would be perfect for the finishing touches, she won second prize with her ingenuity, and the seeds of a business idea were planted.

At Harricana's high-end boutique in Montreal, people can bring in their old fur coats for credit or can arrange to have them refashioned. By recycling old furs, Gagné estimates Harricana has saved the lives of more than 800,000 animals over the past 15 years. Harricana also recycles silk and cashmere scarves and wedding gowns to make its one-of-a-kind collection of coats, vests, hats, scarves, earmuffs and more.

The Sway

The chic leather motorcycle jackets gracing the pages of fashion magazines may seem at odds with the Hawaiian lifestyle of designer Belinda Pasqua, until you know she's originally from Sydney, Australia. These days Maui feels more like home than the bustling streets of NYC that drive her inspiration, and where she lived and worked for eight years. After burning out as a head designer for a fast fashion giant, Pasqua took her pens and sketchpads to Shelter Island for a refresh and recharge. Grappling with the excessive waste she had witnessed in her previous role, she became fixated on creating something out of excess. Pasqua knew that excess leather, unlike other materials, was difficult to break down and that factories had no idea what to do with it. The Sway was born out of the desire to create beautiful, timeless pieces out of available leather.

Pasqua collaborates with a factory partner in India that has enough excess leather on hand that The Sway would never need to purchase any new leather. The collection of jackets and handbags uses leftover cuttings and irregular pieces in a patchwork method Pasqua created to put all sizes to good use — larger pieces for jackets and smaller cuttings for handbags. She was also drawn to this factory because they hire women and pay them an equal wage. While not offering a vegan option, The Sway is cruelty-free.

Vaute Couture

Typically, anything synthetic can be labelled vegan, but designer Leanne Mai-ly Hilgart set out to create a wool-inspired vegan line of winter dress coats for men and women. A vegan herself, and upset with the idea of mulesing, Hilgart wanted the style and chic that traditional wool coats offered but without the wool.

After years of testing and researching, she prototyped a wool alternative called WonderFelt, made of 100 percent recycled plastic bottles, that would offer the same swing and the warmth of a wool dress coat. She adds a wind- and waterproof lining made of closed-loop recycled fibers to ensure that her hometown Chicago fans are protected from the elements.

The line has grown to include menswear and spring/fall waxed canvas coats (using a vegan wax) plus a line of WonderFelt hats.

Shopping Guide

- EcoAlf, ecoalf.com. This Spanish brand produces a line of outerwear, bags, backpacks and shoes for men, women and kids with proprietary fabrics made from "trash." V.A.L.U.E. — (U) Makes its own recycled fabrics from discarded fishing nets, post-consumer plastic bottles, worn-out tires, post-industrial cotton and even used coffee grinds. Flagship store in Madrid plus online with international shipping.
- Fjallraven, fjallraven.com, has produced outdoor apparel and equipment from their base in Örnsköldsvik, Sweden, since the 1960s. V.A.L.U.E. — (E) A member of the Fair Labor Association (FLA), Fjällräven's goal is to make durable products that can be passed down through generations. Fjällräven's quality control system monitors the process by conducting regular inspections, including both announced and unannounced visits. Their down's quality and cleanliness are controlled by the independent International Down and Feather Laboratory (IDFL). Conditions are also checked regularly by an independent Swedish veterinarian. Stores across Europe and in select cities in the US plus online with international shipping.
- Harricana by Mariouche, harricana.qc.ca, is a luxurious eco-fashion label of recycled fur designed by Mariouche Gagné. V.A.L.U.E. — (L) Almost 90 percent of the fur used comes from Quebec. (U) Recycles fur, silk and cashmere scarves and wedding gowns. (E) All items are made in Canada under ethical manufacturing conditions. Available at two stores in Quebec and Montreal, at select boutique in 15 countries and online with international shipping. See also pages 144–145.

- NaturaL Boutique, naturalboutique.ca, is run by husband and wife team Kerry and Jennifer Shears, both Newfoundland Mi'kmaq, and sells handcrafted (fur) products. V.A.L.U.E. — (E) All products are made in communities who depend on fur-bearing animals (like seals) for sustenance. Boutique in St. John's, Newfoundland, and online with international shipping.

- The North Face®, thenorthface.com, is an American outdoor product company owned by the VF Corporation (which also owns Timberland plus 35 other brands). V.A.L.U.E. — (E) The North Face has committed to using 100 percent certified and responsibly sourced down in all of its product lines by 2016–2017; founding member of the Outdoor Industry Association (OIA) Sustainability Working Group; contributed to the Eco Index and the foundation of the Sustainable Apparel Coalition's Higg Index. Stores in the US and select countries plus numerous retail partners and online with international shipping.

- Nunavik Creations, nunavikcreations.com, was created to expand economic opportunities and produce products that reflect the culture, crafts and traditions of Inuit to the outside world. Sells sealskin mittens, kamiks, as well as parkas and other Inuk-designed items. V.A.L.U.E. — (E) Employs Inuit women from various communities in Nunavik to produce products that reflect the traditions of Inuit. Hand-crafted (fur) clothing and accessories. Boutique in Kuujjuaq, QC, or online with international shipping

- TERRA NEW YORK, terranewyork.com, was the first fashion brand focused solely on rainwear. All coats are 100 percent waterproof yet possess unique technical details that allow the body to breathe and move freely. V.A.L.U.E. — (E) The polyurethane is biodegradable in a landfill after 10 years. Available at select boutiques in the US and Canada, plus online store with international shipping.

- Patagonia Inc., patagonia.com, is a Ventura, California-based clothing company focusing mainly on high-end outdoor clothing, with a corporate mission to use business to inspire and implement solutions to the environmental crisis. V.A.L.U.E. — (E) Certified B Corporation, founding member of the Sustainable Apparel Coalition, they base their Code of Conduct on International Labor Organization (ILO) and Fair Labor Association (FLA) guidelines, has its own Traceable Down Standard, which works to prevent the animals from harm and provide content claim assurance to its customers, plus are working on a Sustainable Grazing Protocol for Merino Wool Production in the Patagonia Region. Stores in 15 countries including Canada and the US, plus online with international shipping.

- The Sway, theswaynyc.com, creates timeless leather motorcycle jackets (and handbags) for women. Each piece in this collection is made authentically and sustainably in a small factory that has been handcrafting leather motorcycle accessories and jackets since the 1960s. V.A.L.U.E. — (U) Constructs each piece using genuine motorcycle hardware and upcycled leather excess. (E) Constantly seeking sustainable methods of production, all jacket and bag linings are made using excess materials, and packaging materials are made from recycled paper. Available at select boutiques and online with international shipping. See also page 145.

- Vaute Couture, vautecouture.com, is an independent fashion house by former model Leanne Mai-ly Hilgart, dedicated to taking animals out of the fashion equation for both men and women. V.A.L.U.E. — (L) Coats and hats are produced in NYC. (E) Vegan; uses polyester made from recycled plastic bottles, recyclable and recycled fibers. Seasonal pop-up shops and trunk shows around the globe, plus online store with international shipping. See also pages 145–146.

Chapter 6

Underwear

Consumers get what I put in my mouth, that organic
apple, has a direct impact on my health. But they
haven't got to the point yet what I put on my body
impacts me too.[1]

— LaRhea Pepper,
Organic Farmer Pioneer/Advocate

IF YOU MASH TOGETHER two of the previously referenced reports —
Dirty Laundry (the Greenpeace one about toxic chemical residues on
clothing) and *Chem Fatale: Potential Health Effects of Toxic Chemicals in
Feminine Care Products* (the WVE one about dangerous toxic and allergenic chemicals in feminine care products) — then you can guess where
we are going with this chapter. The things you want closest to your body
— not just underwear but pyjamas, base layers, even bedsheets — are
the fibers and materials that are the cleanest.

The Greenpeace report *Toxic Threads: The Big Fashion Stitch-Up*
found "the presence of a hormone-disrupting phthalate in an item of
Victoria's Secret underwear at levels that would have led to the product being banned in the EU had it been a toy."[2] Limited Brands, parent
company of Victoria's Secret and La Senza, signed on to Greenpeace's
"Detox" campaign (to eliminate hazardous chemicals from supply chains
and products by 2020) and committed to "the total elimination of both
phthalates and perfluorinated chemicals (another hormone-disrupting

chemical group of high concern) long before the 2020 deadline,"[3] but the question lingers — what's lurking in underwear?

Bedding and linens are another place chemicals can hide. In 2010, the US Government Accountability Office (GAO) conducted a study to see how prevalent formaldehyde was in the textiles of day-to-day items. According to the report,

> Some clothing — generally garments made of cotton and other natural fibers — is treated with resins containing formaldehyde primarily to enhance wrinkle resistance. Formaldehyde is toxic and has been linked to serious adverse health effects, including cancer, and some federal agencies have regulations that limit human exposure, which occurs primarily through inhalation and dermal (skin) contact.[4]

Of the nearly 200 items the GAO tested, 6 percent had levels above the recommended limit for formaldehyde and 40 percent of those were bedding or linen products (including a crib sheet). The fabric performance characteristics identified on the labels said things like "wrinkle free, easy care, no ironing needed, eco-friendly soft finish" and, on the crib sheet, "preshrunk."

As consumers, we can read the label and seek specific materials and fibers, but we are often in the dark about whether items were treated with, or are hiding, chemicals. We have to rely on the brand or seek certifications like OEKO-TEX® and GOTS to ensure products don't have any nasty additives.

You'll recall from the Clothing chapter that OEKO-TEX tests for harmful chemicals with a focus on the final use of the item: children up to the age of three require the highest level of safety, and clothes with close skin contact (underwear and bedding) are second. The independent certification system tests for illegal substances, legally regulated substances and known harmful (but not legally regulated) chemicals. When certified, items pose no risk to skin and don't contain any harmful substances in any aspect — from yarns to fabrics, threads, elastics, embroidery, even labels.

GOTS certification ensures the organic status of textiles from harvesting of the raw materials, through environmentally and socially responsible manufacturing up to labeling, in order to provide a credible assurance to the end consumer.[5] Sadly, since only one percent of all cotton produced is currently organic,[6] we need to explore other fibers.

This book has covered many of the *natural fibers* (from plant or animal sources) and several of them would work in this chapter (especially silk), but there are more options in the *manufactured fibers*, specifically cellulose-based fibers — bamboo, viscose/rayon, TENCEL®, modal and micromodal (think of these as the trees, below) — or protein-based fibers — soy, milk and seaweed (and these as the food, also below).

Tree Fibers

Yes, we wear trees: eucalyptus, beech, bamboo (which technically is a grass) and more. Trees make some of the softest, comfiest, environmentally friendly fibers on the planet. It began with **rayon** — a manufactured fiber created from cellulose found in plants and trees and processed with chemicals. When it first appeared in the early 1900s, rayon was referred to as artificial silk. The process was far from environmentally friendly — contamination of the wastewater plus hazardous air pollution — but the resulting fabric was less expensive and more accessible than silk.

There are many methods of producing rayon — viscose, modal and lyocell methods — they all differ in their manufacturing process and in the properties of the finished product. To make matters confusing, each is also a registered textile brand and trademark produced by Lenzing, a fiber production company based in Austria. It is the only company that manufactures all three on an industrial scale: viscose (VISCOSE®), modal (MODAL®) and lyocell (TENCEL®) under one roof. Lenzing products use only sustainably harvested trees either from Program for the Endorsement of Forest Certification (PEFC) or Forest Stewardship Council (FSC) certified European forests, plus their manufacturing is certified OEKO-TEX 100.

Viscose can be made from soft woods like beech trees and often bamboo. Fiber production is similar to the original rayon and has significant environmental implications: it generates air pollution and emissions from the effluent result in high pollution indexes.[7] Viscose on a garment tag is not an indication of a clean fiber.

Modal, a modified version of viscose developed in the 1950s, is made from beech trees. Developed to be a better-wearing, machine-washable improvement over viscose/rayon, it holds more water than cotton and makes a better material for sportswear, according to the manufacturer's claim.

Many people love the softness and feel of **bamboo** and (too) often it is referred to as an eco-fabric, but bamboo is rarely an environmentally friendly material. When it was created in 2002, it entered the market with many claims: eco-friendly, organic, pesticide-free, antimicrobial, and so on. But it wasn't completely true and in 2009 the Federal Trade Commission (FTC) charged companies with "bamboo-zling" consumers with false product claims. The press release reads,

> The Federal Trade Commission has charged four sellers of clothing and other textile products with deceptively labeling and advertising these items as made of bamboo fiber, when they are made of rayon. The complaints also charge the companies with making false and unsubstantiated "green" claims that their clothing and textile products are manufactured using an environmentally friendly process, that they retain the natural antimicrobial properties of the bamboo plant, and that they are biodegradable.[8]

The FTC continues to charge sellers for perpetuating the false marketing. It is true that bamboo grows rapidly and is naturally regenerating, making it a highly renewable source, but more often than not, bamboo is conventionally processed, like rayon. Recently, however, some bamboo is being lyocell-processed in a closed-loop cycle with chemicals replaced by an organic solution. One mark in particular, Monocel®, makes softwear fabrics like French terry and jersey with lyocell bamboo fiber as the main component and is both FSC and OEKO-TEX 100 certified.

Lyocell, is a much more environmentally friendly way to process wood pulp. Developed by Lenzing in the 1980s, it is a closed-loop system, where almost all of the solvent is recovered (no effluent or wastewater), purified and then recycled into the process again. Plus, the solvent itself is non-toxic. Lenzing markets their own lyocell as TENCEL®, which is made from sustainably harvested eucalyptus trees.

Manufacturers claim lyocell has remarkable breathability and can absorb 50 percent more moisture (like perspiration) than cotton, making it an ideal fiber to regulate body temperature and avoid bacteria. These qualities also make it preferable for base layers and moisture-wicking garments.

Sports enthusiasts (anyone from runners to skiers) love moisture-wicking clothes. They have different names depending on the brand, but they almost all have the same thing in common: they are made of polyester. Researchers at the University of Ghent in Belgium, when comparing cotton and polyester shirts from 26 volunteers after a spinning class, discovered the bacteria that flourish on a sweaty polyester T-shirt are different from those that grow on cotton and from what is present in our armpits.[9] The polyester T-shirts seemed to be growing their own bacteria (which might explain why the stench never comes out of some technical or synthetic shirts). Manufacturers have tried to make polyester fabric less hospitable to bacteria by saturating it with antimicrobials like triclosan, but you'll recall from the Beauty chapter that triclosan can pass through skin and has been shown to interfere with thyroid signalling as an endocrine disruption.[10]

The wicking and antibacterial qualities of lyocell and TENCEL® are not just suited for sportswear, they are also good for underwear, sleepwear and bedsheets. TENCEL® is such a pure fiber that it is used by AD RescueWear, a therapeutic clothing company that makes specialty medical undergarments for children suffering from eczema.

Deforestation Concerns

Global forests are at risk from many sectors. If you've read Dr. Seuss's *The Lorax*, then you too possess a small fear about depleted trees. Greenpeace tackles this, in part, with two separate campaigns: one about the ongoing Amazon rainforest clear-cutting for cattle and soy, and another highlighting the ancient forest destruction in Indonesia for palm oil for cosmetics, food, chocolate, etc. When it comes to fashion, Canopy, a Canadian environmental NGO, is targeting global fashion brands in a campaign to raise awareness about their increasing use of rayon and viscose fibres to ensure that ancient forests don't disappear into fast fashion closets.

In the words of Canopy, "Fashion often has a cost that doesn't show up on the price tag. Demand for clothing made with rayon, viscose and other wood-based fabrics is mounting, which means fashion is increasingly behind the devastating loss of endangered forests around the globe."[11] Canopy's research reveals that forests, from the tropical rainforests of Indonesia to the northern boreal forests, were being cut down and pulped to make fabrics at a rate of 70 to 100 million trees each year. They also predict the number could double in the next 20 years.[12]

While Lenzing fabric contains wood from certified forests, the same is not true for every rayon and viscose manufacturer. Through the efforts of Canopy's "Fashion Loved by Forest" campaign, over 25 brands, retailers and designers (such as Zara/Inditex, H&M, EILEEN FISHER, Patagonia, Levi Strauss & Co. and Under the Canopy) have committed to eliminate their use of fabrics containing endangered forest fibers.

Food Fibers

Protein-based fibers are starting to see broader use with designers and brands. I refer to them as "food fibers" only in jest — they might have been edible in their original form (soy, milk and seaweed), but by the time they become a textile, no one would recognize their origins. Designers who use these fibers love the fact that some of the inherent "food" nutrition carries through to the fiber and subscribe to the premise that what we put on our skin matters.

Soybean fiber, often seen as just "soy" or "soy silk" on labels, was first developed in the 1950s and is another textile that can feel like silk or, in a heavier weight, like cashmere. Organic labeling means the chemical process is safe — the waste can even be used as animal feed. Organic soy is also biodegradable. Health claims include the fact that soybean protein fiber possesses amino acids that can be absorbed via the fiber.[13]

Even older than soy is **milk fiber**, first produced from milk casein in the 1930s. Today's milk fiber is considered environmentally friendly and superior to other human-made fibers because it contains amino acids (like soy) and has the same pH as human skin. Both qualities are said to nourish the skin.[14]

The third protein-based fiber that is believed to have positive skin benefits is **SeaCell**™, a seaweed-based fiber processed in the lyocell method. The brown algae in SeaCell™, collected from Icelandic fjords, is rich in antioxidants and believed to offer protection against environmental influences on the skin and to reduce skin damage and premature skin aging caused by free radicals. Plus, algae is rich in vitamins B, A and E and minerals such as magnesium, calcium, potassium and phosphorus, which are set free on contact with the moisture in your skin. This benefit is said to survive washing.[15]

Game Changers
CALIDA

CALIDA of Switzerland launched "guaranteed underwear" (repaired at no cost) in 1941. The line struck a chord and gained immediate favor with women. It was wartime and women had other things to worry about than mending underwear. The brand continued to evolve and has been making ethical, luxury undergarments and nightwear ever since.

CALIDA bills their products as "a delight for your skin" and uses only natural fibers such as cotton, wool, silk or MicroModal®. They also have an "Organic" product line and are OEKO-TEX 100 certified.

Dedication to materials is only one feature of their social responsibility; they also have strict guidelines to protect workers. About a third of CALIDA's finished products come from China and India, and the brand aims to ensure that the basic rights of employees are the same across all countries and that the same consideration is given to the environment in those countries as it is in their native Switzerland.

CALIDA also developed a Code of Conduct that deals with issues such as child labor, discrimination, voluntary labor, working hours and fair pay that apply to all employees and suppliers. To ensure that the Code is also observed in other countries, CALIDA has been a member of the Business Social Compliance Initiative (BSCI) since 2006 and obliges all its suppliers to adhere to the BSCI Code of Conduct.

PACT Apparel Inc.

PACT Apparel came alive in 2009 when UC Berkeley business school classmates Jeff Denby and Jason Kibbey discovered they both wanted to create a socially responsible company that focused on building a sustainable supply chain. They decided to sell clothes that make the world a better place and wanted to start with underwear. PACT Apparel was born. The company tagline is "You change your underwear, we change the world."

PACT manufactures according to the apparel industry's highest environmental and social standards and its emphasis on environmental and social responsibility is supported across its entire supply chain. All cotton is GOTS and in 2014 it announced that most of its production was coming from a Fairtrade Certified facility in India.

In addition to a full lineup of underwear styles, PACT sells "socks with soul" and other everyday essentials for the whole family.

Clare Bare

Los Angeles-based artist and designer Clare Herron launched Clare Bare in 2008 to bring stylish, eco-friendly lingerie to women everywhere. An avid collector of vintage fabrics, Herron began by creating one-of-a-kind pieces that showcased the beauty of the textile. As her line gained attention and boutiques started to request the collections, Herron added fabrics that were more readily available like organic cotton and bamboo jersey.

Not losing her desire to design and play with colors, Herron buys all her material in either black or natural off-white, and any color in the collection is from her hand-dyed efforts with organic dyes and experiments with lac (pinks/reds), logwood (purples/blacks) and Caribbean plants (teal/greens) to create patterns inspired by her treasured fabrics.

Shopping Guide

• Brook There, brookthere.com, has been making sustainable clothing and lingerie in Portland, Maine, since 2007. Sells bras, underwear, garter belts and masks, plus women's basics: tanks, shorts, chemises and slips. V.A.L.U.E. — (L) Everything is made in the US. (E) Materials include US-milled organic cotton and silk, which is dyed in-house. Available online.

• CALIDA, calida.com, of Switzerland has been making luxury undergarments and nightwear for over 70 years. The brand specializes in bras and underwear, as well as sleepwear and loungewear, and offers daywear: tops and knits and swim and beachwear, for men, women and children. V.A.L.U.E. — (E) All products are certified OEKO-TEX 100. A member of BSCI and supports socially and ethically compliant production conditions. Sold across Europe and at select boutiques in the US. See also page 155.

- Clare Bare, clarebare.com, makes local, handmade, stylish, eco-friendly lingerie, including bodysuits, bralettes, garter belts, garter shorts, garter tanks, panties, slips and tops. V.A.L.U.E. — (L) Handmade in LA. (U) Leather remnants are sourced from local designers. (E) Uses sustainable design practices and fabric, including drawing from her collection of vintage fabric and organic dyes. Available at select boutiques and online. See also page 156.

- loup charmant, loupcharmant.com, is a dreamy, ethical line (French for "charming wolf") launched in 2006 by New York-based designer Kee Edwards. Whimsical intimates including bralettes, camisoles, bloomers and slips provide the seasonless foundations of the line that are perfect for lounge, sleep, vacation or honeymoon — and my favorite, the cashmere robe! V.A.L.U.E. — (E) Uses only natural and organic fibers. All cotton is GOTS certified, ethically sourced from around the world. Available at select boutiques worldwide and online.

- PACT Apparel Inc., wearpact.com, is a social enterprise that aims to make the world a better place through "socks with soul, altruistic underwear and other everyday essentials ethically manufactured with fabrics that feel good and go easy on the environment." V.A.L.U.E. — (E) The complete social enterprise, PACT is a business in the business of making the world a better place. It is FairTrade Factory Certified, GOTS and OEKO-TEX 100 Certified, SA8000 Certified and a Certified B Corporation. Sold at retailers such as Whole Foods, as well as online. See also pages 155–156.

- Skin, skinworldwideshop.com, is a lifestyle brand dedicated to sustainable and eco-conscious fashion. Founder Susan Beischel began with lingerie in 2004, but has expanded to include clothing from day to night. Full collection includes underwear, tees, camisoles, chemises, robes, lingerie plus sportswear. V.A.L.U.E. — (E) Champions organic Peruvian pima cotton, uses low-impact dyes, GOTS certified. Works closely with manufacturers to ensure they are treated and paid fairly. Online with international shipping.

- Swedish Stockings, swedishstockings.com. Hoisery shouldn't be forgotten, and founders Linn Frisinger and Nadja Forsberg offer high-fashion luxury, top quality and environmental sustainability with their Swedish

Stockings — standard, patterned, control-top and knee-highs. V.A.L.U.E. — (E) The eco-friendly hosiery is made out of recycled yarn. Online with international shipping.

- Under the Canopy, underthecanopy.com, is a New York-based lifestyle brand offering sleepwear and bedding that is organic and sustainable. Sells an affordable, luxurious, Fair Trade Certified organic cotton kimono robe as well as a full range of GOTS certified bedding. V.A.L.U.E. — (E) The first US apparel and home fashion brand to offer organic/Fair Trade cotton in its products. Has committed to the Canopy Fashion Loved by Forest initiative. Available at select Whole Foods and Bed, Bath and Beyond.

Final Notes

In recent decades, eczema has become two to three times more common.[16] A staggering 10 percent of Americans suffer from it.[17] If you are one, you know what goes against your skin matters and the fact that we have certifications for "chemical-free" is a great consumer advantage.

If chemistry brought us "better living" in the last century, surely it can bring us "cleaner living" in this one. The technological advances that have gone into developing safe, sustainable, manufactured fibers is exciting and gives hope for the future of the entire fashion industry. The textiles outlined in this chapter are just the tip of the iceberg.

Plus, Lenzing is working on making their textiles completely recyclable; this means that the success that Patagonia has seen with Teijin and others have seen with polyester could soon be a reality for cellulose fibers too.

Chapter 7

Shoes and Footwear

> It's about creating products with durable materials and
> a timeless aesthetic — something that's inherently less
> wasteful than "fast fashion."[1]
>
> — Emily Alati,
> Director of Materials Development for Timberland

THIS BOOK IS A HEAD-TO-TOE GUIDE, so naturally we need a chapter for footwear. Such a small item, yet one that can have so much impact. In America, 98 percent of the footwear is imported.[2] All $54 billion of it.[3] According to a closet expert in a recent *Wall Street Journal* article, men tend to have fewer than ten pairs of shoes, whereas women have four to five times that amount.[4] The *Daily Express* reports women will buy 469 pairs of shoes in a lifetime, at an average of seven pairs per year.[5]

The first shoe is over 5,500 years old, so the industry has had some time to evolve and make advances.[6] I'm not referring to the kind of technological advances that can make you jump higher (although those have happened too), but the kind of advances that are relevant to this book: revolutionary recyclable shoes from PUMA, boots creating prosperity for an Aboriginal community, artisanal shoes upcycled from plastic chip wrappers and upcycled tech fibers from TV screens. This section of your closet has it all.

Leather

Leather is one of fashion's most problematic dilemmas. Hides, if left untreated or converted into leather, are a toxic threat. Fashion usage of by-products of the meat industry is necessary until the world reduces (or ends) meat consumption. Even then, an argument could be made to still use hides to avoid waste. Leather is an incredibly durable material (as seen with the 5,000-year-old shoe), so there is a place for leather in an ethical wardrobe. As always, source is everything. There are several issues: the source of the hides, the tanning processes and its effects on workers and the environment in unregulated countries. (One of the tannery regions in Bangladesh made the same list as Chernobyl on *The World's Worst Polluted Places in 2013* by the Blacksmith Institute.[7]) Some brands are leading the way to equitable and ethical leather production, and technology is contributing to environmental safety.

Source of Hides

We know that industrial livestock production is terrible for the planet. In 2006 the Food and Agriculture Organization of the United Nations published *Livestock's Long Shadow* to raise awareness about the "very substantial contribution of animal agriculture to climate change and air pollution, to land, soil and water degradation and to the reduction of biodiversity." The report states,

> The livestock sector is major stress on many ecosystems and on the planet as whole. Globally it is one of the largest sources of greenhouse gases and one of the leading causal factors in the loss of biodiversity, while in developed and emerging countries it is perhaps the leading source of water pollution.[8]

To further highlight the point, especially about biodiversity loss, Greenpeace released their own report, *Slaughtering the Amazon*, in 2009 that revealed that the single largest driver of deforestation of the rainforest is Brazilian beef. Citing "cattle are responsible for about 80 percent of all deforestation in the Amazon region," it documented a three-year investigation that traced beef and other cattle products from ranches involved in deforestation, at the heart of the Amazon rainforest, all the way to the brands using the end product: leather. The research revealed that Amazon cattle products made their way to China, Italy and the US, probably resulting in shoes, handbags, furniture and leather vehicle interiors, making consumers of leather products unknowing supporters of Amazon deforestation.[9]

Immediately following the Greenpeace report, the *Telegraph* reported that leading shoemakers including Adidas, Clarks, Nike and Timberland had demanded suppliers stop sending them leather from illegal ranches in the Amazon.[10]

The leather industry, like others in this book, also needs oversight. In 2005, a group of brands, retailers, product manufacturers, leather manufacturers, chemical suppliers and technical experts recognized that and came together to form the Leather Working Group(LWG). Members include popular mainstream brands like Adidas, Doc Martens, Bata, Burberry, Clarks, Timberland, Geox, H&M, EILEEN FISHER, LVMH, Nike, New Balance, PUMA and Nine West. The group is able to use their collective clout to try to improve the tanning industry by creating alignment on environmental priorities, bringing visibility to best practices and providing suggested guidelines for continual improvement.

Leather to Avoid Waste

Our appetite for meat is greater than it's ever been, resulting in vast amounts of skins and hides that are by-products of the meat industry. Something needs to be done with them, and so far the most environmentally friendly option is to tan and use them.

In 2014, the United Nations Industrial Development Organization commissioned a report titled *The Future for Leather*, which stated,

> If the approximately nine to ten million tons of raw hides and skins as by-products of the meat industry (generated irrespective of the needs of the leather industry) is not processed into leather and subsequently into consumer goods, then it would remain as organic waste. This would be a significant problem — rotting, odour, volume/mass — to be handled or disposed of somehow. It is even claimed that the carbon footprint of disposal footpath would be greater than processing for the short and long term into leather.[11]

This means that, for now, fashion is one of the solutions and not the problem. Or can be, depending where and how it is tanned.

Tanning

Let's be honest, tanning is a disgusting process: separating hair and collagen (the fat and flesh) from a hide in order to produce leather. What was once a natural (woodsmoke and natural oils) and time-intensive process[12] has been replaced by a chemically intensive one. There are three common ways to tan leather: chromium tanning, aldehyde tanning and vegetable tanning, each environmentally challenged. If you're like me, you have probably always thought "vegetables aren't dangerous — this must be the most environmentally friendly way to tan leather." It seems fair, right? Sadly, it's a common misconception, not just among consumers but among brands and designers too. In vegetable tanning, plant tannins replace the chromium, but the other 249 chemicals are still in the process. The BLC Leather Technology Centre, experts who provide audits of the Leather Working Group environmental stewardship program, conducted research to "evaluate the various tanning chemicals, to see if there was an environmentally preferable choice between chrome, vegetable and aldehyde based processes." They share their findings.

The question of Environmentally Preferred Tanning Systems

A question is often asked as to what is the cleanest, greenest or environmentally sustainable tanning method. It is often assumed (without enough understanding) that leather tanned with vegetable extracts must always be better, but the reality is quite different.

Tanning is just one of around twenty major processes that a hide goes through to be converted from a raw pelt to a tanned and finished piece of leather. All the other elements are largely the same whether it be a chrome, vegetable or aldehyde (chrome-free) leather. The residual hair, fats, proteins, pigments and interfibrillary matter still have to be removed using sulphides, lime, acids, alkalis, emulsifiers, enzymes etc. Then the leather is generally dyed, fat-liquored, retanned, ☞

dried and finished. These process elements are generally the same for all tannage types.

To focus on just the "tanning" aspect of the leather making is flawed. To better understand the impacts of the different tannage types, BLC Leather Technology Centre Ltd. contracted an independent company, Ecobilian, to conduct a detailed life cycle analysis of three tanning systems — vegetable, chrome and aldehyde (wet white) — using the ISO14040 standard as a basis. The study concluded that there was no preferred alternative between the tannages as they all had environmental positives and negatives. In fact, it is the leather manufacturing process itself not the tannage type that has the biggest potential for negative environmental effects if not appropriately controlled.

It is this philosophy of appropriate control that underpins the Leather Working Group environmental stewardship program. This program, which has around 200 leather manufacturers, 40 major brands, 40 chemical companies and suppliers, focuses on maintaining an auditing protocol that assesses the environmental stewardship practices of leather makers. More details can be found on leatherworkinggroup.com.

It is only by assessing the complete leather manufacturing process that an informed decision can be made about the environmental credentials of the leather supplied. Unfortunately, in the market place, there are many unsubstantiated (positive and negative) claims about certain tanning systems and processes. There are also many people too quick to accept these promotional claims without fully understanding what they really mean.

Making leather without using chemicals is impossible. To this end, the chemicals used and all other by-products from the process need to be appropriately measured, managed and controlled.

— BLC Leather Technology Centre Ltd., blcleathertech.com, November 2014

Sadly, there's no "greenest" tanning solution. According to the BLC, choosing vegetable-tanned leather over other types succumbs to marketing and not science. The BLC notes that the bigger environmental issues are the overall manufacturing process and the oversight throughout the entire process, not just the tanning. This includes the application of industrially proven low-waste advanced methods and effective effluent treatment.

While the leather industry is making strides to be cleaner and greener, there are many small tanneries that aren't. The Blacksmith Institute points out,

> Even though segments of the industry, especially those connected to large corporations, may be operating responsibly to limit toxic pollution, there are enough polluting tanneries to cause a real and serious health threat to about 1.8 million people, and a black eye to the industry as a whole.[13]

The Dark Side of Tanning

In 2009, Human Rights Watch revealed just how bad, for people and planet, unregulated and unrestricted tanning can be, in their study "Toxic Tanneries." The worst are tanneries located in the far reaches of the globe and in countries that turn a blind eye to the environmental toxicity of the process, especially effluent discharge. Working in tanneries provides a living for many in developing countries like Bangladesh, the Philippines and Zambia; however, the work and the conditions are not without their price. Ninety percent of tannery workers die before the age of 50, revealed an Al Jazeera America exposé called "The dark side of Bangladesh's Leather Trade."[14]

Hazaribagh, a tannery district located in a residential neighborhood of Dhaka, in Bangladesh, is home to more than 150 tanneries over 25 acres (the size of nearly 20 football fields). While the district employs between 8,000 and 12,000 people, another 185,000 live in the district[15] that has been rated "one of the ten most polluted places on earth,"[16] due to antiquated practices, specifically not utilizing effluent treatment. Every day, the tanneries generate 21,000 cubic liters of toxic waste:

> The effluent that pours off tannery floors and into Hazaribagh's open gutters contains animal flesh, dissolved hair, and fats. It is thick with lime, hydrogen sulfide, chromium sulfate, sulfuric acid, formic acid, bleach, dyes, oils, and numerous heavy metals used in the processing of hides. This effluent flows from the open gutters into a stream that runs through some of Hazaribagh's slums, and into Dhaka's main river, the Buriganga.[17]

It's a modern-day tragedy that has no end in sight. Even though the Bangladeshi government has written actions against both the area and the owners, and the government has set aside a new commercial zone for the antiquated tanneries that includes a new effluent treatment plant, production continues where and how it is. They could move — geographically and technologically into safer production, but they haven't. The move was scheduled to happen in 2004, and then rescheduled to 2005, and has continuously been postponed; the next deadline has been pushed to 2016.[18] It's not for lack of money; leather sales from Bangladesh were almost $1 billion in 2012.[19]

The tragic part is that the word "Hazaribagh" will never appear on any label. Because it's the source of the raw material, the leather can be imported to Europe, Japan and North America (the biggest buyers of leather from the zone), and the finished item will say "Made in Italy" or "Made in Japan" or wherever the leather was manufactured into the finished product. [20]

To avoid Hazaribagh and other toxic leathers, choose brands that are members of the LWG, such as:

• Acne	• Deckers	• New Balance
• Adidas	• Deichmann	• Nike
• Dr. Martens	• EILEEN FISHER	• Nine West
• ASOS	• GEOX	• PUMA
• Burberry	• H&M	• Timberland
• Bata	• K-Swiss	• Wolverine
• C&A	• LVMH	
• Clarks	• Marks & Spencer	

Through the LWG, these brands monitor and rate tanneries and their environmental records. The rating system works like the Olympics — bronze, silver and gold — and some companies, like Timberland, have a corporate commitment to work only with silver- or gold-rated tanneries. This positive incentive program seems to work best for activating change. Tanneries who want to get a big contract with a brand like Timberland need to clean up the production. This is a win-win for everyone; cleaner tanneries put less pressure on the environment, and their workers, and effluent plants save the local water supplies. Effluent plants also save money as the tanneries can often recoup and reuse their chemical several times.

Leather: A Material for Longevity

It is estimated that, by 2015, 23 billion pairs of shoes will have been purchased globally.[21] The best way to buy leather sustainably is to do so with longevity in mind. Buy timeless pieces that will last. In 2014, Timberland celebrated the 40th anniversary of their iconic yellow boot. Launched in 1973, the classic boot is an example of the durability of leather in a product that stands the test of time. I asked Timberland to comment on leather, why they use it and how it fits into their view of sustainability. Their response is below.

Leather is our heritage. And sustainability has always been central to the Timberland brand — after all, we're rooted in the outdoors — and we know it matters to consumers worldwide. We have a deep and longstanding commitment to responsible sourcing, in terms of environmental as well as social impact. And we always take into account the broader definition of sustainability, and the importance of designing styles that will literally be around for years to come.

What this all means, is that consumers can be confident that Timberland products are made with the environment in mind. So when they slip on a pair of Timberland boots or a Timberland jacket, they can feel as good as they look. For more than 40 years, Timberland has built its reputation on the careful selection of the finest waterproof and non-waterproof leathers. Material selection is extremely important to making high-quality footwear, and choosing the right leathers is critical to delivering the best possible product to our consumers. Timberland has made the decision to source the finest quality leathers only for footwear from tanneries that have achieved a Silver or Gold rating from the Leather Working Group for its water, energy and waste management practices.

Using leather in our footwear allows us to create classic designs that last season after season and don't go out of style. It's about creating products with durable materials and a timeless aesthetic — something that's inherently less wasteful than "fast fashion."

— Emily Alati, Director of Materials Development for Timberland

End of Life

Tanning is what makes leather so durable but also what keeps it from biodegrading. In *Cradle to Cradle: Remaking the Way We Make Things*, co-author Michael Braungart explains:

> Leather shoes are actually a mixture of biological materials (the leather, which is biodegradable) and technical materials (the chromium and other substances, which have value for industries). According to current methods of manufacture and disposal, neither could be successfully retrieved after the shoe was discarded. From a material and ecological standpoint, the design of the average shoe could be much more intelligent.[22]

Rising to the challenge, in 2009, Sergio Rossi created an eco-friendly shoe called the Eco Pump. It was sleek, beautiful and biodegradable. Its launch coincided with the worldwide broadcasting of the environmental movie *Home* (financed by Kering, the French multinational parent company of Sergio Rossi). According to details released at the time by the development partner Aesop Technologies,

> An innovative sole has been conceived in liquid wood which contains a low percentage of leather waste, chemically clean, which provides the perfect suppleness. The heel, also made in liquid wood gets, thanks to an injection process, high strength. All these materials are biodegradable. For the uppers, Sergio Rossi, renowned for its craft and unique selection of leathers, has worked with an eco-sensitive tanner.[23]

The shoe was proof that shoes, a luxury high heel at that, could be developed with end of life as a consideration. PUMA went on to do the same thing in 2011. PUMA (also in the Kering Group) created the first Cradle to Cradle Certified™ shoe as part of their InCycle line. Partnering with APINAT BIO®, the shoes featured a bioplastic sole that was biodegradable.

Cradle to Cradle certifies products in every sector — including home, beauty as well as fashion — and works with designers and manufactures to create items that, as Braungart calls it, are more intelligent and are created with end of life in mind. (Will it be recycled, repurposed, biodegrable?) Design thinking at its most innovative, applying Cradle to Cradle methodology shows brands and designers are thinking about more than just the sale of the product.

The Cradle to Cradle Certified Product Standard uses a comprehensive approach to evaluating the design of a product and the practices employed in its manufacturing. The materials and manufacturing processes are assessed in five categories:

- Material Health: Knowing the chemical ingredients of every material in a product, and optimizing toward safer materials.
- Material Reutilization: Designing products made with materials that come from and can safely return to nature or industry.
- Renewable Energy and Carbon Management: Envisioning a future in which all manufacturing is powered by 100 percent clean renewable energy.
- Water Stewardship: Manage clean water as a previous resource and an essential human right.
- Social Fairness: Design operations to honor all people and natural systems affected by the creation, use, disposal or reuse of a product.

— The Cradle to Cradle Products Innovation Institute, www.c2ccertified.org

Shopping for V.A.L.U.E.
Vintage

Footwear is a great category to shop for secondhand or second life. Another consumer survey (who knew researchers were so keen on footwear) reported that women wear only a quarter of the shoes in their closets. The reasons they didn't wear the rest will probably sound familiar:

- Too uncomfortable (too tight on feet/too high heels) (64 percent)
- Hard to match with an outfit (55 percent)
- Scared to damage/were very expensive (41 percent)
- Were given as a gift and don't like them (37 percent)
- Didn't like them as much when I got them home (21 percent)[24]

We've all been there. What do you do with your barely worn shoes when you are finally ready to let them go? Donation? Resale?

The Clothing chapter provides a list of online thrift shops, and most of them also resell shoes, but my favorites are eBay and local consignment shops. According to the eBay site, "At any given time there are about 200,000 women's shoes and over 75,000 men's shoes" listed.[25] I love it because often the seller describes why they are selling ("too tight" or "too uncomfortable") and will include the box and/or shoe bag that came with the original purchase. Local consignment is also a good option because you can try the shoes on.

Some people are squeamish about "someone else's shoes." And I get that. Check the soles or treads to see how much wear actually occurred, then turn to the Internet, which has loads of videos on how to clean and freshen old or used shoes.

Providing Customers the Option: Artisan Made or Mass Produced

You might not know the term "mukluk," but chances are you'd know one to see one. Australia has their Uggs and North America has mukluks — the traditional Aboriginal boot made of soft leather and fur, often with fur pompom or with delicate beading. The Manitobah Mukluks story is one of cultural preservation, sustainable growth and adapting to market pressure.

Sean McCormick, a Métis from Manitoba, founded Manitobah Mukluks. He grew up working in a tannery in Winnipeg. While there, he began trading leather with Aboriginal women in the surrounding communities in return for handmade mukluks and moccasins. McCormick developed a business selling the handcrafted boots to hotels and gift shops but recognized a long-term challenge facing both his business and his Aboriginal community.

The artisans who possessed the traditional knowledge were aging, and the younger generation showed little interest in learning the skills and craftsmanship that had been in the community for centuries. McCormick knew he had to do something. As soon as he graduated from business school, he founded Manitobah Mukluks to build capacity to keep the traditions alive.

The first step in developing the "modern" mukluk included a partnership with Vibram™ that led to the creation of a custom tread pattern (designed by a Cree artist) and a new durability for city wear.

Building on the success of the modern mukluk, McCormick turned his focus back to the handmade boots that he knew as a child — traditional boots that had made it possible for his ancestors to survive in the harsh Canadian climate for thousands of years. With this, the Storyboot Project was born — a business building partnership with elders and artisans who crafted mukluks and moccasins the traditional way. Each boot contains a story, both of the artist and of the timeless tradition, with a selling price that reflects the time, skill and knowledge involved. Today, Storyboots sell for up to $1,200, with all proceeds going directly to the artist.

Says McCormick,

> As a company, we work with local artists, showcase successful role models and invest in education and employment through our partnership with the Centre for Aboriginal Human Resource Development (CAHRD). I'm particularly proud of our Storyboot program which aims to help revive traditional arts by creating business building partnerships with elders and artisans who fashion mukluks and moccasins the traditional way.[26]

As business continued to grow, a watershed moment occurred for McCormick: supermodel Kate Moss was photographed wearing his boots. Soon after, demand grew, and McCormick capitalized by opening a factory in Winnipeg. With this growth in production capability, he could further his commitment to three core values: providing jobs, supporting artisans and creating pride in the Aboriginal community.

In his words,

> As an Aboriginal Canadian, authentic to me means being engaged in and contributing to my community. It also means respecting our history while creating positive change for the future. The best way for me to make the biggest impact is to get as many people wearing Manitobah Mukluks as possible. It's simple; for every pair of Manitobah Mukluks we sell, we are able to make a bigger impact.

Research shows that as much as consumers want local production, they aren't really willing to spend more for products manufactured domestically. Boston Consulting reported only 60 percent of Americans would be willing to pay 10 percent more for clothes manufactured domestically.[27] Looking at similar research in Canada, McCormick decided he could build a more sustainable company and create more jobs by finding a manufacturing partner overseas.

McCormick traveled to Vietnam and established a relationship with a small company that could grow as Manitobah grew. He introduced leading human resource and training practices and began transferring materials and production knowledge from those making Manitobah Mukluks and moccasins in Canada to the team in Vietnam.

Production efficiencies in Vietnam meant Manitobah could offer retailers a more competitively priced option. Boots that were previously $299 could now be sold for $199. Alongside the international production, McCormick continued to offer Canadian-made versions. Putting this choice in the hands of consumers, Manitobah Mukluks is better able to focus on other aspects of growing the business, including instituting a training program to help youth learn beading techniques used by elders, reinvigorating the endangered craft and working with local Aboriginal groups to further strengthen and support the community.

"Making some products overseas allows us to reach more people than we would otherwise, thereby contributing to the growth of the brand and to our impact in the community. I believe that our success as an Aboriginal business has been due to our willingness to collaborate and to look to the past while walking forward," says McCormick.

It seems to be working, Manitobah appeared on the 2014 *Profit* magazine list of Canada's fastest-growing companies — achieving a 290 percent growth rate over a five-year period, solidifying it as Canada's fastest-growing footwear brand[28] selling artisan, local and mass-produced products.

Local is a challenge for most footwear brands. The majority of shoe production facilities have been moved offshore, and few have returned. In 1968, there were 233,000 people employed by shoe manufacturers; by 1986, there were 119,000. Today there are 13,900.[29] The Manitobah Mukluk model is new model for some shoe brands: to have a specific model or style manufactured domestically and the rest overseas. Earmarking a "heritage" line or a special edition is often how this hybrid approach appears. Brands like Red Wings, Britain's Dr. Martens and Japan's Onitsuka Tiger sneakers do this, and even Bass[30] and Sperry[31] have reissued "Made in Maine" Collections.

New Balance, the only sportswear shoe company to claim they are "Made in the US," works on a different model. When 70 percent of the materials can be sourced domestically, then the shoe gets this label.[32] If you want domestically made (local) shoes, make sure to check the label before you buy.

Fair Trade

The largest portion (30 percent) of the footwear market is made up of athletic shoes, with the top five players — Nike, Adidas, Reebok, PUMA and Asics — holding around 80 percent market share.[33] A footwear chapter wouldn't be complete without addressing labor, particularly given that some athletic brands can't seem to shake the "sweatshop" moniker.[34]

Manufacturing sneakers is labor intensive. It takes the assembly line at Yue Yuen, a Chinese shoe factory for clients including Adidas and Nike, ten hours to make a single shoe.[35] That's because a running shoe can easily have as many as 50 components, which are assembled by hand.[36]

For all that work, labor accounts for only 0.4 percent of the purchase price. No, that's not a typo; for every $100 shoe, about 40 cents goes towards labor in the manufacturing process. Yet advertising and sponsorship gets 8.5 percent, or about $8.50 of that $100, and product research and development accounts for 11 percent.[37] These data are often cited as an example of how small workers' wages are, as a percentage of retail price, in mass production.

This is why fair trade in this segment is key. Oliberté, a Canadian-based footwear and lifestyle brand, supports workers' rights and sustainable manufacturing in sub-Saharan Africa and is the owner of the world's first Fairtrade Certified footwear factory. Oliberté found they were always pressuring suppliers to provide decent wages and health care, and finally they took control and acquired their own facility in August 2012.[38]

While Oliberté is the first shoe factory to be a certified Fairtrade facility, there are many other small brands that produce shoes under fair trade principles. These brands and designers work with small facilities, ensuring things are being produced in an ethical manner.

French sneaker brand Veja is another example of the fair trade model. They work directly with small producer co-operatives in Brazil, using materials such as organic cotton, wild Amazonian rubber and acacia-tanned leather to create fair sneakers and accessories.[39]

Upcycled

Leather is not the only material for footwear. In addition to the liquid wood and bioplastic mentioned earlier, some other innovative fibers in this category incorporate upcycling. Vegan designer Elizabeth Olsen of Olsen Haus uses an Ultrasuede upcycled from the industrial waste of a television factory in Japan. The process takes the polyester waste from the screen production and creates a non-woven material that is water-resistant, crack-proof and colorfast. She's also found a way to make soles out of recycled rubber tires and sawdust. Being cruelty-free to Olsen means "also being mindful of the planet that she shares with non-human animals."[40]

Game Changers
Brother Vellies

Brother Vellies takes old-world tradition and craftsmanship, adds modern-day innovation and ingenuity, and we are gifted with a modern take on an old African favorite. Taking their name from the original desert boot, the *velskoen* ("vellie" for short), this stylish, quirky shoe and the small group handcrafting them caught the attention of Toronto-raised, Brooklyn-based Aurora James. Brother Vellies was founded by Aurora with the goal of introducing the rest of the world to her favorite traditional African footwear, while also creating and sustaining artisanal jobs within Africa. Never losing its South African roots, Brother Vellies is a collection of boots, shoes and sandals in styles that maintain the spirit and durability of their ancestral counterparts.

Aurora and the Brother Vellies team are skilled at making the most of the opportunities presented by using local sustainable materials and upcyling. Almost every aspect of a Brother Vellies shoe has had a previous life or use; scrap tires are in abundance in Kenya, so they have started appearing as soles on some styles. The leathers and materials, including the distinctive springbok, are by-products from the food industry. Most recently, Brother Vellies inherited donated scrap denim from Morocco, which is also being incorporated into select styles. Plus, all scraps and leftovers from production of the men's and women's collections get repurposed in the adorable "mini" line for kids.

The collections are adored by *Vogue* (both French and American), *Harper's Bazaar* and *Nylon*.

LOVE IS MIGHTY

LOVE IS MIGHTY is more than just the name of designer Monisha Raja's brand; it's also an expression about her profound love for people, planet and animals. She launched her vegan footwear and accessory line in 2011 after successful stints as a freelance designer on footwear lines for Tory Burch, Max Azria, Banana Republic and BCBG. In creating LOVE IS MIGHTY, New York-based Raja wanted to create a brand that would support endangered communities in her native India.

Her journey led her to the northern deserts of India, where she developed partnerships with skilled local tribes. Together they are reviving embroidery techniques, showcasing and developing metal weaving on non-leather materials with the community and marrying ancient weaving techniques with modern innovative designs using recycled plastics. A beautiful example is the Heera shoe; chip and biscuit wrappers are retrieved from the landfill and handwoven by artisans on looms, creating a unique textile with unexpected bursts of color resulting in an incredible vegan shoe. The LOVE IS MIGHTY design ethos bridges the gap between luxury fashion and ancient mastery.

NINA Z

The NINA Z collection of traditional Swedish clogs is like their designer, "Made in Sweden, based in Brooklyn." Nina Ziefvert has been making her New York-inspired versions of Swedish clogs since 2008. In addition, the stylish line includes sandals and boots. Each pair is designed by Ziefvert and made by her partner, in business and life, in their Crown Heights, Brooklyn, studio.

Ziefvert says, "It's really rewarding to be able to oversee production from a customer's order to final packaging. I love the sound of the staple gun as the finishing nails seals the shoe."

A good clog base should be made of wood from the birch or alder family; the wood has to be durable yet light enough to be comfortable to walk on. The wood bases are made in Sweden, the traditional way, but the leather is sourced locally from smaller vendors or hide houses in Brooklyn or Queens. Ziefvert chooses to source in small batches so each production looks a little different.

Shopping Guide

- Aurora Shoe Co., aurorashoeco.com, an upstate New York shoe company, has been handcrafting shoes since the early 1990s. These simply styled shoes for men and women come with Vibram soles. V.A.L.U.E. — (L) Made in the US with locally sourced materials. (E) The company aims to make shoes that people can wear for years to come (even offers repair services for the shoes they produce). Purchase from their factory or online.

- BHAVA NY, bhavastudio.com, is a vegan footwear and accessory brand that travels the globe in search of ethical, vegan fabrics for its contemporary collections of sandals, flats, wedges, boots and belts. V.A.L.U.E. — (E) Dedicated to ethical production, the BHAVA team hand selects suppliers who match their ethics. Uses cruelty-free, organic and recycled components. At select boutiques and online.

- Brave GentleMan, bravegentleman.com, might sound familiar from the Special Occasions chapter. Based in New York, it makes high-end, sustainable and ethical suiting to go with its premium, vegan men's footwear line. V.A.L.U.E. — (E) PETA vegan fashion award-winner; uses luxurious, recycled or organic textiles free of animal fibers. Produced in Portugal under fair labor conditions. At select boutiques or online.

- Brother Vellies, brothervellies.com, was founded by Aurora James with the goal of introducing the rest of the world to her favorite traditional African footwear, while also creating and sustaining artisanal jobs within Africa. V.A.L.U.E. — (A) Hires local artisans of all genders, sexual orientation, backgrounds and tribes, and gives them fair wages and skills training from other experienced artisans. (U) Upcycles everything from tires for soles, to bones for beads. Recently, it has worked with a brass artisan in Kenya who hand-casts the sandal buckles from recycled brass padlocks and keys. (E) Most of the production process is done by hand, keeping energy consumption low; and Brother Velllies believes in the concept of slow fashion, using the best practices and materials to make "forever shoes" that will last many years. They believe that good-quality leather shoes are an investment that should be thought of as a long-term purchase. Available at select boutiques and online. See also pages 173–174.

- Calleen Cardero, calleencordero.com, had a vision of creating hand-made artisan quality footwear, handbags and accessories in the US. She opened her factory in 1999 and employs nearly 40 artisans in North Hollywood, California. V.A.L.U.E. — (A) From sculptors of wooden soles, hand-lasters and sewers, each piece is passed through the hands of talented artisans the old-school way. (L) Made in California. (E) All heel woods used are from sustainable forests or recycled plywood, and every attention is paid to using the best and safest materials. Available at select boutiques and online.

- Cri de Coeur, cri-de-coeur.com, is a collection created using the highest-quality vegan materials. In addition to seasonal collaborations with Arden Wohl, the New York design duo offers boots, shoes, sandals, handbags, wallets and jewelry collaborations. V.A.L.U.E. — (E) The brand is PETA approved, cruelty-free and is committed to choosing vendors who abide by their ideals of earth-friendly manufacturing processes and fair treatment of workers. Sells direct to customer with free shipping and free returns.

- LOVE IS MIGHTY, www.loveismighty.com, was born from a desire to create beauty without harming any living beings while promoting traditional arts and crafts. The line of high-quality, handcrafted unique women's footwear and accessories puts those values into action. V.A.L.U.E. — (A) Made by various artisan communities in India. (U) Melding old-world craftsmanship with the abundance of waste, creates new textiles out of plastic. (E) Uses other ethical textiles like organic canvas. Won *Most Stylish Women's Flat* in PETA USA's first Vegan Fashion Awards. Available at select boutiques and online. See also page 174.

- Manitobah Mukluks, manitobah.ca, is an Aboriginal-owned Canadian brand creating original handcrafted mukluks and moccasins. Provides authentic products that support an endangered craft and community. V.A.L.U.E. — (A) The handcrafted Storyboots support local artisans. (L) Produces in their factory in Winnipeg, creating jobs and work for the local Aboriginal community. (E) Also ethically and fairly produces in Vietnam. Available at select boutiques and online. See Shopping for V.A.L.U.E. for more information.

- NINA Z, ninaznyc.com, is a collection featuring traditional Swedish clogs and is, just like the designer, "Made in Sweden, based in Brooklyn." Includes small-batch production of contemporary clogs, boots and sandals. V.A.L.U.E. — (L) Made in Brooklyn. (E) Sources locally, produces in small batches, makes by hand. Available at select boutiques and weekly at the Brooklyn Flea or online. See also pages 174–175.

- Oliberté, oliberte.com, is a sustainable brand supporting workers' rights in sub-Saharan Africa and is the first Fair Trade shoe brand. Offers shoes, bags and wallets for men and women. V.A.L.U.E. — (E) They have their own Fair Trade certified factory. Use locally sourced material, such as natural rubber and free range leather. Certified B Corporation. Wide distribution throughout Canada and online, including Zappos and Amazon. See also page 172.

- Olsen Haus, olsenhaus.com, designer Elizabeth Olsen is a strong voice for animal rights, healthy vegan lifestyle and eco-consciousness. She created Olsen Haus to offer pure vegan footwear: boots, heels, flats and sandals. V.A.L.U.E. — (U) Fabric is made from recycled products: TVs, plastic water bottles, milk jugs and rubber from tires. (E) 100 percent vegan: no animal skins, animal products, by-products or testing used in the making of products. Works closely with factories to ensure they are following fair trade principles. Available at select boutiques and online.

- Osborn, shoposborn.com, makes "small-batch, direct trade footwear that ties the worlds of weaving and textiles, eco-materials, and socially conscious production into a thoughtful one-of-a-kind shoe." Sells women's ankle boots, flats and oxfords. V.A.L.U.E. — (A) Collaborates with teams of traditional weavers, embroiderers, spinners, block printers and dyers in the handcrafting of custom textiles. (E) Uses eco-friendly leathers recycled and remnant materials. Available online.

- PUMA, puma.com, is a multinational sportswear brand that offers lines of shoes and sports clothing. V.A.L.U.E. — (E) Has not used PVC since 2003. Collaborated with Greenpeace on Chemicals Management in 2005. Environmental initiatives include: Cradle to Cradle Certified, Sustainable Apparel Coalition, AFIRM Group, Leather Working Group. Member of Fair Labor Association (FLA). Stores in 46 countries including Canada and the US, plus online with international shipping. See also page 167.

- Sydney Brown, sydney-brown.com, is a luxury footwear label founded on Sydney Brown's conviction that luxury can be produced in an environmentally friendly way. V.A.L.U.E. — (L) Handmade by artisans in the Los Angeles atelier. (E) Uses eco-friendly materials such as coconut insoles, recycled and sustainable uppers and reclaimed wooden soles, creating shoes with "cradle to cradle" in mind. Available at select boutiques and online.

- Timberland, shop.timberland.com, are makers of boots, shoes, clothes and gear. Launched the EarthKeepers® line in 2007, which use environmentally responsible materials. V.A.L.U.E. — (E) Uses materials that incorporate recycled PET, including SmartWool® faux shearling (made from merino wool and recycled PET), Polartec® fabric and Bionic® canvas. Timberland has even developed its own material: ReCanvas™ fabric, with the look and feel of cotton canvas, that's made from 100 percent recycled PET. Over 128 million used plastic bottles have made their way into shoes and boots. Stores in over 60 countries including Canada and the US, plus online with international shipping. See also page 166.

- Veja, veja-store.com, is a French ecological and fair trade brand of sneakers and accessories. V.A.L.U.E. — (E) Veja works with cooperatives of small producers and social associations in Brazil and France. Uses organic and fair trade cotton plus wild rubber from the Amazon. Cotton is monitored by Instituto Biodinâmico for Rural Development. Veja does not advertise; instead those resources are integrated into the production chain. Farmers and producers Veja works with are fairly remunerated — to accommodate their social and environmental requirements. Available in select boutiques worldwide, plus online.

Final Notes

I love shoes, and this category has so many choices. There are only15 brands listed in this shopping guide, and it was hard to cut it down to just that. There are even two e-commerce sites dedicated strictly to vegan and eco-friendly shoes:

MooShoes: www.mooshoes.com
PlanetShoes: www.planetshoes.com

The research cited earlier — women have about 20 pairs of shoes in their closet, yet only wear about 5 pairs — bears the truth of my closet. I've sold some on consignment, and am trying, like all things, to limit my purchases. At the risk of sounding like a broken record — the best way to change is to buy less, buy better and take care of them. A cobbler is my shoe collection's greatest asset. (More about shoe care in Chapter 9.)

Chapter 8

Handbags

> It could be made of leather or canvas or nylon. It
> could be a tiny clutch in her hand or a backpack slung
> over her shoulder. Never mind what's in it. More than
> anything else today, the handbag tells the story of a
> woman: her reality, her dreams.[1]
>
> — Dana Thomas,
> author of *Deluxe: How Luxury Lost Its Luster*

THERE ARE CLUTCHES, satchels, purses, backpacks and of course, *the
bag.* Handbags are more than holders of phones and lipsticks — they
are the holders of secrets and can often form part of our personal brand.
The size, shape and color all say something about us. So does our choice
of brand or designer. Luxury designer "It" bags can show our wealth and
status or be an aspirational purchase driven by glossy magazine ads and
celebrity sightings; a Chanel wardrobe might not be affordable, but the
handbag may be within reach.

Similar to diamonds, the rise of the "It" bag desirability was created
through marketing initiatives by luxury brands. And its success is not
hard to understand: handbags come in every price point, they don't need
to be tried on and are available around the world.[2] This has led to $20
billion in sales,[3] and because the profit on handbags can be ten times the
cost (or more), handbags are often the engine that funds designers and
design houses.

The dark side of this obsession with status bags and logos has fuelled a subculture of imitations and knockoffs. According to the Department of Homeland Security, 500 million fake handbags, belts and wallets worth $1 billion on the street were confiscated in 2012.[4] While buyers think they are getting a harmless replica, the counterfeit industry is anything but harmless and has been linked to child labor[5] and terrorism.[6] INTERPOL reports that a "wide range of groups — including Al-Qaeda, Hizbullah, Chechen separatists, ethnic Albanian extremists in Kosovo and paramilitaries in Northern Ireland — have been found to profit from the production or sale of counterfeit goods."[7]

The brighter side of this quest for status through handbags has also created a niche for social enterprises and the savvy businesses who understand that, beyond logos, the modern role of handbags is about values. Whether cruelty-free, artisan or handcrafted, for the ethical shopper, handbags provide an opportunity to display those values (at every price point). Even traditional luxury gets a makeover as the descendants of Fendi and Mulberry make handbags with a mission.

The Rise of the Social Enterprise "It" Bag

A new business model appearing at an ever-increasing rate is the social enterprise. The concept isn't that new: social enterprises have formed the backbone of non-profits for ages. Also referred to as the "missing middle," social enterprises sit between the work of governments and NGOs (focused mainly on social impact) and traditional businesses (focused mainly on profit). They use the methods and disciplines of business and the power of the marketplace to advance social, environmental and/or human justice agendas. What makes them "new" is how brands are engaging in business activities for profit *and* for the common good.

These brands can be recognized as Certified B Corporations, publicly highlighting their objectives as social enterprises; or certified Fair trade, highlighting their attention to fair trade principles; or as a Social Enterprise (often abbreviated to SocEnt), which aligns brands with the growing, socially conscious movement.

You can see it in the case of Lauren Bush Lauren's **FEED Projects**: creating good products that help feed the world. Every FEED item, whether it's a purse, messenger, tote or wallet, has a number attached to it, indicating how many meals that purchase pays for. The effort to provide meals to programs around the world is built into the purchase price. And the bags are clearly identifiable with FEED branding, highlighting the wearer's philanthropic values.

In the case of **Bottletop**, the fashion company and registered charity launched by Cameron Saul and his father Roger (founder of British luxury fashion brand Mulberry), each bag supports disadvantaged youth. The luxury bags are clearly identifiable by their upcycled aluminum ring pulls (the type that open a soda or beer can) crocheted together. Each handbag purchase supports the work of the foundation, annually empowering over 35,000 young people to tackle delicate teenage health issues including: the prevention of HIV/AIDS, unplanned pregnancy, drug abuse and gender equality.

These new ethical "It" bags have value woven into the model. The purchase of each bag serves a mission: end hunger or empower youth.

Bridging with Artisans

For Ilaria Venturini Fendi's socially conscious luxury brand **Carmina Campus**, each bag is made by artisans from reused and repurposed materials, creating both a social and environmental impact. A handwritten tag provides a detailed list of the materials and where each bag was made. The brand recently collaborated with the Ethical Fashion Initiative (see below) to create a 100 percent "Made in Africa" collection designed with locally sourced materials.

A flagship program of the International Trade Centre (ITC), a joint agency of the UN and the WTO, the Ethical Fashion Initiative was founded by Simone Cipriani in 2009. Under its slogan, "Not Charity, Just Work," this ITC initiative advocates a fair and responsible fashion industry and makes it possible for fashion designers (like Fendi) to embrace the skills of artisans in the developing world. Of particular focus for the Ethical Fashion Initiative is empowerment of women artisans, many of whom have worked on handbags not just for Carmina Campus but also Sass & Bide, Stella Jean, United Arrows, Stella McCartney, Vivienne Westwood and more.

Just like the old days at the beauty counter when you bought something and got a "gift with purchase," all of these brands and their forms of social enterprise offer a gift of "social good" with purchase.

Materials

Leather is a common material for handbags, and just as in shoes, provenance is key. Purchasing from members of the Leather Working Group or from makers who know the source of their leather will help ensure you get an ethical bag and support healthy, ethical supply chains. However, leather is far from the only choice — there's fish leather, canvas, horn, beading plus many upcycling options such as excess leather, truck tarps, seat belts, gum wrappers and aluminum cans.

Other options include faux, vegan leather and pleather, usually polyvinyl chloride (PVC) or polyurethane. Thanks to California's Proposition 65, things made of PVC that might be sold there have to carry this wording "WARNING: This product may contain a chemical known to the state of California to cause cancer or birth defects or other reproductive harm."[8] That's because PVC contains phthalates (see page 13). Even if you don't see a warning, fake leather and vinyl products have been known to be high in lead. In 2009, the Center for Environmental Health (CEH), a watchdog out of Oakland, CA, released a study called *Pretty but Poisonous: Lead in Handbags and Wallets.* Like other studies cited in this book, the CEH purchased dozens of inexpensive, brightly colored, fashionable, faux-leather handbags, purses and wallets at over 20 California outlets of national chains, such as Kohl's, Target, Macy's, JC Penney, H&M and Wal-Mart. Most of the bags were made of PVC or vinyl but some were made from other materials such as polyurethane. Tests of the outer surfaces of the bags (the part we most often touch) found high lead levels in all but five. Lead was found in bags of every color tested, but the worst offenders were yellow or yellow-tinted bags. [9]

The report went on to highlight that recent medical research shows lead causes a wide spectrum of health problems in adults including cancer. Low-level lead exposures are linked to a greater risk of heart attacks and strokes, increases in blood pressure problems and an increased risk of ALS (Lou Gehrig's disease) and accelerates kidney failure in patients with chronic kidney disease. The effects of lead are worse on children, who often love to play with old purses. Not all low-cost purses are toxic, but like costume jewelry, please consider limiting direct contact with skin and keeping out of the hands of children.

Game changers
CARMINA CAMPUS

The tagline from a 2011 *W Magazine* article describes it best: "With her new line of bags, fashion scion Ilaria Venturini Fendi is spinning cast-off materials into chic carryalls — and changing lives in Africa in the process."[10]

Fendi had stepped away from her brand legacy (under the LVMH umbrella since 1999) to run an organic farm outside of Rome when a chance gift from some Cameroonian visitors — a hat she could immediately picture as a handbag — captured her imagination, and she was back in the handbag business: CARMINA CAMPUS. This time it was on her own terms: upcycling and recycling materials and teaching her skills to communities of craftspeople in Africa. A partner and supporter of the Ethical Fashion Initiative since 2009, Fendi has brought expert Italian artisans to Kenya to share knowledge, train and build the capacity of local artisans.

CARMINA CAMPUS has also delved into collaborative upcycling, working with MINI (making bags from leftover seating fabric and using car visors as makeup mirrors) and Campari (making bags from marketing billboard PVC). CARMINA CAMPUS bags plus other accessories, objects and designs exclusively made with recycled or reused materials are available at RE(f)USE, the Milan boutique and workshop also owned by Fendi.

Looptworks

Looptworks, an innovative brand from Portland, OR, is breaking the mold in modern manufacturing — as a company, they have vowed to never use any new materials. Every product they produce is upcycled: iPad cases made from excess belt leather, backpacks from upcycled polyester and laptop cases from excess neoprene from the wetsuit industry.

In 2014, when Southwest Airlines underwent a large-scale redesign that included replacing leather seats with a more lightweight material (lighter planes mean less fuel and less pollution), they found themselves with discarded leather from 80,000 airline seats. Looptworks has taken the 40 acres of leather and, "repurposing with a purpose," is creating a line of fashionable and functional bags.

Shopping Guide

- **Bottletop**, bottletop.org, founded in 2002 by Cameron Saul and his father Roger (founder of British luxury fashion brand Mulberry), creates luxury purses, clutches, shoulder bags, cross-body bags, totes and belts from recycled bottle tops. V.A.L.U.E. — (A) Production supports artisans and their families in Brazil. (U) The products have a distinctive aspect: the upcycled aluminum ring pulls crocheted together. (E) Sales fund the operation of the Bottletop Foundation, which uses contemporary art and music to raise money and awareness for education projects that tackle delicate teenage health issues such as HIV/AIDS, drug abuse and teenage pregnancy. The Bottletop Foundation supports young people in Malawi, Mozambique, Rwanda, Brazil and the UK. Available at select boutiques and online.

- **CARMINA CAMPUS**, carminacampus.com, the luxury bag concept of Ilaria Venturini Fendi, uses sustainable creativity to cope with the present social and environmental crises, making clutches, purses and shoulder bags. V.A.L.U.E. — (A) Supports and includes the work of artisans. (U) Works only with existing materials such as reclaimed wood, soda cans, PVC, fabric and leather remnants. Available at select boutiques, online retailers and at the RE(f)USE showroom in Milan. See also page 185.

- **Dutzi Design**, dutzishop.com. Ariane Dutzi started the Dutzi workshop in Valladolid, Yucatan, in 2009 to make one-of-a-kind bags and accessories with indigenous Mayan artisans. V.A.L.U.E. — (A) Works with artisans, most of them women. (L) Artisans and workers are from Valladolid and the surrounding communities and are free to work from home or in the workshop. (U) Many of the bags are made from recycled burlap. (E) Also uses local and natural materials. There is no mass production. Available at select boutiques, from her showroom in Valladoid and online.

- **Erin Templeton**, erintempleton.com. A vintage buyer by trade, Erin Templeton always found masses of unloved leather inspiring. After studying shoemaking, she came back to leather and the myriad opportunities for bags and accessories she could make from excess, vintage and unused leather. V.A.L.U.E. — (L) All productions done in her Vancouver, BC, studio. (U) Most pieces made from recycled leather.

(E) As demand grew, Templeton also started sourcing exclusive and locally tanned elk and bison hide. Available at boutiques in Canada, US and Australia, plus online.

- **Far & Wide Collective**, farandwidecollective.com. The goal of this collective is to empower artisans from emerging economies. The Canadian-based e-commerce site is filled with an edited selection of handmade products such as bags and wallets (in addition to jewelry, home goods and other artisan wares). V.A.L.U.E. — (A) Each item is artisan handmade from emerging economies. (E) Works on fair trade principles. Profits are reinvested threefold: to help artisan partners grow their businesses, to help sourcing new products and to develop new artisan networks and channels.

- **FEED Projects**, feedprojects.com. Lauren Bush Lauren created the first FEED Bag, a reversible burlap and organic cotton bag reminiscent of the bags of food distributed by the World Food Program (WFP), to help raise funds and awareness for WFP school feeding programs. Every FEED bag, wallet, backpack and tote (and new artisanal leather) bag has a measurable donation attached to it. V.A.L.U.E. — (E) Through the non-profit FEED Foundation, the social business has been able to provide over 87 million meals globally through the WFP and Feeding America. FEED has also supported nutrition programs around the world, providing over 3.6 million children with vitamin A supplements through the WFP and the US Fund for UNICEF.

- **From the Road**, fromtheroad.com. Founder and designer, Susan Easton travels the globe collaborating with master artisans on one-of-a-kind creations using heritage techniques that are nearing extinction. Fish leather clutches and Turkana hand-beaded bags from Kenya join jewelry and home decor offerings from far-flung places such as Nepal, Kyrgyzstan and Ecuador. V.A.L.U.E. — (A) Each product is artisan made. (E) Ethical production, seeks natural dyes and use of traditional, local materials. Follows fair trade principles. Available at select boutiques and online.

- **Global Goods Partners**, globalgoodspartners.org, a fair trade non-profit organization founded in 2005, provides support and market access to women-led cooperatives in the developing world. This US e-commerce site is filled with an edited selection of artisan and hand-crafted handbags, purses, wallets (in addition to jewelry, home goods and other artisan wares). V.A.L.U.E. — (A) Works with artisan groups and producer partners in the Global South. (E) Vets each organization to ensure that artisans receive a fair living wage and work in safe conditions. Available online.

- **Kempton & Co.**, kemptonandco.com. British-raised, Brooklyn-based designer Fiona Kempton creates heritage-inspired, technology-friendly handbags made in washed leathers, waxed canvas or vintage textiles. V.A.L.U.E. — (L) Bags are made in the studio connected to the Red Hook shop. (U) Bags are made from upcycled, vintage materials. Available at select boutiques in Italy, Japan and the US, its Brooklyn boutique and online.

- **FREITAG**, freitag.ch, was founded by Swiss brothers Markus and Daniel Freitag who wanted to give used materials a new life. They devised a way to transform used truck tarps into over 40 highly functional, unique bags and accessories for men and women. V.A.L.U.E. — (L) Made in their own factory in Zürich. (U) All products made of upcycled truck tarps, inner tubes and seat belts. Available at boutiques in Asia, Europe and North America plus online.

- **Looptworks**, looptworks.com, a Portland, OR, brand, creates premium upcycled laptop, tablet and smartphone cases from rescued excess. V.A.L.U.E. — (L) Everything is made in the US. (U) The brand identifies and rescues high-quality materials that are left over from premium good manufacturers. (E) 100 percent of Looptworks' products are crafted in factories that employ fair labor practices. Certified B Corporation. Available online. See also page 185.

- **MATT & NAT**, mattandnat.com, short for MAT(T)ERIAL + NATURE, this familiar Canadian brand has been offering vegan choices since 1995. Creates a full line of men's and women's bags and wallets. V.A.L.U.E. — (E) In addition to being vegan, uses sustainable materials such as cork and rubber, plus linings are always made out of 100% recycled plastic bottles. Available at select boutiques and online.

- **Mercado Global**, mercadoglobal.org, empowers indigenous women to overcome poverty and become agents of change in their communities and offers handmade weekenders, totes and clutches in distinctive patterns. V.A.L.U.E. — (A) Works with over 300 artisans in more than 30 cooperatives across Guatemala. (E) Fair trade initiatives include providing education, tools and access to international markets so that women can build their own businesses and invest in their own communities. Available in retail stores throughout North America and online.

• **Shannon South**, shop.shannonsouth.com. Shannon South designs and produces her eponymous line of handbags in her Brooklyn studio using luxury remnant nubuck leather from the furniture industry. V.A.L.U.E. — (L) Made in NYC. (U) Uses excess leather. (E) An additional line, Remade USA, offers custom handbags created from clients' old leather coats and jackets.

Shopping for V.A.L.U.E.

Well-made (and luxury) handbags retain their value and can be bought vintage and second-hand through consignment and vintage shops as well as eBay. (See page 94 for more.)

You can also rent luxury "It" bags, on one-month leases, from Bag Borrow or Steal (bagborroworsteal.com), an online boutique for women and men to borrow, collect and share luxury accessories.

Final Notes

The *Wall Street Journal* wrote that Carmina Campus bags "are gaining traction with luxury customers who see themselves as socially conscious — and already have the requisite stock of Céline and Bottega Veneta bags in their closets,"[11] showing one perception that ethical handbags are the "in addition to" purchase.

I don't agree; I think they are the "instead of" and carry the same craftsmanship and cache as heritage "It" bags but with added value.

Chapter 9

Cleaning, Tending and Mending

"Care for your clothes, like the good friends they are."[1]

— Joan Crawford,
Academy Award-winning actress, author

UP TO THIS POINT, this book has been about giving you the background and deeper information to help you choose better and buy better with V.A.L.U.E., but that's only part of the puzzle.

How and where things are made make up only a small portion of their overall footprint. Research shows most of the carbon footprint of a garment happens *after* it is bought. The energy and resources of growing the fibre, turning the fibre into textile, cutting and sewing, dying, washing and transporting the finished garment to the store (or to you) don't hold a candle to the energy that will be expended by simply washing it.

Washing Clothes

Washing, and in most cases over-washing, is an extension of marketing and our need for garments to have a specific smell. Dr. Kate Fletcher, lecturer at the Centre for Sustainable Fashion, London College of Fashion, puts it this way: "Keeping clean used to be about disease prevention, but now the culture of whiter than white has weakened our immune systems, lined the pockets of detergent manufacturers and led to the startling fact that the energy needed to wash your favorite garment is about six times that needed to make it."[2]

Yes, you should wash the garment initially. Research cited earlier indicated that chemical residue from production might remain on the garment, and much of that can be removed through washing (for new clothes labelled "dry-clean only," they should be thoroughly aired outside before use).[3] Then after the initial wash, maybe your garments don't need as much laundering as you think. Most organic and ethical denim companies are cautioning against washing selvage denim often — if at all. In those cases, they are suggesting a yearly or twice-yearly wash or better yet — try "never wash."

If this is the first-time you've heard of "never wash," it is just that: never wash your jeans. Modern denim makers stress that the quality of denim, and in particular selvage denim, will wear better and last longer if you do not wash it. Rather let the oils of your body and the environment help shape the denim to your body, allowing the jeans to wear and discolor at specific stress points (knees, key pockets, etc.) so that each pair becomes as unique as the wearer.

It is an interesting concept and one that helps shape the idea about washing in general. If you can "not" wash your jeans, what else can you "not" wash? Where once we laundered clothing and bedding to avoid illness and disease, now we have bought into soap makers' propaganda about scent and odor. Through over-washing and harmful soap, we create our own vicious circle of needlessly expanding our carbon footprint and the degradation of our favorite garments. We wear, we wash, until we wear and wash right out, and then back to the store we go.

Trying to preserve garments as long as possible is another aspect of sustainability. But what about germs and bacteria, you say? Several studies have shown that "never wash" jeans don't have any higher bacteria or fecal count than jeans that are washed weekly or bi-monthly.[4]

Sunshine is a natural bacteria and germ killer; it works for everything and can even brighten whites. Often, a brief stint outside in the sun will do what you hoped for from a cycle in the washing machine: kill bacteria and freshen odors, but without any of the footprint.

Can't bring yourself to "never wash"? Using energy-efficient machines and cold water are other ways to lessen the footprint of laundering. *Good Housekeeping* reports, "The best way to save water, energy, and trim your utility bills is to wash full loads of laundry in an Energy Star washer, using cold water."[5]

You've heard it before, but if you want to save money, and prolong the life of your clothes — ditch the dryer. And the conventional dryer sheets and fabric softeners while you are at it. Both can be loaded with chemicals that accumulate on clothes, adding a toxic layer you can't wear off.

The Environmental Working Group (EWG) says,

> Fabric softeners and dryer sheets coat our clothes with a subtle layer of slimy chemicals — in fact, that's why they feel a little softer. The most common softening chemicals are called "quats" (short for quaternary ammonium compounds) and include such chemical mouthfuls as diethyl ester dimethyl ammonium chloride, dialkyl dimethyl ammonium methyl sulfate, dihydrogenated palmoylethyl hydroxyethylmonium methosulfate and di-(palm carboxyethyl) hydroxyethyl methyl ammonium methyl sulfate.[6]

Quats are "asthmagens" — substances that can cause asthma to develop in otherwise healthy people. Chemical-free households often use vinegar in the rinse cycle for the same soft effect (without any smell). Ditching fabric softeners and dryer sheets also lessens the toxic load from too much fragrance (as discussed in Beauty).

Dry Cleaning

Dry cleaning, discovered by accident in the late 1880, is another chemical process that brought convenience and then concern. French dyer Jean Baptiste Jolly realized that the kerosene spilled on his tablecloth managed to leave it cleaner. Dry cleaning has evolved from kerosene to tetrachloroethylene or perchloroethylene (known as PCE or PERC).

PERC is toxic, carcinogenic and should be avoided. The Natural Resources Defense Council (NRDC) doesn't mince words: "Used to dry-clean clothes, perchloroethylene (PERC) is a danger not only to dry-cleaning workers but also to consumers who bring dry-cleaned clothes into their homes."[7]

Estimates show that 85 percent of dry cleaners in the US still use this process,[8] and as a $9 billion industry, dry cleaning and the use of PERC does not seem to be going away.[9] Two new versions of dry cleaning are commonly marketed as "eco-friendly," "green" or "organic": hydrocarbon and GreenEarth washing, both of which are cautioned for their chemical PERC replacements. The United States Environmental Protection Agency (EPA) suggests professional wet cleaning as the preferred method, stating that "wet cleaning chemicals are biodegradable and generally benign."[10]

It might be nerve-racking the first time you go against the care label instructions, but if you are going to go with "wet cleaning," why not consider doing it yourself? Silk, wool and rayon need special care with soap choice and agitation. Wet wash doesn't necessarily work well for those fibers, but with care, they can be washed at home. Many items we feel need to be dry cleaned don't. They can be spot cleaned, hand washed or steamed. I love my hand steamer; it takes just a few minutes, and the garment looks dry cleaned without any of the chemical load. Special note: if you are steaming clothes that have been dry cleaned in the past or were produced using conventional dyes, make sure to steam in a well-ventilated space (ideally outdoors).[11]

Make Do and Mend

During WWII, the British Ministry of Information released a pamphlet titled "Make Do and Mend." It provided housewives with tips on how to be both frugal and stylish in times of harsh rationing. Readers were advised to create pretty "decorative patches" to cover holes in warn garments, unpick old sweaters to reknit into new styles, turn men's clothes into women's, as well as darn, alter and protect against the "moth menace."[12]

Times have changed. We've lost those skills — seven out of ten young adults don't know how to sew on a button.[13] It works when "grunge" and "distressed" are in fashion, but often clothes end up in the discard pile because they need a simple mend. If you are one of the seven, Martha Stewart has an extended list of how-to tutorials on her site under "Homekeeping Solutions." There are tips on sewing on a button, patching a hole, fixing a hem, even darning a sock. Another website with repair manuals for almost every item in your closet, iFixit even includes a full section on repairing Patagonia items. Alternatively, your neighborhood dry cleaner is also usually your local tailor and can do repairs at affordable prices.

The same is true for footwear. The life of shoes and boots can be extended by a little home care, proper storage and regular visits to the cobbler (shoe repair shop). Waterproofing and wiping surface dirt, snow or salt off boots before you put them away are good first steps to keeping them as long as possible, as is storing them in shoe bags. Cobblers can significantly extend the life of your footwear by resoling, reheeling and conditioning leather.

Before you give up on an item, consider if any of the above advice could help extend its life. Here are some additional salvage and repair services that can help preserve the life of your favorites:

- Cashmere: Stella Neptune, stellaneptune.com, sells iron-on cashmere patches in unique shapes and styles for self-mending.
- Denim: Denim Therapy, denimtherapy.com. Ship them your favorite jeans, and they will repair and reconstruct.
- Knits and sweaters: Knit Alteration & Design, knitalteration.com. Mail them your treasured knits or sweater to have moth holes, burn holes and tears repaired by reknitting. Other types of damage like snags, runs and breaks in seams are also repaired.
- Leather coats and jackets: Leather CARE Specialists, greatleather.com, will repair, re-dye and restore all jackets.
- Shoes: NuShoe, nushoe.com, are masters at handcrafted shoe or boot renewal; they also rebuild shoes.

Think your garment is beyond repair but you are reluctant to part with it? What about a refit? These designers and brands that will help you reshape existing pieces into new treasures:

- Deborah Lindquist, deborahlindquist.com (also in Special Occasions) will take your cashmere sweater and design a unique, reincarnated, bespoke sweater for you, your child or a beloved pet.
- Shannon South, remadeusa.shannonsouth.com (also in Handbags) runs Remade USA, a custom service that repurposes individual vintage leather jackets into handbags.

- Project Repat, projectrepat.com, will help you wrap yourself in your T-shirt memories. Send them your collection of T-shirts, and they'll send back a quilt or blanket.

What to Do When You Are Done

You've done it; you read the whole book! Congratulations! By now you are thinking about all the ways you are going to buy better and buy with longevity and durability in mind. Maybe you're even thinking about the decades you'll be passing in your new garments. Great! The average American throws away 70 pounds of clothing and other textiles a year.[14] Part of that is due to our disposable culture, but another part might be because no one knows what to do with garments when they're done. Here are some ideas:

- Restyle: Have your tailor change a long sleeve to a short sleeve, shorten a hem, change the flares to a skinny or a dress to a tunic. DIY books and video tutorials have lots of ideas to refashion existing pieces, giving them extended life.

- Gift: If someone you know covets a particular piece, when you are ready to retire it from your wardrobe, gift it to them.

- Swap: Have several friends in the same boat? Host a clothing swap or join one in your community.

- Sell: Make your contribution to the resale and second-hand inventory, list on eBay, with any of the online thrift shops listed at the end of the Clothing chapter or at your local consignment shop.

- Return to vendor: Retailers like PUMA, Patagonia and EILEEN FISHER will take their clothes back and recycle them into new products.

- Donate: If you choose a known charity, your donation will likely be sold by them to raise money for their endeavors or resold to garment pickers who will resell the best pieces to vintage stores and package up the rest for resale to other markets, including clothing markets in Africa. Individual items of clothing can go to specific needs: Nike recycles sneakers into playground surfaces;[15] cities in colder climates are always seeking coats (check with your local fire hall); and women's homeless shelters will take bras.

We are still buying far too much and discarding far too often. Whichever afterlife option you seek, it is far better than putting textiles into the trash where they'll end up in a landfill. In a last note about chemicals in our clothing: decomposing clothing can release methane, and the dyes and chemicals in the fabric can leach into the soil, contaminating both surface and groundwater.[16]

Final Notes

Natural resources and water shortages are part of our 21st-century realities, resulting in brands thinking very proactively about afterlife. The future is very bright for textile recycling, and although most brands aren't thinking about reducing our consumption, many are thinking about the afterlife of their garments. Whether it's using cradle to cradle methodology (like PUMA) or creating designs for 3-D printing with recyclable materials (like Bruno Pieters), soon the afterlife possibilities will be yet one more criteria with which to evaluate a new purchase and another element to add to shopping with V.A.L.U.E — we can stick "end-of-life" considerations under the letter "E" with other ethical considerations. As the industry and brands evolve, I'll be there, tracking and updating. Want to stay on top of the future of fashion? See you in the digital realm at Magnifeco.com.

Acknowledgments

THIS BOOK SITS ON THE SHOULDERS OF GIANTS. I'm incredibly indebted to the work of the NGOs and advocacy groups who tirelessly research, publish and put pressure on the industry to change, and to the authors, many listed in the bibliography, who have tackled this issue before me.

This book would not be possible without the chain of introductions and support that started with Anthony and Celeste Lilore, Eric Henry and Lyle Estill that then led to Ingrid Witvoet and everyone at New Society Publishers who gave this book life. Thank you to Judith Brand for editing.

So many generous people gave me their time, shared resources or gave me feedback, and for that I am extremely grateful. Thank you especially to Janet Ackerman, Emily Alati, Jennifer Barckley, Rona Berg, Eve Blossom, Lisa Biswell, Leah Borromeo, Ariana Boussard-Reifel, Nina Braga, Howard Brown and Karen Stewart, Tricia Carey, Stacey Davis, Tal Dehtiar, Katey Denno, Edward Jay Epstein, Natalie Frigo, Jeff Garner, Bryce Gracey, Annie Gullingsrud, Leila Hafzi, Amy Hall, Alexandra Hart, Alan Herscovici, Adam Hughes, Titania Inglis, Aurora James, Reema Keswani, Jennifer Krill, Anjelika Krishna, Rajaiah Kusuma, Safia Minney, Maggie MacDonald, Samuel Moore, Andrew Morgan, Chloe Mukai, Marie Veronique Nadeau, Joseph Nakashian, Jay Nalbach, Elizabeth Olsen, Belinda Pasqua, Brian Paulson, Richard Pearshouse, Bruno Pieters, Sasha Plavsic, Cassidy Randall, Matt Reynolds, Patricia

Ronning, Damien Sanfilippo, Tara Sawatsky, Mark Sejvar, Tara St James, Kiran Stordalen, Pat Syvrud, Rebecca van Bergen, Diana Verde Nieto and Marci Zaroff.

This book is based on the work of the Magnifeco.com blog, which has been enhanced greatly by the vision and gifts of talent from Liezel Strauss, Genevieve Sawtelle, Elie Yoo, Chie Oishi, Katharine Wynkoop, Lynn Duffy, Melissa Chong. Special thanks to Sæunn Kjartansdóttir, who brought her incredibly diligent research skills to this book and joined this incredible list of people to whom I will always be grateful.

Book writing is an incredibly solitary process, and I'm blessed to have friends like Swati Argade, Stephanie Benedetto, Susan Easton, Jennifer Gootman, Yoshiko Matsuhisa, Victoria Clark, Sarah Seatherton and Lily Strauss checking in (and checking up) on me.

Thank you to my family: the two in my pocket — Babs and Fraz; my far-flung, extended family; and my family through marriage, especially Gerry and Larraine. The love and support from each of you is wonderful and greatly appreciated, especially the unconditional and never-ending mantra that I "can do anything" from you, Mama. Every child should be so lucky and so loved.

Over two decades ago, I was asked to be the godmother of a beautiful baby girl. That honor, and the opportunity to be involved with the intelligent, creative woman she has become, fuels me to work harder, be better and inspire her to believe that anything (including writing a book) is possible. Thank you to Amanda for proofreading, commenting and giving insight; you are a delight in my life.

Lastly, incredible and indescribable amounts of gratitude to my spouse, partner and true love, who is a tireless champion of Magnifeco and its mission. Steve, thank you especially for the constant belief that I could do it and that I could take the tragic stories and shocking research and share it in a way that would communicate hope and optimism. You are such a talented artist, and you inspire me constantly. My life with you is a gift, and I'm ecstatic each and every day I get to wake up and share with you.

Bibliography

Alba, Jessica. *The Honest Life: Living Naturally and True to You*. New York: Rodale, 2012.

Baker, Nena. *The Body Toxic: How the Hazardous Chemistry of Everyday Things Threatens Our Health and Well-being*. New York: North Point Press, 2008.

Black, Sandy. *The Sustainable Fashion Handbook*. New York: Thames & Hudson, 2013.

Blanchard, Tamsin. *Green Is the New Black: How to Save the World in Style*. London: Hodder Paperbacks, 2008.

Bloom, Stephen G. *Tears of Mermaids: The Secret Story of Pearls*. New York: St. Martin's Press, 2009.

Brown, Sass. *Eco Fashion*. London: Laurence King, 2010.

Chang, Leslie T. *Factory Girls: Voices from the Heart of Modern China*. London: Picador, 2010.

Cleveland, Todd. *Stones of Contention: A History of Africa's Diamonds*. Athens: Ohio University Press, 2014.

Cline, Elizabeth L. *Overdressed: The Shockingly High Cost of Cheap Fashion*. New York: Portfolio/Penguin, 2013.

Craik, Jennifer. *Fashion: The Key Concepts*. Oxford, UK: Berg, 2009.

Devinney, Timothy M., Pat Auger and Giana M. Eckhardt, *The Myth of the Ethical Consumer*. Cambridge: Cambridge University Press, 2010.

Eagan, Greta. *Wear No Evil: How to Change the World with Your Wardrobe*. Philadelphia: Running Press, 2014.

Earth Pledge, *Future Fashion White Papers: White Papers*. Chelsea Green, 2008.

Epstein, Edward Jay. *The Rise and Fall of Diamonds: The Shattering of a Brilliant Illusion*. New York: Simon and Schuster, 1982.

Fletcher, Kate. *Sustainable Fashion and Textiles: Design Journeys*, 2nd ed. New York: Routledge, 2014.

Freinkel, Susan. *Plastic: A Toxic Love Story*. Boston: Houghton Mifflin Harcourt, 2011.

Gunn, Tim. *Tim Gunn's Fashion Bible: The Fascinating History of Everything in Your Closet*. New York: Gallery Books, 2012.

Hawthorne, Fran. *Ethical Chic: The Inside Story of the Companies We Think We Love*. Boston: Beacon Press, 2012.

Herscovici, Alan. *Second Nature: The Animal-Rights Controversy*. Montreal: CBC Enterprises/Les Entreprises Radio-Canada, 1985.

Hoffmann, Jonas and Ivan Coste-Manière. *Global Luxury Trends: Emerging Markets, Digital Innovations and the Future of the Luxury Industry*. Basingstoke, UK: Palgrave Macmillan, 2012.

Jenkins, McKay. *What's Gotten into Us?: Staying Healthy in a Toxic World*. New York: Random House, 2011.

Malkan, Stacy. *Not Just a Pretty Face: The Ugly Side of the Beauty Industry*. Gabriola Island, BC: New Society, 2007.

McDonough, William and Michael Braungart. *Cradle to Cradle: Remaking the Way We Make Things*. New York: North Point Press, 2002.

McDonough, William and Michael Braungart. *The Upcycle: Beyond Sustainability: Designing for Abundance*. New York: North Point Press, 2013.

Minney, Safia, Emma Watson, Lucy Siegel and Livia Firth. *Naked Fashion: The New Sustainable Fashion Revolution*. Oxford, UK: New Internationalist, 2011.

Mukherjee, Siddhartha. *The Emperor of All Maladies: A Biography of Cancer*. New York: Scribner, 2010.

O'Connor, Siobhan and Alexandra Spunt. *No More Dirty Looks: The Truth About the Toxins in Your Beauty Products and the Safe Must-haves to Keep You Looking Hot*. New York: Da Capo Lifelong Books, 2010.

Raichur, Pratima and Marian Cohn. *Absolute Beauty: Radiant Skin and Inner Harmony Through the Ancient Secrets of Ayurveda*. New York: Harper Perennial, 1999.

Shell, Ellen Ruppel. *Cheap: The High Cost of Discount Culture*. New York: Penguin, 2010.

Sunstein, Cass R. and Martha Nussbaum Craven. *Animal Rights: Current Debates and New Directions*. Oxford: Oxford University Press, 2004.

Thomas, Dana. *Deluxe: How Luxury Lost Its Luster*. New York: Penguin, 2008.

Tseëlon, Efrat. *Fashion and Ethics*. Bristol, UK: Intellect, 2014.

Uliano, Sophie. *Gorgeously Green: Every Girl's Guide to an Earth-friendly Life*. New York: Collins, 2008.

Vartan, Starre. *The Eco Chick Guide to Life: How to Be Fabulously Green*. New York: St. Martin's Griffin, 2008.

Winter, Ruth. *A Consumer's Dictionary of Cosmetic Ingredients: Complete Information About the Harmful and Desirable Ingredients Found in Cosmetics and Cosmeceuticals*. New York: Three Rivers Press, 2009.

Endnotes

Introduction

1   Williams, Austin. "Fashionable Dilemmas," as quoted in *Fashion and Ethics*, p. 70.

Chapter 1

1   Carson, Rachel. *Silent Spring*, Boston: Houghton Mifflin, 1962.

2   "Lipstick & Lead: Questions & Answers," FDA, March 3, 2015, website accessed May 15, 2015. "FDA has not set limits for lead in cosmetics," and lead is not the only heavy metal in lipsticks, according to Sa Liu, S. Katharine Hammond and Ann Rojas-Cheatham, "Concentrations and Potential Health Risks of Metals in Lip Products," *Environmental Health Perspectives*, June 2013.

3   Referring to parabens, a common ingredient. Darbre, P.D., et al., "Concentrations of Parabens in Human Breast Tumours," *Journal of Applied Toxicology*, 2004, 24(1), pp. 5–13; and *THE MANSCAPE: The Dirt on Toxic Ingredients in Men's Body Care Products*, Environmental Defense Canada, 2012.

4   Corby-Edwards, Amalia K. FDA Regulation of Cosmetics and Personal Care Products, Congressional Research Service Report for Congress, July 9, 2012.

5   Amended by the Color Additive Amendments Act of 1960 and the Poison Prevention Packaging Act, see above, and most recently by the Sunscreen Innovation Act (SIA), signed into law by Obama on November 26, 2014. See Gaffney, Alexander, "Obama Approves Bill Reforming Regulation of Sunscreen Ingredients, Other Drugs," December 1, 2014, Regulatory Affairs Professionals Society, website accessed May 15, 2015.

6   Jenkins, McKay. *What's Gotten into Us?: Staying Healthy in a Toxic World*, New York: Random House, 2011.

7   Bhopal Disaster, Greenpeace, n.d., website accessed May 15, 2015.

8   The Bhopal reference was used as an example of toxic chemical overload in both Baker, Nena *The Body Toxic: How the Hazardous Chemistry of Everyday Things Threatens Our Health and Well-being*, New York: North Point Press, 2008, p. 43, and *What's Gotten into Us?*, p. 24.

9   Cosmetics: Prohibited & Restricted Ingredients. FDA, January 26, 2015, website accessed May 15, 2015.

10 Madsen, Travis, and Elizabeth Hitchcock. *Growing Up Toxic: Chemical Exposures and Increases in Developmental Disease*, March 2011, US PIRG Education Fund.

11 Chustecka, Zosia."Cancer Strikes 1 in 2 Men and 1 in 3 Women," *Medscape Medical News*, February 9, 2007.

12 "BRCA1 and BRCA2: Cancer Risk and Genetic Testing." Cancer.gov, National Cancer Institute, n.d., website accessed April 1, 2015.

13 *Growing Up Toxic.*

14 Alexander, Brian. "Special Report: The New Boys' Health Scare." *Redbook*, May 25, 2011, website accessed May 15, 2015.

15 *The Manscape.*

16 Breast Cancer Statistics, Canadian Cancer Society, n.d., website accessed May 25, 2015.

17 "Asthma and a Common Household Chemical: New Research on Pre-natal Exposure," Environmental Defence, May 26, 2014, website accessed May 15, 2015.

18 Bergman, Åke, Jerrold J. Heindel, Susan Jobling, Karen A. Kidd and R. Thomas Zoeller (Eds). State of the Science of Endocrine Disrupting Chemicals 2012, Inter-Organization Programme for the Sound Management of Chemicals: A Cooperative Agreement Among FAO, ILO, UNDP, UNEP, UNIDO, UNITAR, WHO, World Bank and OECD. Geneva; 2012, with permission. This number is an estimate of what the UN calls "the lack of chemical constituent declarations in products, materials and goods."

19 "That's a Killer Look: A Study of Chemicals in Personal Care Products," Alliance for a Clean and Healthy Maine, 2010 report.

20 Exposures Add Up: Survey Results. Environmental Working Group, n.d., website accessed May 19, 2015.

21 Rachel Carson, American biologist. *Encyclopædia Britannica*, n.d., website accessed May 30, 2015.

22 Ibid.

23 Ibid.

24 *What's Gotten into Us?*

25 Malkan, Stacy. *Not Just a Pretty Face: The Ugly Side of the Beauty Industry*, Gabriola Island, BC: New Society, 2007.

26 *What's Gotten into Us?*

27 For more information, refer to the Agency for Toxic Substances & Disease Registry website. This information from the Toxic Substances

Portal: "Polychlorinated Biphenyls (PCBs)," www.atsdr.cdc.gov/toxfaqs/tf.asp?id=140&tid=26.

28 *What's Gotten into Us?* "Synthetic chemicals circle the globe like the winds" suggests McKay Jenkins.

29 "High PCB Levels Found in Eskimo Breast Milk." *New York Times*, February 7, 1989, website accessed May 30 2015.

30 *What's Gotten into Us?*

31 "The Just Beautiful Personal Care Products Pocket Shopping Guide," Environmental Defence Canada, n.d., website accessed May 30, 2015.

32 "'Dirty Dozen' Cosmetic Chemicals to Avoid," David Suzuki Foundation, n.d., website accessed May 30, 2015.

33 Lipstick & Lead: Questions & Answers. FDA, n.d., Website accessed May 30, 2015.

34 Houlihan, Jane, Charlotte Brody and Bryony Schwan. "Not Too Pretty," Environmental Working Group, May 2002.

35 *The Manscape.*

36 Wilson, Michael P., et al., *Green Chemistry in California: A Framework for Leadership in Chemicals Policy and Innovation*, California Policy Research Center, May 2006. This is not exclusive to differing personal care products. "Without comprehensive and standardized information on the toxicity and ecotoxicity for most chemicals, it is very difficult even for large firms to identify hazardous chemicals in their supply chains.... Meanwhile, evidence of public and environmental health problems related to chemicals continues to accumulate."

37 Campaign Victories & History page, Campaign for Safe Cosmetics, n.d., website accessed May 30, 2015.

38 Ibid.

39 "Environmental Defence, Just Beautiful Campaign Launch," *Globe and Mail*, September 22, 2010, website accessed May 30, 2015.

40 *The Manscape.*

41 Dodson, R.E., M. Nishioka, L.J. Standley, L.J. Perovich, J.G. Brody, R.A. Rudel. "Endocrine Disruptors and Asthma-associated Chemicals in Consumer Products," *Environmental Health Perspectives*, March 8, 2012, website accessed May 30, 2015.

42 Raichur, Pratima, and Marian Cohn. *Absolute Beauty: Radiant Skin and Inner Harmony through the Ancient Secrets of Ayurveda*, New York: HarperPerennial, 1999.

43 "Scented Secrets," Environmental Working Group, February 12, 2007, website accessed May 30, 2015.

44 "Science and Policy: Fragrance and Parfum," David Suzuki Foundation, n.d., website accessed May 20, 2015.

45 "Scented Secrets."

46 Sigurdson, Tina. "Expert Panel Confirms That Fragrance Ingredient Can

Cause Cancer," Environmental Working Group, August 7, 2014, website accessed May 30, 2015. Carcinogens are broken into two groups, *known* to be human carcinogens or *reasonably anticipated* to be human carcinogens, by the US National Toxicology Program.

47 Winter, Ruth. *A Consumer's Dictionary of Cosmetic Ingredients: Complete Information about the Harmful and Desirable Ingredients Found in Cosmetics and Cosmeceuticals*, New York: Three Rivers, 2009.

48 "Chemicals of Concern." Campaign for Safe Cosmetics, n.d., website accessed May 30, 2015.

49 "Science and Policy Update: Chemicals in Our Cosmetics," David Suzuki Foundation, n.d., website accessed May 30, 2015.

50 Ibid.

51 Congleton, Johanna. "Chemicals That Should Disappear from Cosmetics," Environmental Working Group, January 6, 2014, website accessed May 30, 2015.

52 Smith, Kristen W., Irene Souter, Irene Dimitriadis, Shelley Ehrlich, Paige L. Williams, Antonia M. Calafat and Russ Hauser. "Urinary Paraben Concentrations and Ovarian Aging among Women from a Fertility Center," Environmental Health Perspectives, online August 2, 2013, website accessed May 30, 2015.

53 "Science and Policy Update: Chemicals in Our Cosmetics."

54 Ibid.

55 1,4-DIOXANE. Skin Deep® Cosmetics Database, Environmental Working Group, www.ewg.org, reprinted with permission.

56 Adapted from Chait, Jennifer. "Why Certify Organic Personal Care Products If You Don't Have to?" Organic/About.com, n.d., website accessed May 30, 2015.

57 For more details on USDA labels for beauty, refer to the USDA Agricultural Marketing Service, National Organic Program PDF.

58 See more from the Center for Laboratory Animal Welfare on the MSPCA site, website accessed May 30, 2015.

59 *Absolute Beauty*, p. 120.

60 Katey Denno, personal interview, November 26, 2014.

61 O'Connor, Siobhan, and Alexandra Spunt. *No More Dirty Looks: The Truth about the Toxins in Your Beauty Products and the Safe Must-haves to Keep You Looking Hot*, New York: Da Capo Lifelong Books, 2010.

62 "Hair Dyes," American Cancer Society, May 27, 2014, website accessed May 30, 2015.

63 "Chemicals That Should Disappear from Cosmetics."

64 "Science and Policy Update: Coal Tar Dyes," David Suzuki Foundation, n.d., website accessed May 30, 2015.

65 "Coal Tar Hair Dyes: Bladder Cancer and Non-Hodgkin's Lymphoma," Environmental Working Group, June 2004, website accessed May 30, 2015.

66 "Not So Pretty: Toxic Products Marketed to Black Women," Environmental Working Group, 2011, Brochure.

67 *Not Just a Pretty Face*, citing a 2006 analysis by researchers at the University of Pittsburgh Cancer Institute Center for Environmental Oncology and the Graduate School of Public Health.

68 "Not So Pretty: Toxic Products Marketed to Black Women."

69 Vitello, Paul. "Horst Rechelbacher, 'Father of Safe Cosmetics,' Dies at 72," *New York Times*, February 23, 2014, website accessed May 30, 2015.

70 *No More Dirty Looks.*

71 Denno, personal interview. For more information see her website, www.thebeautyofitis.com.

72 Marie Veronique Nadeau, personal interview, December 20, 2014.

73 Scranton, Alexandra. "What's the Smell: How the Pine Forest in Your Cleaning Product May be Hazardous to Your Health," Women's Voices for the Earth, June 2010.

74 Ibid.

75 Thomas, Dana. *Deluxe: How Luxury Lost Its Luster*, New York: Penguin, 2008.

76 Wendlandt, Astrid. "Perfume Makers Adapt to EU Rules," *Women's Wear Daily*. July 2014, website accessed May 30, 2015.

77 Olczyk, Nicolas. "La guerre des nez," *Economie du Nouvel Observateur*, December 2011.

78 "Essential Oil Basics," *Aura Cacia*. Frontier Co-op, n.d., website accessed May 30, 2015.

79 *Deluxe: How Luxury Lost Its Luster.*

80 Patricia Ronning, personal interview, June 19, 2014.

81 Ibid.

82 Wendlandt, Astrid. "Insight: What's in a scent? Perfume Makers Adapt to EU Rules," Reuters UK, July 7, 2014, website accessed June 1, 2015.

83 "What's the Smell."

84 Ibid.

85 "Teen Girls' Body Burden of Hormone-altering Cosmetics Chemicals: Cosmetics Chemicals of Concern," EWG, September 24, 2008, website accessed June 1, 2015.

86 *A Consumer's Dictionary of Cosmetic Ingredients.*

87 "Sodium Laureth Sulfate," EWG, Skin Deep® Database, n.d., website accessed June 1, 2015.

88 "'Dirty Dozen' Chemicals to Avoid."

89 "Antiperspirants/Deodorants and Breast Cancer." Cancer.gov, National Cancer Institute, January 4, 2008, website accessed June 1, 2015.

90 *The Manscape.*

91 Ibid.

92 Robinson, J.K. "Sun Exposure, Sun Protection, and Vitamin D," *Journal of the American Medical Association*, September 28, 2005.

93 "Cancer Facts & Figures 2015," Atlanta: American Cancer Society, 2015, website accessed June 2, 2015.

94 Holick, Michael F., and Tai C Chen. "Vitamin D Deficiency: A Worldwide Problem with Health Consequences," *American Journal of Clinical Nutrition*, April 2008, website accessed June 2, 2015.

95 O'connor, Anahad. "Low Vitamin D Levels Linked to Disease in Two Big Studies," *New York Times*, April 1, 2014, website accessed June 2, 2015.

96 "Vitamin D: Fact Sheet for Health Professionals," National Institutes of Health, US Department of Health & Human Services, November 10, 2014, website accessed June 2, 2015.

97 "Research and Markets: Suncare in the United States," *Business Wire*, July 05, 2012, website accessed January 12, 2015.

98 Gaffney, Alexander. "Regulatory Explainer: Understanding the Regulation of New Sunscreen Ingredients," Regulatory Affairs Professionals Society, March 19, 2014, website accessed June 2, 2015.

99 "Sun Safety Campaign: How to Pick a Good Sunscreen," EWG, n.d., website accessed June 1, 2015.

100 Ibid.

101 Ibid.

102 "Benzophenone & Related Compounds," Campaign for Safe Cosmetics, n.d., website accessed June 2, 2015.

103 Buck Louis, G.M., K. Kannan, K.J. Sapra, J. Maisog and R. Sundaram. "Urinary Concentrations of Benzophenone-Type Ultraviolet Radiation Filters and Couples' Fecundity," *American Journal of Epidemiology*, November 13, 2014, website accessed June 2, 2015.

104 Ibid.

105 "Benzophenone & Related Compounds."

106 "What's the Safest and Eco-friendliest Sunscreen?" David Suzuki Foundation, n.d., website accessed June 2, 2015.

107 Nazzaro, F., F. Fratianni, L. De Martino, R. Coppola and V. De Feo. "Effect of Essential Oils on Pathogenic Bacteria," *Pharmaceuticals* (Basel), December 6, 2013, website accessed June 2, 2015.

108 *The Body Toxic.*

109 Scranton, Alexandra. *Chem Fatale: Potential Health Effects of Toxic Chemicals in Feminine Care Products.* Women's Voices for the Earth, November 2013, with permission.

110 Ibid.

111 "Guidance for Industry and FDA Staff, Menstrual Tampons and Pads: Information forPremarket Notification Submissions," FDA, July 27, 2005, website accessed June 2, 2015.

112 *Chem Fatale*, with permission.

113 *Chem Fatale.*

114 *No More Dirty Looks.*

115 "DW Staff, German Study Says Condoms Contain Cancer-causing Chemical." *Deutsche Welle*, May 29, 2005, Website accessed June 2, 2015.

116 *Chem Fatale.*

Chapter 2

1   Westwood, Vivienne in conversation with Deborah Orr at Chelsea Old Town Hall, October 29, 2014. *Guardian* website.

2   Ahmed, Imran. "Let's Show the World That Fashion Is Serious Business." Business of Fashion, April 9, 2013, website accessed April 15, 2015.

3   Challa, Lakshmi. "Impact of Textiles and Clothing Industry on Environment: Approach Towards Eco-friendly Textiles," Fibre2Fashion.com, n.d., website accessed April 15, 2015.

4   Danish Fashion Institute. "Changing the World Through Fashion at Rio+20," Fibre2Fashion.com, n.d., website accessed April 15, 2015.

5   American Apparel and Footwear Association, website accessed April 15, 2015.

6   "Young Consumers' Guide to Eco-friendly Living," YouthXchange, UNEP and UNESCO, n.d., website accessed April 15, 2015.

7   Tagline from Cotton Inc., an organization funded by cotton growers in the United States, www.cottoninc.com.

8   Said in many places, but specifically: *The Deadly Chemicals in Cotton*, Environmental Justice Foundation in collaboration with Pesticide Action Network UK, London, UK, 2007.

9   Ferrigno, Simon. "Cotton Scape," *The Cotton Conundrum*, Forum for the Future, July 2013. These are global averages of cotton production account.

10 Turney, Jon. "Crop Challenge," *The Cotton Conundrum*.

11 Rowland, Katherine." A Grower's Guide," *The Cotton Conundrum*.

12 *The Cotton Conundrum*. The full sentence, as it appears: "But cotton does not just clothe and feed us: it is the stuff of livelihoods. For many resource-poor farmers from the global South, it is a gateway to organised markets, cash, and hopes for a better future."

13 "Cotton Scape."

14 "History of Bollgard Cotton," Monsanto, n.d., website accessed April 15, 2015.

15 Center for Human Rights and Global Justice. *Every Thirty Minutes: Farmer Suicides, Human Rights, and the Agrarian Crisis in India*, New York: NYU School of Law, 2011.

16 Ibid.

17 Ibid., with permission.

18 Ibid., with permission.

19 "Cotton Scape."

20 Ibid.

21 Chemicals Programme of the United Nations Environment Programme, with the assistance of UNEP's Information Unit for Conventions, "Childhood Pesticide Poisoning Information for Advocacy and Action," 2004.

22 WHO and Healthy Environments for Children Alliance. "Issue Brief Series: Pesticides," n.d., website accessed April 15, 2015.

23 "Children Are Facing High Risks from Pesticide Poisoning," joint note for the media WHO/FAO/UNEP. WHO, September 24, 2004, website accessed April 15, 2015.

24 *The Deadly Chemicals in Cotton*, Environmental Justice Foundation in collaboration with Pesticide Action Network UK, London, 2007.

25 Ibid.

26 Inspired by Schwab, Jennifer, "Slipping Sustainability Through the Back Door," Green Home, SierraClub, n.d., website accessed April 15, 2015.

27 This is documented on the Wikipedia page for the Aral Sea, and received mass press coverage in the summer of 2014; a good piece is Hoskins, Tansy, "Cotton Production Linked to Images of the Dried up Aral Sea Basin," *Guardian*, October 1, 2014, website accessed April 15, 2015.

28 "Cotton Production Linked to Images of the Dried up Aral Sea Basin."

29 "The Impact of a Cotton T-Shirt: How Smart Choices Can Make a Difference in Our Water and Energy Footprint," WWF, n.d., website accessed April 15, 2015.

30 "Cotton Scape."

31 Ibid.

32 Pepper, LaRhea (Textile Exchange). "How much cotton is organic?" Email to the author, October 10, 2014.

33 "Among all consumers, 80% say better quality garments are made from natural fibers like cotton, according to Monitor™ data," reported by Cotton Inc.'s Lifestyle Monitor™ Survey. "The Touch, The Feel… Time to Break Out the Silver for Fabric of Our Lives." Lifestyle Monitor, Cotton Inc., December 1, 2014, website accessed April 15, 2015.

34 "Why Natural Fibres? Five Good Reasons," NaturalFibres, 2009, FAO n.d., website accessed April 15, 2015.

35 Ibid.

36 Ibid.

37 Wynters, Sharyn, and Burton Goldberg. *The Pure Cure: A Complete Guide to Freeing Your Life from Dangerous Toxins*, Berkeley: Soft Skull Press, 2012.

38 "Guide to Greener Fibers," Natural Resources Defense Council, November 11, 2011, website accessed April 15, 2015.

39 "Impact of Textiles and Clothing Industry on Environment."

40 "How Polyester Is Made," MadeHow, Avameg, Inc., n.d., website accessed April 15, 2015.

41 "REALITY LAB: How Can Design Provide a Solution to the Problems the Society Is Facing?" Exhibiton, Tokyo 2010, included an extensive presentation about Teijin and ECO CIRCLE® as part of the exhibit.

42 "Patagonia's Common Threads Garment Recycling Program: A Detailed Analysis," a whitepaper, n.d.

43   "What Is the Gyre," Environmental Cleanup Coalition, n.d., website accessed April 15, 2015.

44   McDonough, William, and Michael Braungart. *Cradle to Cradle: Remaking the Way We Make Things*, New York: North Point Press, 2002.

45   Ibid.

46   Beauchamp, Emilie. "Fibre to Fabric," *The Cotton Conundrum*.

47   Friends of Nature Institute of Public & Environmental Affairs, Green Beagle Environmental Protection, Commonwealth Association, Nanjing Green Stone Environmental Action Network, "Cleaning up the Fashion Industry," 2012 report.

48   Ibid.

49   Greenpeace. *Dirty Laundry: Unravelling the Corporate Connections to Toxic Water Pollution in China*, 2011.

50   "Nonylphenol and Nonylphenol Ethoxylates," EPA, n.d., website accessed April 15, 2015.

51   "Calvin Klein, Zara Among Worst Chemical Users, Greenpeace Says," *Environmental Leader*, Business Sector Media, LLC, November 21, 2012, website accessed April 15, 2015.

52   Muthu, Subramanian Senthilkannan, ed. *Roadmap to Sustainable Textiles and Clothing: Eco-friendly Raw Materials*, Singapore: Springer, 2014.

53   Rangair, N.T., T.M. Kalyankar, A.A. Mahajan, P.R. Lendhe and P.K. Puranik. "Ayurvastra: Herbal Couture Technology in Textile," *International Journal of Research in Ayurveda and Pharmacy*, 3(5), 2012, 733–736.

54   Smithers, Rebecca. "Benetton Admits Link with Firm in Collapsed Bangladesh Building," *Guardian*, April 29, 2013, website accessed April 15, 2015.

55   Ibid.

56   "Post Rana Plaza: A Vision for the Future. ILO Director-General Guy Ryder's address," ILO, April 3, 2014, website accessed April 15, 2015.

57   Johnson, Kay. "Bangladesh Disaster: Can US Brands Repair Their Reputations?"*Christian Science Monitor*, May 6, 2013, website accessed April 15, 2015.

58   "One Year after Rana Plaza," op-ed, *International New York Times*, April 27, 2014, website accessed April 15, 2015.

59   "Bangladesh Disaster."

60   Lopez Acevedo, Gladys, and Raymond Robertson, eds. "Sewing Success?: Employment, Wages and Poverty Following the End of the Multi-fibre Arrangement," World Bank, 2012.

61   Kristof, Nicholas D. "Where Sweatshops Are a Dream," *New York Times*, January 14, 2009, website accessed April 15, 2015.

62   Williams, Austin. "Fashionable Dilemmas," *Fashion and Ethics: Critical Studies in Fashion and Beauty*, Volume II, Efrat Tseëlon, ed., Bristol: Intellect, 2014.

63 "Post Rana Plaza."

64 "Origins and History," ILO, n.d., website accessed April 15, 2015.

65 "Post Rana Plaza."

66 "Towards 2017: Better Work Phase III Strategy," ILO and IFC, n.d.

67 "10 Principles of Fair Trade," WFTO, n.d., website accessed April 15, 2015.

68 Minney, Safia, Emma Watson, Lucy Siegel and Livia Firth. *Naked Fashion: The New Sustainable Fashion Revolution*, Oxford, UK: New Internationalist, 2011.

69 Fonseca, Felicia. "Navajo Nation Sues Urban Outfitters Over Goods," *USA Today*, February 29, 2012, website accessed April 15, 2015.

70 "Meet the Aspirationals: Shifting Sustainability from Obligation to Desire," BBMG and GlobeScan, 2014.

71 *Naked Fashion: The New Sustainable Fashion Revolution*.

72 Siegel, Lucy. "Obsessed with Fleeting Trends and Seduced by Bargains, We've Never Bought So Much: But a New Book Says It All Adds up to More Clothes, Less Style," May 16, 2011, *Daily Mail*, website accessed April 15, 2015, *adjusted for 2% industry growth.

73 "We Wear the Facts," American Apparel and Footwear Association, n.d., website accessed April 15, 2015.

74 "Average Price per Apparel Article Worldwide in 2011," Statista, n.d., website accessed April 15, 2015.

75 "Clothing Sector Agrees Challenging Targets to Cut Environmental Impact by 15%," WRAP UK, February 11, 2014, website accessed April 15, 2015.

76 "Fashion Xchange," Global Fashion Exchange, Danish Fashion Institute and Intandem Creatives, n.d., website accessed April 15, 2015.

77 Shell, Ellen Ruppel. "Cheap: The High Cost of Discount Culture," New York: Penguin, 2010.

78 Ibid.

Chapter 3

1 Bruno Pieters, personal interview, September 30, 2014.

2 Doran, Sophie, "What the 2014 BrandZ™ Top 100 Means for Luxury," Luxury Society, Digital Luxury Group, May 21, 2014, website accessed April 15, 2015.

3 Roberts, Fflur. "Luxury Goods Sales to Reach $405 Billion by 2019," Luxury Society, Digital Luxury Group, October 7, 2014, website accessed April 15, 2015.

4 Tsui, Enid. "The Luxury That Dare Not Speak Its Name," *Financial Times*, October 3, 2012, website accessed April 15, 2015..

5 Weber, Caroline. "The Devil Sells Prada," *New York Times*, August 26, 2007, website accessed April 15, 2015.

6 Mavrody, Nika. "At a Glance: See How These Six Corporations Control the Luxury Fashion Industry," Fashion Spot, April 30, 2014. Mavrody's note:

Created based on a table in *Stitched Up: The Anti-Capitalist Book of Fashion* by Tansy E. Hoskins.

7   "History of Silk," Wikipedia, website accessed April 15, 2015.

8   "The History of Silk," Silkroad Foundation, n.d., website accessed April 15, 2015.

9   "The Alliance for Artisan Enterprise: Bringing Artisan Enterprise to Scale." The Aspen Institute, n.d. The Alliance is a platform enabling companies, non-profits, governments and international organizations to collaborate to support and grow artisan enterprises, provide best practice services to the organizations that support them and to support the broader recognition of the importance of the artisan sector to development, economic growth and preservation of cultural heritage.

10   Ibid.

11   Lopez Acevedo, Gladys and Raymond Robertson, eds. "Sewing Success?: Employment, Wages and Poverty Following the End of the Multi-Fibre Arrangement," World Bank, 2012.

12   "Improving the Livelihoods of Cambodian Silk Entrepreneurs." *ITC News*, International Trade Centre, March 1, 2013, website accessed April 15, 2015.

13   "Silk Weavers in Varanasi Hang on by Thread, Plead for Rescue." Agence France-Presse, NDTV, May 4, 2014, website accessed April 15, 2015.

14   Ibid.

15   Ibid.

16   "The Alliance for Artisan Enterprise."

17   Localwisdom.info, an international fashion research project exploring the "craft of use," with permission.

Chapter 4

1   *Blood Diamond*. Edward Zwick, Director, 2006, DVD, quote from director's commentary.

2   Hart, Matthew. "Is There a Way Around the Sale of 'Blood Gold'?" December 13, 2013, Reuters, website accessed April 15, 2015.

3   "What Is Artisanal and Small-scale Mining?" *Mining Facts*, Fraser Institute, n.d., website accessed April 15, 2015.

4   Ibid.

5   "Learn More About Child Labour in Mining." ILO, n.d., website accessed April 15, 2015.

6   "Mali: Artisanal Mines Produce Gold with Child Labor." Human Rights Watch, December 6, 2011, website accessed April 15, 2015.

7   "Peru: Child Labour in Gold Mines." ILO, June 23, 2005, website accessed April 15, 2015.

8   Mottaz. "Child Labour in Gold Mining: The Problem," ILO, International Programme on the Elimination of Child Labour, 2006.

9   "Dirty Gold's Impacts." *No Dirty Gold,* Earthworks, n.d., website accessed April 15, 2015.

10   Rastogi,Nina Shen. "Production of Gold Has Many Negative Environmental Effects." *Washington Post,* September 21, 2010, website accessed May 15, 2015.

11   "New Fairtrade Gold and Precious Metals Standards Published." Fairtrade International, November 12, 2013, website accessed April 15, 2015.

12   Perlez, Jane and Kirk Johnson. "Behind Gold's Glitter: Torn Lands and Pointed Questions," *New York Times,* October 24, 2005, website accessed April 15, 2015.

13   "Production of Gold Has Many Negative Environmental Effects."

14   Epstein, Edward Jay. *The Rise and Fall of Diamonds: The Shattering of a Brilliant Illusion,* New York: Simon and Schuster, 1982.

15   Garfield, Bob. "Ad Age Advertising Century: The Top 100 Campaigns," *AdAge,* Crain Communications, March 29, 1999, website accessed April 15, 2015.

16   "N.W. Ayer & Son (N.W. Ayer & Partners)." *AdAge Encyclopedia of Advertising,* Crain Communications, September 15, 2003, website accessed April 15, 2015.

17   "The Truth About Diamonds." *Global Witness,* November, 2006, website accessed April 15, 2015.

18   Hill, Amelia. "Bin Laden's $20m African 'Blood Diamond' Deals," *Guardian,* October 20, 2002, website accessed April 15, 2015. www.theguardian.com/world/2002/oct/20/alqaida.terrorism

19   "Credibility of Kimberley Process on the Line, Say NGOs." *IRIN,* June, 2009, website accessed April 15, 2015.

20   Zwick, Edward. "The Sad Truth About the Fight Against Blood Diamonds." *Huffington Post,* December 4, 2011, website accessed April 15, 2015.

21   Reema Keswani, personal interview, August 30, 2014.

22   World Vision Australia, "Beyond the Bling," 2013.

23   Cleveland, Todd. *Stones of Contention: A History of Africa's Diamonds.* Athens: Ohio University Press, 2014.

24   Epstein, Edward Jay. "Have You Ever Tried to Sell a Diamond?" *Atlantic,* February 1982, website accessed April 15, 2015.

25   "The History of Pearls." *NOVA,* PBS, December 1998, website accessed April 15, 2015.

26   Bloom, Stephen G. *Tears of Mermaids: The Secret Story of Pearls,* New York: St. Martin's Press, 2009.

27   "CIBJO President Outlines Sustainability Framework for Pearl Sector, Says Economic, Environmental and Social Elements Must Be Incorporated." CIBJO, World Jewellery Confederation, June 14, 2014, website accessed April 15, 2015.

28   "5 Sustainability Principles for Marine Cultured Pearls." *Sustainable Pearls,* July 2, 2014, website accessed April 15, 2015.

29 "Capim Dourado." EcoArte Brazil, n.d., website accessed April 15, 2015.

30 Natalie Frigo, personal interview, August 28, 2014.

31 "Wildlife in the Jewelry Trade." Office of Law Enforcement, U.S. Fish & Wildlife Service, February 2013, website accessed April 15, 2015.

32 "Stopping Illegal Wildlife Trade." International Federation of Animal Welfare, 2011, website accessed April 15, 2015.

33 Lambo, Turquil. "Campaign to Ban Use of Coral Picks Up Steam," *Shine Times*, April 21, 2014, website accessed April 15, 2015.

34 Gomelsky, Victoria. "Jewelers Divided Over Use of Coral," *New York Times*, December 8, 2009, website accessed April 15, 2015.

35 Gearhart, Jeff. "Low-Cost Jewelry Ranks HIGH for Toxic Chemicals," HealthyStuff.org, March 13, 2012, with permission.

36 D'Urso, William. "16 L.A. Businesses Accused of Selling Jewelry Tainted with Lead," *Los Angeles Times*, July 17, 2012, website accessed April 15, 2015.

Chapter 5

1 Hilary Alexander, in preface to Sandy Black, *The Sustainable Fashion Handbook*, Thames and Hudson, 2012, with permission.

2 Gregoire, Lisa. "The Hunt Revisited: Greenpeace Makes Nice with Inuit Communities," *Walrus*, November, 2014, website accessed April 15, 2015.

3 This concept was raised by Lucy Siegle in her article, "Should I Worry About Cheap Cashmere," Guardian.com, December 7, 2014, website accessed April 15, 2015.

4 "Natural fibres: Alpacca." International Year of Natural Fibres, Food and Agriculture Organization (FAO), n.d., website accessed April 15, 2015, with permission.

5 "Natural fibres: Angora." International Year of Natural Fibres, FAO, n.d., website accessed April 15, 2015, with permission.

6 Siegle, Lucy. "Should I Worry About Cheap Cashmere?" Guardian.com, December 7, 2014, website accessed April 15, 2015.

7. Jacob, Pearly. *Cashmere Story*, Documentary, online, Vimeo, July 9, 2012, website accessed April 15, 2015.

8 "Natural fibres: Wool." *International Year of Natural Fibres,* FAO, n.d., website accessed April 15, 2015, with permission.

9 "Mulesing in Sheep: Legal, Welfare and Ethical Issues." NSW HSC Online, NSW Department of Education and Communities, and Charles Sturt University, n.d., website accessed April 15, 2015.

10 Rubeli, Ella. "The End of the Sheep's Back." *Australian Wool Growers Association News*, December 20, 2012, website accessed April 15, 2015.

11 Sneddon, Joanne. "How the Wool Industry Has Undercut Itself on Mulesin," *Conversation*, May 2, 2011, website accessed April 15, 2015.

12 Gunther, Marc. "Down Smackdown: The North Face v Patagonia on Ethical Feather Standards," Guardian, August 27, 2014, website accessed April 15, 2015.

13 Schumpeter. "Adventures in the Skin Trade: How the Danes Became Masters of the Global Fur Business," *Economist*, May 3, 2014, website accessed April 15, 2015.

14 Alexander, Ella. "The Fur Trade Is Valued at $40 Billion," Voque.co.uk, March 28, 2014, website accessed April 15, 2015. *Based on statistics from 2012 and 2013.

15 O'Connor, Joe, Andrew Barr, Mike Faille and Richard Johnson. "Graphic: The Canadian Beaver and Our Furry Heritage," *National Post*, June 28, 2013, website accessed April 15, 2015.

16 Alan Herscovici, Personal interview, August 1, 2014.

17 "Wild Fur Trapping in North America." *Truth About Fur*, North American Fur Industry Communications group, n.d., website accessed April 15, 2015.

18 Herscovici, Alan. *Second Nature: The Animal-rights Controversy*, Montreal: CBC Enterprises/Les Entreprises Radio-Canada, 1985. 19 "FICA Facts." Fur Information Council of America, n.d., website accessed April 15, 2015.

19 "FICA Facts." Fur Information Council of America, n.d., website accessed April 15, 2015.

Chapter 6

1 As spoken in *Thread: A Documentary* (trailer), Michelle Vey, Director, with permission.

2 Crawford, Tommy. "Victoria's Secret: From Fallen Angel to Detox Leader?" Greenpeace International, January 22, 2013, website accessed May 15, 2015, with permission.

3 Ibid.

4 "Formaldehyde in Textiles." United States Government Accountability Office, GAO-10-875, August 13, 2010, with permission.

5 "General Description." Global Organic Textile Standard, December 30, 2014, website accessed May 15, 2015.

6 Pepper, LaRhea (Textile Exchange). "How much cotton is organic?" Email to the author, October 10, 2014.

7 Fletcher, Kate. *Sustainable Fashion and Textiles: Design Journeys*, 2nd ed., New York: Routledge, 2014.

8 "FTC Charges Companies with 'Bamboo-zling' Consumers with False Product Claims." Federal Trade Commission, August 8, 2009, website accessed May 15, 2015.

9 Callewaert, Chris, Evelyn De Maeseneire, Frederiek-Maarten Kerckhof, Arne Verliefde, Tom Van de Wiele and Nico Boon. "Microbial Odor Profile of Polyester and Cotton Clothes after a Fitness Session," *Applied and Environmental Microbiology*, August 2014.

10 "Chemicals That Should Disappear from Cosmetics: Triclosan." David Suzuki Foundation, n.d., website accessed April 15, 2015.

11 Sawatsky, Tara (Canopy Planet). "Fashion brands and designers protect en-dangered forests — given it is now in clothing." Email to the author, October 29, 2014.

12 "Canopystyle Media Backgrounder: Fashion Loved by Forests," n.d.

13 "Soybean Protein Fiber Properties." Swicofil, n.d., website accessed April 15, 2015.

14 Saluja, Mohit. "An Introduction to Milk Fiber: A Review," *Fibre2Fashion*, November 15, 2010, website accessed April 15, 2015.

15 "SeaCell™: The Natural Fiber with the Skin-caring Properties of Pure Seaweed." *Smartfiber Ag*, September 18, 2014, website accessed May 15, 2015.

16 Brody, Jane. "Understanding Eczema to Treat It," *New York Times*, June 29, 2013, website accessed May 15, 2015.

17 Silverberg, Jonathan I. "Adult Eczema Prevalence and Associations with Asthma and Other Health and Demographic Factors: A US Population-based Study," *Journal of Allergy and Clinical Immunology*, May 2013.

Chapter 7

1 Emily Alati, personal interview, August 13, 2014

2 "ApparelStats 2014 and ShoeStats 2014 Reports." American Apparel & Footwear Association, January 9, 2015, website accessed May 16, 2015.

3 "About NSRA." National Shoe Retailers Association, n.d., website accessed May 16, 2015.

4 Smith, Ray. "A Closet Filled with Regrets," *Wall Street Journal*, April 17, 2013, website accessed May 16, 2015.

5 "Women's £16k Shoe Bill." *Daily Express*, June 28, 2010, website accessed May 15, 2015.

6 Belluck, Pam. "This Shoe Had Prada Beat by 5,500 Years," *New York Times*, June 6, 2010, website accessed May 15, 2015.

7 "Top Ten Toxic Threats in 2013: Cleanup, Progress, and Ongoing Challenges." Blacksmith Institute, November 4, 2013, website accessed May 15, 2015.

8 "Livestock's Long Shadow: Environmental Issues and Options." FAO/LEAD. Food and Agriculture Organization of the United Nations, 2006, with permission.

9 Greenpeace. "Slaughtering the Amazon," 2009, with permission.

10 "Adidas, Clarks, Nike and Timberland Agree Moratorium on Illegal Amazon Leather." *Telegraph*, August 4, 2009, website accessed May 14, 2015.

11 Král', I., F. Schmél and J. Buljan. "The Future for Leather," United Nations Industrial Development Organization, 2014, with permission.

12 Richards, Matt, Rowan Gabrielle and Stacie Wickham. "Leather for Life," Future Fashion White Papers, New York: Earth Pledge Foundation, 2008.

13 Sim, M. "'Sensationalist' Claim About Tanneries and Pollution," Pure Earth Pollution Blog, Blacksmith Institute, website accessed May 15, 2015.

14 "Inside Story: The Dark Side of Bangladesh's Leather Trade." *Al Jazeera*, December 3, 2013, website accessed May 14, 2015.

15 "Toxic Tanneries: The Health Repercussions of Bangladesh's Hazaribagh Leather." Human Rights Watch, 2012, with permission.

16 "The World's Worst 2013: The Top Ten Toxic Threats." A joint report from Blacksmith Institute and Green Cross Switzerland, 2013.

17 "Toxic Tanneries."

18 "Moving The Toxic Tanneries: Another Wait Starts." Research Initiative for Social Equity Society. March 6, 2014, website accessed May 15, 2015.

19 Aulakh, Raveena. "Bangladesh's Tanneries Make the Sweatshops Look Good," *Toronto Star*, October 12, 2013, website accessed May 15, 2015.

20 "Inside Story."

21 BLC Leather Technology Centre. "Biodegradability of Leather Report," *Leather Mag*, Leather International, April 2011, website accessed May 15, 2015.

22 McDonough, William and Michael Braungart. *Cradle to Cradle: Remaking the Way We Make Things*, New York: North Point Press, 2002, pp 13-14.

23 "NEWS: Sergio Rossi Launches an Eco-friendly Shoes, the Eco Pump," Aesop Innovation, June 2009, website accessed May 15, 2015.

24 "You Probably Own Way Too Many Pairs of Shoes, Study Says." *Huffington Post*, August 19, 2013, website accessed May 15, 2015.

25 "Guide to Safely Buying Shoes on eBay by Shoe Metro." eBay, July 2, 2007, website accessed May 15, 2015.

26 Sean McCormick, personal interview, June 19, 2014.

27 "Knowing Which Products Are Truly Made in America: How to Know Which Flag-waving Products Are True Red, White, and Blue." *Consumer Reports*. February 2013, website accessed May 15, 2015.

28 Aarts, Deborah. "A Look Inside Canada's Fastest-Growing Companies," *Profit Guide*, June 12, 2014,website accessed May 15, 2015.

29 Marsh, Steve. "Wings of Desire," *Mpls.St.Paul Magazine*, April 25, 2014, website accessed May 15, 2015.

30 Berlinger, Max. "Now Available: G.H. Bass & Co.'s Made In Maine Collection," *Esquire*, October 29, 2013, website accessed May 15, 2015.

31 Williams, Michael. "Sperry Top-Sider: Made in the USA," *A Continuous Lean*, May 17, 2013, website accessed May 15, 2015.

32 Wording on the New Balance site in early 2015 read: "We're proud to be the only major company to make or assemble more than 4 million pairs of athletic footwear per year in the USA, which represents a limited portion of our US sales. Where the domestic value is at least 70%, we label our shoes Made in the USA."

33 "Global Athletic Footwear Market Is Expected to Reach USD 84.4 Billion in 2018: Transparency Market Research," PRNewswire, September 26, 2012, website accessed May 15, 2015.

34 Refers to a quote made to *New York Times* in the 1990s by Nike co-founder Phil Knight who said the brand had "become synonymous with slave wages, forced overtime, and arbitrary abuse." Cited often over the years and most recently in Felicity Carus, "Will Nike Deliver on Its 2015 Performance Standards?" *Guardian*, February 15, 2013, website accessed May 15, 2015. Plus the 2012 Adidas scandal around the Olympics; Conal Urquhart, "Olympics Sportswear by Adidas Made in 'Sweatshop' Conditions: Reports," *Guardian*, April 14, 2012, website accessed May 15, 2015.

35 Chang, Leslie T. *Factory Girls: Voices from the Heart of Modern China*, London: Picador, 2010.

36 "Running Costs." Consumers International, n.d., website accessed May 16, 2015.

37 Graph, Clean Clothes Campaign, 2004, in "Running Costs."

38 Tal Dehtiar, personal interview, September 23, 2014.

39 Beavis, Lynn. "Veja: An Ethical Passion for Fashion," *Guardian*, May 30, 2012, website accessed May 15, 2015.

40 Olsen, Elizabeth. Personal Interview. August 26, 2014.

Chapter 8

1 Thomas, *Deluxe: How Luxury Lost Its Luster*, New York: Penguin Books, 2008, with permission.

2 Ibid.

3 Ibid. *Thomas states $11.7 billion in 2004. I have adjusted for 5% growth.

4 Pohlman, Jeff and Andrea Day. "Behind the Billion-dollar Counterfeit Bag Market", CNBC, August 1, 2013, website accessed June 1, 2015.

5 "Criminal Activity." Don't Buy Fakes, Authentics Foundation, June 8, 2013, website accessed June 2, 2015.

6 "Growing Evidence of Links Between Counterfeit Goods and Terrorist Financing." INTERPOL, April 6, 2004, website accessed June 2, 2015.

7 Ibid.

8 You can view the CURRENT PROPOSITION 65 LIST [01/23/15] on the OEHHA (one of six agencies under the umbrella of the California Environmental Protection Agency) website: http://oehha.ca.gov/prop65/prop65_list/newlist.html

9 Cox, Caroline. "Pretty but Poisonous: Lead in Handbags and Wallets," Center for Environmental Health, 2009.

10 Hume, Marion. "Ilaria Venturini Fendi's Eco-friendly Bags," *W Magazine*, August 2011, website accessed June 1, 2015.

11 Binkley, Christina. "Fendi Scion Makes Trash into Luxury Handbags," *Wall Street Journal*, October 31, 2012, website accessed June 2, 2015.

Chapter 9

1 Crawford, Joan. *My Way of Life*, New York: Simon & Shuster, 1971.

2   Fletcher, Kate. "No Wash," n.d., website accessed June 10, 2015, with permission.

3   "Formaldehyde in Clothing." Consumer Affairs New Zealand, November 14, 2013, website accessed May 1, 2015.

4   Betkowski, Bev. "Jeans Remain Surprisingly Clean After a Year of Wear." University of Alberta, January 21, 2011, website accessed June 1, 2015.

5   Peterson, Christina. "Can Cold Water Get Your Clothes Clean," *Good Housekeeping*, September 23, 2011, website accessed June 1, 2015.

6   Sutton, Rebecca. "Don't Get Slimed: Skip the Fabric Softener." EWG, November 1, 2011, www.ewg.org, with permission.

7   "Smarter Living: Chemical Index, Perchloroethylene (Tetrachloroethylene, PERC, PCE)." Natural Resources Defense Council, December 27, 2011, website accessed June 1, 2015.

8   Dos Santos, Alissa. "Green "Dry" Cleaning," *Green American*, September 2007, website accessed June 1, 2015.

9   Neff, Jack. "P&G Plots Growth Path Through Services," *Advertising Age*, March 22, 2010, website accessed June 2, 2015.

10   LaMonica, Lorne. "A Greener Option to Dry Cleaning," Greening the Apple blog, EPA, September 18, 2012, website accessed June 10, 2015.

11   Garner, Jeff. Shared on the Green Festival stage, June 7, 2015.

12   "Make Do and Mend," British Library Board, 1943, website accessed May 30, 2015.

13   Ward, Alex. "It's a Stitch Up! How Seven Out of 10 Young People Don't Know How to Sew a Button," *Daily Mail*, October 6, 2012, website accessed June 15, 2015.

14   "The Facts About Textile Waste." Council for Textile Recycling, n.d., website accessed June 1, 2015.

15   "Nike Reuse-A-Shoe Program." Nike.com, n.d., website accessed May 30, 2015.

16   Wallander, Mattias. "Why Textile Waste Should be Banned from Landfills," Triple Pundit, January 2, 2012, website accessed June 2, 2015.

Index

About the Author

KATE BLACK HAS LIVED AND WORKED in the major fashion centers of the world and written over 1,000 articles about designers and ethical fashion from her decidedly global perspective. She is the founder and editor-in-chief of Magnifeco.com, the digital source for eco-fashion and sustainable living. Kate is also the founder of EcoSessions®, a global platform bringing together designers, industry, and consumers to discuss change. She is regularly featured on the *Huffington Post* and is highly in demand as a speaker on ethical fashion at regional and national green living events.

ROMP PHOTOGRAPHY

If you have enjoyed *Magnifeco* you might also enjoy other

BOOKS TO BUILD A NEW SOCIETY

Our books provide positive solutions for people who want to
make a difference. We specialize in:

**Food & Gardening • Resilience • Sustainable Building
Climate Change • Energy • Health & Wellness • Sustainable Living**

**Environment & Economy • Progressive Leadership • Community
Educational & Parenting Resources**

New Society Publishers

ENVIRONMENTAL BENEFITS STATEMENT

New Society Publishers has chosen to produce this book on recycled paper made
with **100% post consumer waste,** processed chlorine free, and old growth free.
For every 5,000 books printed, New Society saves the following resources:[1]

25	Trees
2,264	Pounds of Solid Waste
2,491	Gallons of Water
3,249	Kilowatt Hours of Electricity
4,115	Pounds of Greenhouse Gases
18	Pounds of HAPs, VOCs, and AOX Combined
6	Cubic Yards of Landfill Space

[1]Environmental benefits are calculated based on research done by the Environmental Defense Fund
and other members of the Paper Task Force who study the environmental impacts of the paper
industry.

For a full list of NSP's titles, please call 1-800-567-6772 *or check out our website* at:

www.newsociety.com

new society
PUBLISHERS